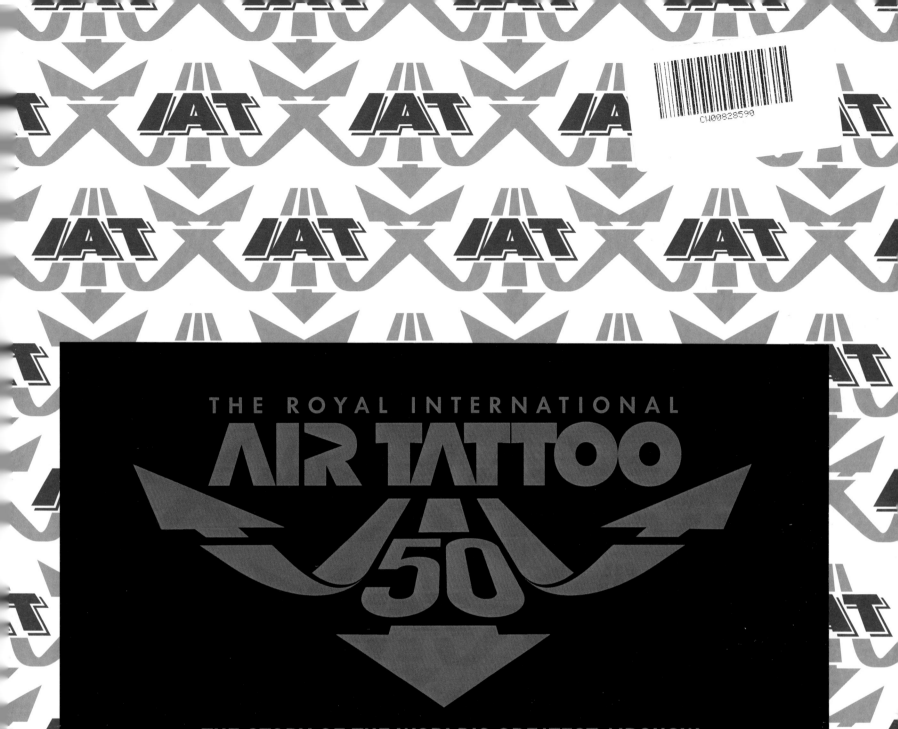

THE ROYAL INTERNATIONAL
AIR TATTOO
50

THE STORY OF THE WORLD'S GREATEST AIRSHOW

Kindly gifted at the RIAT 2022 Gala Dinner by

LOCKHEED MARTIN

NORTHROP GRUMMAN

THE ROYAL INTERNATIONAL
AIR TATTOO
50

Foreword

Over the years much has been written about the amazing story of the Air Tattoo and its loyal, hardworking, talented family of people from all around the world who have been behind it. The airshow has featured in print and broadcast media worldwide, as well as more recently online, reporting both the good times and occasionally when circumstances challenged this world-renowned gathering of military aviators and their aircraft.

Within this 50th anniversary book, important and memorable aviation milestones are recorded, as the Air Tattoo continually developed as the meeting place for like-minded military aviators and their supporting personnel. It is an occasion when valuable professional relationships are established and learned lessons shared in a warm and friendly atmosphere — an aspect so generously praised by air forces around the world, and which I have witnessed first-hand. Defence diplomacy opportunities are equally highly valued — providing many informal opportunities for senior military officers to further relationships with counterparts from other air forces. Letters reproduced within this book provide testament to the importance of the Air Tattoo to the UK, the USA, NATO and other allies from across the globe and of course, the Royal Air Force.

Such is the regard in which the Air Tattoo team is held that, over the years, many countries have asked for its assistance when planning their first airshows or anniversary celebrations. South Africa, the Czech Republic, Slovakia, Romania, the Netherlands, Switzerland, Canada, the USA and Spain come to mind. The team has also arranged significant flypasts for the opening of the Eurotunnel and the 50th anniversary of Heathrow Airport, pre-race flying displays for the Formula 1 Grand Prix at Brands Hatch and the management of the World Aerobatic Championships in 1986 — all undertaken with the support of the volunteer team. Likewise were the long-running RAF Bands concert tours and the SkyHigh trading operation at airshows in the UK and Europe. Our combined skills were also put to good use when the MOD turned to us for the hugely complex data and ticket management for D-Day and VE-Day celebrations, and the Royal Military Tattoo 2000.

My own involvement began in 1970, having been a trainee civilian air traffic controller along with Paul Bowen. We had both been posted to the Aircraft and Armament Experimental Establishment [A&AEE] at Boscombe Down. Shift patterns and working hours there were surprisingly relaxed and so, when Squadron Leader Jack Currie and Paul's father asked if a volunteer aviation operations team could be brought together to organise the flying at an airshow at North Weald Aerodrome in support of the Royal Air Forces Association, the answer was easy. Along with about ten other A&AEE colleagues, Air Tattoo '71 became the start of my eight years as a volunteer followed by 35 years on the permanent staff, retiring as chief executive after RIAT 2014. I now enjoy an honorary vice-patron role, again on the volunteer team. Paul and I worked alongside each other for 33 years until his untimely death in 2004. Like many others, the Air Tattoo has been a very significant part of my life, as it has been for my wife and two sons, each of whom has played their part in its success over the years.

This book has been written by Ben Dunnell and designed by Graham Finch, both of whom are suitably credited by editor David Higham in his acknowledgements. David's background as a past RAFCTE finance director, and more recently editing the RIAT souvenir programme, made him eminently qualified for the role of editor. The task for these three wise and experienced men of squeezing into this book the whole life story of the Air Tattoo, with all of the people from so many different walks of life who have given so very much over the 50 years to make it what it is today, was always going to be an emotionally challenging and somewhat impossible task.

For those past and current members of the wide Air Tattoo family and, whether or not you or your team, military unit, organisation or company are mentioned within this book, I do hope you will be appropriately proud of being a part of this truly amazing team that has worked so well together over the years. The Air Tattoo brand has been built into one that is world famous and which has contributed, in no small way, to strengthening bonds between military and civilian aviators across the globe, whilst furthering the understanding of the importance of military aviation to us all. There is also no doubt that the Air Tattoo has inspired many youngsters to pursue a career in aviation, whilst raising millions of pounds for its parent charities, nowadays the Royal Air Force Charitable Trust.

Clearly there is so much more to the airshow than the aircraft. The Air Tattoo team's proposed activities have to be agreed with the civil and military aviation authorities, and the list of overseas invitations to be extended cleared with the UK Foreign Office and its US counterparts; the showground and static aircraft park has to be designed and built, whilst satisfying rigorous health and safety and aviation regulations; external and internal traffic routings and management have to be co-ordinated with local authorities and have the support of the local community; security and emergency/safety plans need to be drawn up and agreed with numerous outside agencies; souvenirs, programmes and ticketing have to be designed and sourced; marketing and publicity material has to be designed and implemented; sponsorships, guest invitation and hosting arrangements managed; exhibiting facilities need to be sold and delivered; contracts for tents, toilets, showers, generators, cabins, fencing, trackway, PA systems, etc, have to be planned and agreed; thousands of cones laid out and roped together to a dynamic plan that changes day on day; a vast network of radios, telephones, wi-fi and computing facilities have to be installed; flying operations ops rooms and a flight centre have to be built and operated; risk assessments for all activities have to be undertaken; and budgeting and careful financial management and the welfare of everyone involved — their accommodation, feeding, transport and social facilities — taken care of. These are just some examples of the work the team has to undertake for the Air Tattoo every year. And of course, when the show is over, everything has to be dismantled quickly so that control of the airfield can be returned to the United States Air Force, our highly supportive and generous hosts of some 37 Air Tattoos since 1973.

So, as I write this foreword, I would like to convey my heartfelt thanks to everyone who makes this happen so efficiently year-on-year, including those behind the scenes such as our brilliant unpaid non-executive directors. My very best wishes also go to Paul Atherton, his fellow executive directors, Stu, Steve, Kate, Caroline and everyone on the permanent staff as they tirelessly work their way through all that COVID-19 is throwing at them, whilst setting off on the next 50 years of the Air Tattoo.

The Air Tattoo has created enduring friendships and touched so many people over the years. I am confident that this book will rekindle memories and demonstrate just how much has been achieved by what started out as a small acorn event just north of London that has now grown into an oak tree in the Cotswolds.

Tim Prince
Air Tattoo founder member and RIAT Honorary Vice-Patron

Contents

PHOTO: CAZ CASWELL/AIRTEAMIMAGES.COM

Introduction	4
Patron's Message	5
A Royal Tribute	6
A Very Special Thank You	7
Timeline: 50 Years of the Air Tattoo	8
1971-1979	**10-47**
1980-1989	**48-81**
1990-1999	**82-137**
2000-2009	**138-213**
2010-2020	**214-299**
RAFCTE Permanent Staff	300
Roll of Honour	302
Acknowledgements	304

Editor: David Higham
Author: Ben Dunnell
Assistant Editor: Graham Finch
Contributing Editors: Tim Prince, Ben Dunnell, Peter R March, David Halford
Design: Graham Finch Design

airtattoo.com

Introduction

It is a unique privilege to be the new Chairman of the RAF Charitable Trust, the parent charity of RAF Charitable Trust Enterprises and the Royal International Air Tattoo, and I am immensely grateful to my predecessor, Sir Kevin Leeson, for his outstanding stewardship of the RAF Charitable Trust Group. During his tenure, we have collectively gone from strength to strength, staging the unique Air Tattoo that is known across the world while steadily increasing our charitable activity for the RAF and young people. Indeed, that record of success made the pandemic-induced cancellation of RIAT20 all the more difficult.

However, we have been working tirelessly to ensure that the Air Tattoo can return safely and that the essential work of the Trust can continue. We are now confident that RIAT21 will not just mark the return of the world's best air show, modified appropriately for these times, but that it will also be a fitting focus for our 50th Anniversary celebrations. This confidence comes from the hard work of many, many people from across our Group, and our volunteers and supporters. Of particular note has been the unstinting support of the RAF, the USAF, our other international partners, our major industry sponsors and of course our customers. To you all, I want to offer my sincere thanks and my heartfelt appreciation for your support during this difficult period.

We have also been looking to the future. Despite these challenging times, we have real ambition for the RAF Charitable Trust and the Air Tattoo. We want the Tattoo to continue to celebrate the history and present day achievements of the RAF, air power and aviation technology, while looking firmly to the future; to that end, we will increasingly embrace Space and sustainable aviation, as well as offering many more opportunities to take part in the RIAT experience. As importantly, we want to deepen our charitable work to not just promote and support the RAF, but to also really inspire young people to fulfil their potential in air and space, and hence supercharge their interest in the wonder of aviation.

The future of the Charity and the Air Tattoo is as compelling as our history, and we should celebrate both to the full during our 50th Anniversary.

Air Marshal Phil Osborn
Chairman, Royal Air Force Charitable Trust

Patron's message

I remember first visiting the International Air Tattoo when it was at RAF Greenham Common in the 1970s. Since then, I have enjoyed watching this incredible event grow in both size and stature. Not only does the airshow consistently feature an impressive range of international participation each year but also often stages unique and dramatic aerial set pieces that one would never see anywhere else.

Throughout its 50 years, the Air Tattoo has served to provide the focal point for national and global commemorations marking key RAF landmarks and anniversaries, most recently in 2018 when the Royal Air Force Centenary was celebrated at the airshow with an RAF Review and parade of the new Queen's Colour for the RAF in the United Kingdom.

The Air Tattoo has grown to become one of the world's greatest airshows, which also provides the main source of income for the RAF Charitable Trust, the newest member of the Royal Air Force's family of charities.

It was an honour to be asked in 2005 to become Patron of the Trust and, during the past 15 years, I have had the privilege to see first-hand the excellent work it does in promoting the Royal Air Force, most directly through the staging of the Air Tattoo. It is primarily through money raised by this event each year that the Trust has been in a position to support many initiatives and flying scholarships that have had such a significant and positive impact on people's lives.

Finally, much of the airshow's appeal and success is due to the dedication and hard work of the team of volunteers who each year come together from around the globe and from many different backgrounds. I warmly thank and commend all who have given their time to make the Air Tattoo one of the world's most thrilling aviation spectacles.

His Royal Highness The Duke of Kent KG
Patron, Royal International Air Tattoo and the Royal Air Force Charitable Trust

When two Pitt S-2A Specials, flying as the Royal Jordanian Falcons aerobatic team, displayed at RAF Greenham Common in 1979, it marked the start of a strong and enduring relationship between the Royal Jordanian Air Force and the Royal International Air Tattoo.

This friendship was a natural extension of the historical ties that existed between the Royal Air Force and the Hashemite Kingdom of Jordan. My late father was taught to fly by the RAF which also assisted in the formation of the Royal Jordanian Air Force in 1956.

Shortly after the death of Battle of Britain flying ace Sir Douglas Bader in 1982, my father took over as Air Tattoo President and I have many fond memories of attending the airshow both at Greenham Common and latterly RAF Fairford.

When the IAT Flying Scholarships scheme was set up in 1983 in honour of Sir Douglas, we were keen to join those helping to fund flying training for disabled people and I remember accompanying my family at the Air Tattoo to present wings to the latest group of disabled fliers.

Following my father's death in 1999, his wife Queen Noor then I proudly followed as Patron of the Flying Scholarships scheme (now Flying Scholarships for Disabled People) and it remains one of the highlights of my year to attend the Air Tattoo to continue the charity's excellent work and award scholars with their certificates and wings.

The Air Tattoo remains one of the most unique and exciting aviation spectacles held anywhere in the world bringing together first-class aviators in the spirit of friendship and collaboration. I remain proud of the small but precious part the Royal Jordanian Air Force – and my family – has played in the success of the Royal International Air Tattoo during the past half century.

His Royal Highness Prince Feisal Ibn Al-Hussein
Honorary Vice-Patron, Royal International Air Tattoo
Patron, Flying Scholarships for Disabled People

A Very Special Thank You

The Air Tattoo would not exist without the generous, unwavering and exceptional support of our sponsors and commercial customers. The show has attracted corporate participation from its very early years to the significant group of companies that we work with now that you see on this page. We are not a trade event and have worked hard to maintain the Air Tattoo's unique atmosphere. Bringing together the air chiefs of the world and our own senior military heads provides a hugely valuable environment for these critical stakeholders but above all, everyone who has come together over these July weekends comes to celebrate and bask in the spirit of aviation, past, present and future.

There are too many companies over fifty years to list all of them here but we would like to pay tribute to a few special cases. WD & HO Wills was the first commercial partner under its Embassy brand and the support continued for 30 years from its parent, Imperial Tobacco,

until legal restrictions forced the relationship to end. Marshall of Cambridge and Lockheed (now Lockheed Martin) came on board as the first aerospace sponsors in 1979 and their support continues, unfailingly, each year. They have been joined along the journey by Boeing, Northrop Grumman, Rolls-Royce, Airbus and all the others here.

Our non-executive board members have brought incredible support through their contacts and other 'hats', not least Lloyds, Nationwide, Alliance & Leicester, Victoria Wine and Ind Coope. Other companies with which we have had happy and successful relationships are Shell, TVS, SAGA, Waitrose, Serco and Mitel.

And finally, a very special tribute to our title sponsor, BAE Systems. As British Aerospace, the company became involved in 1991 and their long-term and multi-year contracts form the backbone of this extraordinary contribution.

BAE SYSTEMS

  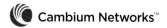 

Timeline: 50 Years of the Air Tattoo

1971

The beginning – First Air Tattoo held at North Weald.

1973

The Air Tattoo moves to Greenham Common.

1976

Sir Douglas Bader becomes President of IAT.

1983

Salute to Douglas Bader. Last IAT at Greenham Common.

1985

IAT moves to its new home at RAF Fairford.

1987

IAT Patron HM King Hussein of Jordan attends the 1987 event.

1990

Boscombe Down used for Battle of Britain 50th anniversary.

1991

Aircraft from the Eastern Bloc attend IAT for the first time.

1993

RAF's 75th anniversary. First appearance of Russian Tu-95 Bear.

1995

The Victory Airshow tribute and 'Theatre of the Air'.

1996

IAT celebrates its silver jubilee and gains royal assent.

1997

The Air Tattoo celebrates the USAF's 50th anniversary.

2000

RIAT moves temporarily to RAF Cottesmore.

2003

100 Years of Flight. Named world's largest military airshow.

2004

RIAT loses its founding father, Paul Bowen.

2005

The RAF Charitable Trust becomes RIAT's parent charity.

2008

RAF's 90th anniversary and first ever cancellation of show.

2014

Red Arrows 50th display season. Founder member Tim Prince retires.

2018

RAF100 — the RAF's flagship event — hosted by RIAT.

2020

RIAT hosts a 'Virtual' show due to the COVID-19 pandemic.

"Boy, we're

"Tim and I had seen a lot of airshows in England as spectators and we really felt, even at that stage in the early 1970s, that they needed some imagination and a whole new style."

PHOTO: DENIS J CALVERT

PHOTO: LINDSAY PEACOCK

'71

NORTH WEALD
31 MAY

out of our depth..."

That's what Tim Prince remembers thinking during Air Tattoo 71, when a new team of enthusiastic volunteers young and old came together at North Weald, Essex, to breathe new life into the Royal Air Forces Association (RAFA) South-Eastern Area's annual air display.

Hindsight shows us that Air Tattoo 71, the one that started it all, was amongst the most significant events in the more than century-long history of air displays. At the time, there were few overt thoughts of that. For Tim Prince, "just getting through the week safely was the key", but he acknowledges that his late colleague Paul Bowen, "very much a character who liked reaching for the stars" in Tim's words, may have thought differently. "Paul saw it as a great opportunity to do something special in life, and he was always looking for new ideas."

It was through Paul's father Pat Bowen that the two friends who went on to become the Air Tattoo's co-directors first got involved. "Paul and I had joined the Board of Trade as air traffic control cadets", recalls Tim. "At the end of our three-year 'sandwich course', we were posted to [the Aeroplane and Armament Experimental Establishment at] Boscombe Down, and Paul's father, who was a member of the South-Eastern Area of RAFA, asked for some help in the staging of this event at North Weald. They'd been running a show there, and they wanted a bit more help in general". What they got was rather more — a rejuvenated, revamped event, and the precursor to far bigger things.

The annual RAFA display on the Spring Bank Holiday Monday was generally dominated by British involvement, military and civilian. The RAF's support was paramount, both in terms of flying and static aircraft and provision of air traffic controllers for the tower. However, the shows were fairly limited in scope, and as a result did not generate a great deal of income for RAFA.

A key figure in changing that was Sqn Ldr Jack Currie DFC, a wartime Bomber Command veteran. As of 1970, he was employed as registrar of Nottingham College of Further Education, and was, in his own words, "rather bored" when he spotted an advertisement for the post of area secretary for RAFA's South-Eastern Area. He decided to apply, and was successful. Currie went along to the 1970 event at North Weald as an observer. He decided on a radical change of approach.

AIR TATTOO "71"

SOUVENIR PROGRAMME

NORTH WEALD

MONDAY

31st MAY, 1971

GATES OPEN 10.00 a.m.
DISPLAYS COMMENCE 11.00 p.m.
GATES CLOSE 8.00 p.m.

Organised by
THE
ROYAL AIR FORCES
ASSOCIATION

IN AID OF THE
R.A.F.A. WELFARE FUND
AND
SPONSORED BY
THE DAILY EXPRESS

"We have a slight problem with the French..." Famously, the Patrouille didn't much care for the accommodation they were offered in a disused barrack block.

"But all credit to the French; they flew a great display, as did everybody else, the crowds rolled in, and everyone was happy — including several chambermaids at the Harlow motel!"

Peter Bramley and his 'Follow Me' Land Rover.

Sqn Ldr Jack Currie, organising secretary (second from right), with colleagues.

"Being run by a volunteer group on a disused airfield was pretty much pioneering. I'm sure that if we tried to do it today, 'the system' would quickly find ways of saying 'no'!"

This was to involve putting together a volunteer team to run all aspects of the show that did not require the bringing-in of professional expertise. The enthusiasm of these volunteers would, he felt, be key to transforming the North Weald display's fortunes.

Under Currie's leadership as organising secretary, meetings of the first group of volunteers started to put together the 1971 show. They met in the conference room of St Margaret's Hospital in Epping, volunteer managers being appointed for the apron, public relations, the arena, trade and static displays and the like. Further like-minded helpers were brought in, and gradually the team grew. It was perhaps an unlikely combination, bringing together — amongst others — the RAFA team from Epping, Paul Bowen, Tim Prince, colleagues of theirs from Boscombe Down, fellow aviation enthusiasts and some of Paul's old school friends — but it worked.

To mark the show's 25th anniversary, Paul Bowen looked back on the Air Tattoo's genesis to *Aircraft Illustrated* writer Mark Ashley. "Tim and I had seen a lot of airshows in England as spectators", he said, "and we really felt, even at that stage in the early 1970s, that they needed some imagination and a whole new style. We saw the opportunities were there to provide an event that was much more involved in providing family entertainment. We followed the example of the major county shows in providing entertainment on the ground. Where the airshow was concerned we felt the international element was the key that would successfully change the style of the event."

PHOTO: DENIS J CALVERT

One of the first changes the team adopted was to introduce a new, distinctive name. "If my memory serves me well, it was Richard Holmes who suggested Air Tattoo to make it rather special — more than just another airshow", says Tim. The venue helped when it came to expanding the show's horizons, too. "Having it at North Weald, given its historical roots in the Battle of Britain and so on, meant that many saw it as a great opportunity to come back. So, the Dutch came, the French came, the Norwegians with their F-5s, and so on. This was

Spitfire LFIX MH434 provided perhaps the day's most spectacular individual display, flown by former Red Arrows leader Ray Hanna.

quite something, because when we invited them, perhaps without having the right authority to do so, they just turned up."

As for the venue, North Weald was still in Ministry of Defence ownership, but the former Battle of Britain fighter station near Epping had been kept in care and maintenance status for six years before the RAF moved out in 1964, and the site had fallen into increasing disuse by the time of that inaugural Air Tattoo. "Being run by a volunteer group on a disused airfield was pretty much pioneering", Tim reflects. "I'm sure that if we tried to do it today, 'the system' would find ways of quickly saying 'no'!"

As some of Tim's recollections of 1971 demonstrate, the infrastructure was far from ideal, even by the standards of the time. "I remember the General Post Office coming to install just two telephones, Epping 5010 and Epping 5020. Someone else turned up with a small suitcase that had two hand-portable radios in it, and that was it. There were no other radios. And I remember when the first aeroplanes landed, thinking, 'My goodness, we're now actually running an airfield as opposed to just being air traffic controllers', with the responsibility for fuel, aircraft start units, and all the rest of it.

"An ATC colleague from Boscombe Down, an assistant called Peter Bramley — no longer alive, sadly — was driving the 'follow me' truck, a rather tired Land Rover belonging to one of the RAFA guys who was a farmer, leading in the *Patrouille*

de France, and the door fell off the back. All very embarrassing. There was an excitement that we were in charge of something, because we didn't really know what we were in charge of..."

Sponsored by the *Daily Express*, Air Tattoo 71 opened at 10.00hrs on that Bank Holiday Monday. As Currie recalled, "Paul Bowen and Tim Prince had got a great programme together, we had cleared the runway and the peritrack, and cleaned one of the barrack blocks to accommodate the people flying in. Bob Basing was our engineering officer, Richard Holmes was in charge of reception, Paul's father Pat was on publicity, dear John Blake was on the microphone, and Bill Newby-Grant and Chris Hammerbeck were engaged in — well, I can't quite remember, but something really useful". There was plenty of time for visitors to explore the extensive range of ground attractions — this was, after all, a tattoo — before the flying started at 13.15.

The first act was a Seventies favourite. Born in the USA, Formula One air racing had been introduced to Britain the previous year. For 1971 there was to be a four-race season, with a trophy donated by Rolls-Royce, and its opening round was staged at the Air Tattoo. Joining the Rollason Betas and Cassutt Racers that had hitherto dominated proceedings, Ian McCowen had imported from America the first ever LeVier Cosmic Wind, *Little Toni*, while Farm Aviation's Owl Racer *Ricochet* was newly completed. McCowen finished first, being presented with the Duke of Edinburgh Trophy by RAFA South-Eastern Area president ACM Sir John Baker and

Jack Currie (in white jacket) with the Air Tattoo's original management team on the control tower at North Weald. Paul is to the right of Jack, and Paul's dad is third from the right.

actor Kenneth More. In contrast, the Owl Racer came to grief on its way home after the event, crashing into the Thames at Greenwich after a propeller failure tore the engine out, killing pilot P. T. Gent Eggert.

What of the rest of the show? The RAF provided solo appearances by a Lightning F1A, Nimrod MR1, Andover C1, Belfast C1, Britannia C1 and Comet C4, together with a four-strong Phantom FGR2 flypast and an air-to-air refuelling demonstration by a Victor K2 and two Lightning F6s. Two of the service's then current Jet Provost T5 teams, the *Gemini Pair* from No 3 Flying Training School at Leeming and the four-ship *Blades* of No 1 FTS at Linton-on-Ouse, were on the bill, as were the *Falcons* parachute team (jumping from an Argosy C1) and the Historic Aircraft Flight with Hurricane IIc LF363 and Spitfire PRXIX PM631. Their own routine aside, the *Gemini Pair*'s 'JPs' took part in a ground attack demonstration alongside members of the Royal Anglian Regiment supported by the Royal Armoured Corps Parachute Squadron. According to one period account, this didn't go quite according to plan: "the controller of the ground explosions was seen smouldering gently and shaking his fists as he emerged from his straw-bale command post". Another British military display team in the programme was the Army Air Corps' *Blue Eagles* with six Sioux AH1s.

A second Spitfire provided perhaps the day's most spectacular individual display, this being LFIX MH434 flown by former *Red Arrows* leader Ray Hanna. The New Zealander was then relatively new to Spitfire display flying, having begun his association with MH434 during 1970, but his show-closing aerobatic performance — many 'daisy-cutting' low passes included — was already setting the standard. Personal Plane Services' Fokker E.III replica represented the fighting machines of the previous world war, while the Old Warden-based Shuttleworth Collection offered some 1930s nostalgia with its Avro Tutor and Gloster Gladiator.

Overseas participation included a pair of Royal Norwegian Air Force F-5s (a single-seater for the flying and a two-seater on static display), a Royal Netherlands Air Force NF-5A, four Royal Danish Air Force A 35XD Drakens (one of which flew for the first time at a British event) with their support C-47 Skytrain, and the French Air Force *Patrouille de France* with its CM170 Magisters. US Air Force support, a central feature of the Air Tattoo's future, came courtesy of a four-ship F-4D Phantom flypast from the 81st Tactical Fighter Wing at RAF Bentwaters. Surpassing them all for rarity value, however, was the Austrian Air Force's first visit to a British display, with a Sikorsky S-65OE transport

helicopter. "They [the Austrians] came over out of novelty, I think, more than anything else", says Tim. "From that point we made some very good friendships. The nice thing was it was all very small, so there were barbecues, there was drinking, and we were all pioneering together."

Famously, the *Patrouille* didn't much care for the accommodation they were offered in a disused barrack block. In the official book published in 1996 to celebrate 25 years of the Air Tattoo, Jack Currie recounted the tale of how aircrew reception manager Richard Holmes (later famous as a military historian, not least for his *War Walks* television series, and as a brigadier) "strolled into my office. 'We have a slight problem', he told me, 'with the French...' The team manager was a captain, who spoke a little English, and we contrived to reach an understanding. It amounted to this — no VIP accommodation, no display. Well, I was on a budget, as we always were, but what's money, after all? I took Richard aside. 'Call the motel in Harlow', I said, 'and lay on a coach'... When the Austrians came in, we wondered what their reaction to the barrack block might be. We need not have worried: 'We are soldiers', said their leader, 'and we sleep where we are put'. We all

Air Tattoo Memories: Peter R. March

Peter March has been a volunteer since the first Air Tattoo at North Weald, editor of the show programme from 1973 until 2013, and is still a member of the RIAT photo team.

Aviation photo-journalist Peter March had applied to publicity officer Pat Bowen for press accreditation on behalf of *Aircraft Illustrated* magazine and, suitably impressed by the rarities on show, was photographing away happily during the flying display. Then, Peter recalls, "Paul Bowen arrived in a Land Rover and invited me to go with him to the north side of the airfield where the Drakens were parked. That was my first meeting with Paul, whose title then was air operations manager. I got some very nice pictures, including memorable ones for me of Ray Hanna in Spitfire MH434. Subsequently, Pat Bowen 'phoned me up and asked me if I'd be prepared to let them have some of the photos I'd taken, because they didn't have a photographer there of their own. I did, and they soon invited me to become their photographer at the next Air Tattoo". Having stayed in this role, and fulfilled many others over the years, Peter became the only member of the North Weald volunteer team to still be with the show following Tim Prince's retirement in 2014.

SEVEN AIR FORCES SHOW OFF THEIR TALENT

THE flying display, which was truly international, was among the best seen at North Weald.

Seven foreign air forces were originally expected to participate but the Belgian aerobatics team did not get as far as the final flying programme.

The Royal Netherlands Air Force Freedom fighter did not fly in the display, but was on show in the static aircraft park. The French, Austrian, Danish, American and Norwegian air forces were also represented, as well as our own RAF and Army Air Corps.

For the first time ever there was an air race round a course bordering that part of the airfield in front of the crowd, and this extended the flying programme to something like four and a half hours.

Following the first two heats of the Formula I air race, the aerial show proper opened with the Patrouille de France aerobatics team of the French Air Force. The nine blue Fouga Magisters provided a spectacular 20-minute opening and their close-knit formations equalled anything performed by the RAF's famous Black Arrows and Red Arrows teams of previous years.

The mirror formation, in which one aircraft flies inverted just above another, was shown to perfection by the French and, later, by the Gemini Pair, two Jet Provosts from RAF Training Command. The French pair even executed a slow roll without breaking their mirror formation.

Another aerobatics display was provided by the Blades—four Jet Provosts from RAF Linton.

The Royal Danish Air Force sent four Saab Drakens, but only one was flown during the display. It was the first public appearance of the Swedish designed Draken, which is capable of flying at twice the speed of sound, and from the noise it made it was probably just as well that the other three stayed on the ground.

Almost as noisy were the Phantom ground attack fighters demonstrated by the American Air Force and the RAF. Coming in close third was the Freedom fighter of the Royal Norwegian Air Force.

In contrast, the vintage aircraft of yesteryear brought back nostalgic memories for many of the days when aircraft pop-popped along at speeds now common on the roads.

The most interesting of these—although she was not a genuine "oldie" but a replica with a modern engine—was the Fokker Eindekker. It was this aircraft that gave the Germans command of the skies in 1915—although, set against today's 1,000 mph flying armouries, it looked pretty impotent as it chugged along at all of 50 mph !

Of more modern vintage were the Avro Tutor trainer and Gloster Gladiator fighter from the Shuttleworth Collection—and, of course, the Spitfire and Hurricane.

A Spitfire, flown by Ray Hanna, a former leader of the RAF's Red Arrows aerobatics team, later showed off its beautiful lines in a solo aerobatics spot.

There were plenty of helicopters, from the Sioux light observation "choppers" of the Army Air Corps Blue Eagles display team to the CH53A Sea Stallion of the Austrian Air Force, one of the largest helicopters in the world.

The RAF demonstrated the Andover, Comet, Britannia, Nimrod, Wessex helicopter, and, its biggest aircraft, the 100-ton Belfast.

A Victor bomber and two Lightning fighters of RAF Strike Command also demonstrated in-flight refuelling—although this was not so much a demonstration as a slow fly-past.

The RAF's parachute display team, the Falcons, gave its usual immaculate display of controlled descent, the 11 parachutists showing that with modern equipment, and particularly in Monday's ideal conditions, it is possible to land on a sixpence (or even a new halfpenny) from 5,000 feet.

The grand finale—before the final of the air race—was a tactical assault and ground attack demonstration by the Royal Anglian Regiment, supported by Ferret scoutcars and two Jet Provosts, which produced a lot of smoke and pyrotechnics even if the tactics were a little obscure.

■ Organising secretary Squadron Leader Jack Currie with two attractive air hostesses.   ★(161)

The greatest aeroplane in the world — and he should know!

THE appearance of the Spitfire must have brought back memories for many people at the show and not the least of these was ex-Luftwaffe pilot Anton Honniger. For Herr Honniger had the misfortune to be shot down, not once, not twice, but seven times by Spitfires during the last war.

Herr Honniger, along with about 20 of his police colleagues from Freiburg and their wives and families, visited the show during an International Police Federation-sponsored trip to this country.

"Seeing the Spitfire really made his day," said one of the Romford policemen who were acting as hosts to the German party. "When it came over he was clapping his hands and saying 'There goes the greatest aeroplane in the world.' He was really chuffed."

After being shot down for the seventh and final time in the Middle East, Herr Honniger was taken prisoner and sent to a PoW camp in Canada and later to England. On this occasion there were 170 bullet holes in his plane.

Following the visit to the show, the German party were entertained at a social at Harlow police station where Herr Honniger received and accepted a dinner invitation for Wednesday from Special Constable Harry Matthews of 42 Pennymead, Harlow, who was an RAF wireless operator during the war.

Profit and loss

THREE stalls selling hot dogs and coke had their profits cut.

During the afternoon two of the stalls were slit open at the back and bowls containing the takings were raided. A hand appeared through the join in the material at the back of a third stall—and disappeared with the bowl and all its contents.

The total haul, the property of PC Catering of Oxford was around £145.

HIGH FLYING

JOY FLYING moved into the big time this year with flights in a Viscount airliner of Channel Airways and two BEA Ferranti helicopters.

The helicopter flights were "high" and of very short duration, but there seemed no shortage of passengers at £2 a head (£1.50 for children).

For a family of four—Mum, Dad and two children—the bill for a two minute trip over the car park was £7.

A bit cheaper, and much better value, was the 7-8 minute flight in the Viscount, which cost £1.25.

■ Fighters, transports, helicopters, bombers . . . just a few of the many aircraft that took part in the display.
★ (163, 164, 165, 166, 167)

50 LOST CHILDREN

THE Essex Police mobile caravan reported a "huge trade" in lost children.

"We have had more than 50 of them lost and claimed, and two children have been here all day" said a policewoman.

"It seemed to work out that those parents who came to report a missing child hadn't had their child brought in and the children already here just were not being claimed."

But by 7pm only a handful of unclaimed children remained including the two who had watched the day's events from the inside of the caravan.

THE LARGEST

SPECTATORS were able to go inside and inspect the largest aircraft on display, a Canadair CL 44 of Trans Meridian Airways.

There was also a model aircraft exhibition of more than 150 planes made by three enthusiasts from Farnborough, and these filled a marquee.

---

liked the Austrians. But all credit to the French; they flew a great display, as did everybody else, the crowds rolled in, and everyone was happy — including, as I gathered, several chambermaids at the Harlow motel!"

Apart from the need to give the *Patrouille de France* a decent bed for the night, what lessons did Tim learn from that first Air Tattoo? "Get sleep when you can, because you're effectively on duty all the time. There was no-one we could hand over to. We were all there whether it was the team running aircrew reception, looking after accommodation, flight operations, air traffic — you had to be ready to catch whatever fast ball came your way.

"Because we were relying very much on the goodwill of others, there was one aircraft start unit for the whole lot, and as the show finished, the battery went flat before the last F-5 got out. It was a matter then of contacts, so the biggest lesson to me out of all of that was to never make enemies, but always make friends, because you never know when you might need to pick up the 'phone and say, 'Hey, OC engineering wing at Wattisham, can I borrow an aircraft start unit? I'll come and pick it up in my Ford Escort', or whatever."

Air Tattoo 71 had been a learning experience for everyone, and a very positive one. Best of all, perhaps, it generated a net profit of £10,413 for RAFA, a new record for the North Weald display. Clearly the crowds had not been put off by "a substantial increase in admission charges" — rather, they had proved willing to pay more in order to see an event of demonstrably greater quality. In its annual report, the South-Eastern Area branch said it had been "the most successful" show in its history, one that halted "the decline in public attendance which had been noticed over recent years". In many ways, the die had been cast and the groundwork laid for the growth of the Air Tattoo.

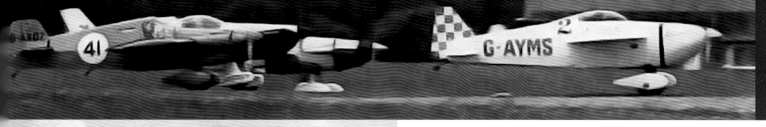

PHOTO: DENIS J CALVERT

AIR DISPLAY REPORT

Policy Committee: Air Chief Marshal Sir John W. Baker, Air Marshal Sir Edouard Grundy, Mr A. R. Kendrick, Mr T. V. McGarey, Mr. R. A. F. Collins, Mr. D. Willis.

The decline in public attendance which had been noticed over recent years was halted by Air Tattoo 71 at North Weald on 31st May. Despite a substantial increase in admission charges, income from all sources more than trebled that of 1970. The Area Council's decisions a) to employ professional agencies throughout the public control functions, and b) to detail the management of the display to a local working committee under the directions of the Area Secretary, were amply justified by results.

The publicity campaign went as planned, and received a high level of support from the Daily Express, the Evening Standard, the local press and cinemas, London Transport, trade journals, R.A.F.A. C.H.Q. and Branches, and Eastern Area Headquarters.

The air traffic control tower was manned by a professional control team working voluntarily, and provided by the R.A.F. with full communications and control facilities. A barrack block and the mess were reactivated, furnished and equipped. A service apron with refuelling, start-up and basic servicing facilities was developed. A static aircraft park, a trade display and a ground arena were established. Security, crash, medical and catering organisations were set up.

Aircraft from Norway, Austria, Denmark, France, the Netherlands and the U.K. arrived and rehearsed during 28th, 29th and 30th May. On 31st May alone, 260 aircraft movements took place on the airfield. The flying display ran non-stop from 1315 to 1830 hrs with 29 items, including the heats and final of the Formula One Air Race for the Duke of Edinburgh and Daily Express Trophies, formation aerobatics by La Patrouille de France, the Gemini Pair, the Blades, and the Blue Eagles, demonstration by the Fokker Eindekker replica, the Shuttleworth Collection Avro Tutor and Gloster Gladiator, the giant Austrian Sikorsky helicopter, R.A.F. and U.S.A.F. Phantoms, the Norwegian Freedom Fighter, the Danish Saab Draken, the breathtaking free-fall act of the Falcons, the tactical assault and battle-scene, and the brilliant solo aerobatics of Ray Hanna's Spitfire.

Meanwhile, in the ground arena, performances were given by the Royal Military Police, with their magnificent tent-pegging display on horseback and motor-cycle, and by the R.A.F. Central Band and Queen's Colour Squadron detachment; the arena entertainments also included an A.T.C. Assault Course competition and a motor-cycle display by 64 Squadron A.T.C.

PHOTO: DENIS J CALVERT

PHOTO: DAVID WHITWORTH

Operations team and participants at North Weald (Tim Prince at left).

Building a reputation

With a year's experience under the team's collective belt, it was back to North Weald for Air Tattoo 72, but this time the Spring Bank Holiday weather was nowhere near as favourable. In fact it was downright poor.

Nevertheless, an excellent show was put on, again featuring some very rare foreign visitors. Already, the airshow was building a reputation for attracting the new and unusual. The Austrian Air Force was back, giving a UK debut display with a Saab 105OE as well as the return of an S-65OE, while the Belgian Air Force *Diables Rouges* team of Magisters made its first Air Tattoo visit, the Royal Netherlands Air Force flew an NF-5A and the Royal Netherlands Navy an SP-13A Atlantic. US military support was strong, with a refuelling demo by an HC-130N and HH-53C from the USAF's 67th Aerospace Rescue and Recovery Squadron at Woodbridge, very seldom-seen displays by a US Army OV-1B Mohawk and CH-54A Tarhe, and a US Navy C-1A Trader in the static park. Adding to the mix, there were even flying appearances from a Britannia Airways Boeing 737-200 and a Transmeridian Air Cargo CL-44D — civil airliners and freighters have always been an occasional feature of the Tattoo line-up.

The 1972 show also introduced an innovation. One of the Air Tattoo's first commercial sponsors was W. D. & H. O. Wills, part of the Imperial Tobacco group, which agreed to sponsor the Embassy Trophy for

the best solo jet aerobatic display. Fg Off Rod Dean from No 79 Squadron, RAF took the spoils for his dashing routine in a Hunter F6. "I think it was my second or third display", says Rod. "I've still got the silver salver. My fondest recollection was of the late Russ Pengelly, a lovely man, who displayed the Lightning at the same show but not operating out of North Weald as the runway wasn't long enough. He flew after me, and I thought that he would win it, because I'd heard by then that there was a trophy going. The sight that's stayed with me is Russ coming along on his final run, pulling up into the vertical in full reheat and disappearing into the biggest, blackest thunderstorm you've ever seen in your life..."

No fewer than three RAF Jet Provost displays might be considered excessive, but the returning *Gemini Pair*, the four T5s of the Central Flying School's *Red Pelicans* and a singleton T3, also from the CFS, put on contrasting performances. Being operated from RAF Waddington prior to allocation to the Battle of Britain Flight, Lancaster I PA474 made the first of countless Air Tattoo appearances. Again there was a Formula One air race, and again it was won by Ian McCowen aboard Cosmic Wind *Little Toni*. The day was a good one for rotary-wing participants to show their versatility in the face of the elements, a particular star being Maj Mike Somerton-Rayner of the Army Air Corps in his privately owned Skeeter AOP12.

For some of the Air Tattoo team, there were — as unthinkable as it seems today — opportunities to get airborne in visiting military aircraft. On the rehearsal day, a large group went aloft in the Dutch Atlantic, a sortie which began, according to Bill Newby-Grant in his 1983 book *Air Tattoo*, with "a take-off with a gusting 35-knot cross-wind and included a close survey of the 620 feet tall masts of the nearby aerial array". Paul Bowen said, "We found ourselves hurtling low-level across Epping Forest, doing simulated anti-submarine-style attacks on vehicles driving along the A11!"

Even more memorable was the offer by the US Army CH-54 crew, from the

Embassy Solo Jet Aerobatic Trophy winner, Rod Dean.

"The sight that's stayed with me is Russ coming along on his final run, pulling up into the vertical in full reheat and disappearing into the biggest, blackest thunderstorm you've ever seen in your life..."

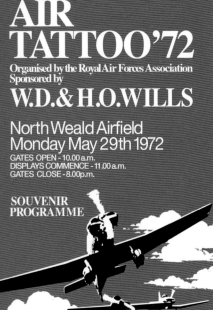

AIR TATTOO '72

Organised by the Royal Air Forces Association
Sponsored by

W.D.& H.O.WILLS

North Weald Airfield
Monday May 29th 1972

GATES OPEN - 10.00 a.m.
DISPLAYS COMMENCE - 11.00 a.m.
GATES CLOSE - 8.00p.m.

SOUVENIR PROGRAMME

PHOTOS: DAVID WHITWORTH

FLYING PROGRAMME

AIR TATTOO 72

Commences 12.30.   Finishes 18.15

Item	DISPLAY

1. W.D. & H.O. Wills Formula 1 Air Race—Heat.
2. B.A.C. 1-11—Flypast.
   Court Lines, Luton Airport.
3. Blue Eagles—Display Team.
   6 Sioux Helicopters of the Army Air Corps, Middle Wallop.
4. Hawker Tom Tit—Demonstration.
   Shuttleworth Trust, Old Warden Airfield.
5. Morane N—Demonstration.
   Personal Plane Services, Wycombe Air Park.
6. Hawker Sea Fury and Fairey Swordfish—Demonstration.
   R.N.A.S. Yeovilton.
7. Sikorsky S.62—Helicopter Demonstration.
   Austrian Air Force.
8. Westland Puma—Helicopter Demonstration.
   33 Squadron, Royal Air Force.
9. Red Pelicans—Aerobatic Display Team.
   Central Flying School, Royal Air Force.
10. Saab 105—Aerobatic Display.
    Austrian Air Force.
11. Saunders-Roe Skeeter—Helicopter Demonstration.
    Major Somerton-Rayner.
12. Les Diables Rouges—Aerobatic Display Team.
    7th Squadron, Royal Belgian Air Force.
13. Spitfire and Hurricane—Demonstration.
    Battle of Britain Flight, Royal Air Force.
14. North American Harvard—Demonstration.
    Mr. Bevan of Strathair.
15. Short Skyvan—Demonstration.
    Mr. Warner of Short Bros. & Harland.
16. Gemini Pair—Synchro Aerobatic Display.
    Flying Training Command, Royal Air Force.
17. The Falcons—Free-fall Parachute Display Team.
    No. 1 Parachute Training School, Royal Air Force.

18. Lockheed C130K Hercules—Demonstration.
    Air Support Command, Royal Air Force.
19. Avro Vulcan—Demonstration.
    Strike Command, Royal Air Force.
20. Northrop F5A Freedom Fighter—Aerobatic Display.
    332 Squadron, Royal Norwegian Air Force.
21. De Havilland Chipmunk—Aerobatic Display.
    Central Flying School, Royal Air Force.
22. Bristol Britannia—Demonstration.
    Air Support Command, Royal Air Force.
23. Grumman Mohawk 0P-1—Demonstration.
    122 Aviation Company, United States Army Air Force.
24. Four McDonald F4E Phantoms—Flypast.
    92 Squadron, 81st Tactical Fighter Wing, United States Air
    Force.
25. Avro Lancaster—Demonstration.
    Strike Command, Royal Air Force.
26. D. H. Vampire and Gloster Meteor—Demonstration.
    Central Flying School, Royal Air Force.
27. Hawker Siddeley Nimrod—Demonstration.
    Strike Command, Royal Air Force.
28. Canadair NF5A Freedom Fighter—Aerobatic Display.
    315 Squadron, Royal Netherlands Air Force.
29. Breguet SP13A Atlantic—Demonstration.
    321 Squadron, Royal Netherlands Navy.
30. Lockheed C130H Hercules and Sikorsky HH53D—In-flight
    refuelling Demonstration.
    67th Aerospace Rescue and Recovery Squadron, United
    States Air Force.
31. B.A.C. Lightning—Aerobatic Display.
    Strike Command, Royal Air Force.
32. Hawker Hunter—Solo Aerobatics.
    229 O.C.U., Royal Air Force.
33. B.A.C. Jet Provost TMK5—Aerobatic Display.
    Central Flying School, Royal Air Force.
34. Tactical Assault Demonstration.
    5th Royal Anglian Regt., supported by 332 Squadron, Royal
    Norwegian Air Force.
35. Supermarine Spitfire Mk. 9—Aerobatic Display.
    Squadron Leader Ray Hanna.
36. W.D. & H.O. Wills Formula 1 Air Race.

This programme was correct on going to press on Wednesday,
24th May. The Organisers cannot guarantee the accuracy on
the actual day.

Air Tattoo Memories: Bill Newby-Grant

Bill was reception manager from 1971-74 and then facilities manager in 1976.

Among Bill's many happy memories as an IAT volunteer, he fondly remembers a couple of occasions... "Having adopted the callsign Merlin for our Collie cross dog to include him in the proceedings, he graced the tower and went flying in several aircraft in the run-up to the display at North Weald. His name did not celebrate the engine as much as the fact that Rolls-Royce was in straitened times in the early seventies, and I believe the callsign is still used at RIAT. Talking of dogs, Chris Hammerbeck's spaniel, Willie, lived with Richard Holmes and me in one of the small cabins in one of the blocks there. Richard got up and put his foot in what Willie had produced during the night — which enlivened the start to the day somewhat! Happy memories."

295th Aviation Company at Mainz-Finthen, to go flying the day after the show. Newby-Grant wrote, "a number of the organisers — including as many of the crash rescue crews as could fit into it — were taken for a flight in the Crane's vast underslung container, and their pale faces could be seen at the small window by the two more cunning organisers who flew in the main body of the machine, which, incidentally, seemed almost as insecure". Newby-Grant was one of that pair, Paul Bowen the other. What's more, as Bowen recalled to *Aircraft Illustrated's* Mark Ashley in 1996, the CH-54 was involved in a 'race' with an F-4 Phantom. "On the party night after the show they had taken on a bet with the Phantom crew that they could get to 10,000ft faster than the F-4 — and they would take on board 40 passengers at the same time... We beat the Phantom to 10,000ft! It was just a vertical up-lift. But in the cab we found this big red handle which said, 'Pod Jettison'. I will always remember Tim's face in the pod when Bill kept moving his hands towards the handle!"

Despite the far worse weather, Air Tattoo 72 made as much money for RAFA as had the 1971 event, and attracted a crowd in the region of 14,000. There had been difficulties, not least the continued deterioration of North Weald's airfield surfaces and traffic congestion at the end of the day, but nothing that couldn't be examined and overcome. "The team had shaken down into a happy and effective group", Newby-Grant recalled, "and there seemed no reason to stop organising shows now that its abilities had been proved. Besides, for all the hectic nature of the events and the countless hours spent trying to forestall potential problems and resolve actual ones, the whole thing was fun". Has there ever been a better description of the Air Tattoo's ethos?

The pattern for future events was apparently set, but they would not be held at North Weald. As Tim Prince says, "They were building the M11 across the end, and the Kia-Ora Café was about to disappear. It was our place of sustenance during the show. The M11 made us think that it wasn't possible to continue. We looked at many possible venues. Of course, what we wanted was someone to give us free rein. Although going to a disused airfield was ideal in

> "A number of the organisers — including as many of the crash rescue crews as could fit into it — were taken for a flight in the Crane's vast underslung container."

some respects, because there was no kit there it was a bit of a nightmare". The list included such places as Bournemouth Hurn (apparently an especially serious contender), Dunsfold, Manston, Odiham, Tangmere, Thorney Island and West Malling. But prospects looked rather better, says Tim, "when we came to Greenham Common, which was under the control of the USAF's 7551st Combat Support Group as a stand-by base, with the 'Busy Brewer' B-52 deployment arrangements and an airfield that was in very good order with a hangar full of what they call war readiness materiel, all the aircraft start units and the other kit you need, and a willing commander who saw it as an opportunity to turn the base over and keep the place working well."

Bill Newby-Grant recounted how, "After listening to an outline of the aims and scope of the proposed future displays for some twenty minutes", the base commander "nodded his consent, and with one word — 'Sure' — began the long and happy association between the Tattoo Team and Greenham Common". Its vast expanses would permit the Air Tattoo to grow beyond the hopes of its founders — even, perhaps, those of Paul Bowen. But it is no cliché to say that the first two years at North Weald had laid the foundations.

The pattern for future events was set, but they would not be held at North Weald.

Goodwood Air Show
19 August 1972

The aerodrome at the old Goodwood racing circuit, the former RAF Westhampnett, was the scene of two shows staged by the Air Tattoo team under Jack Currie. "South-East Area RAFA saw the opportunity", remembers Tim Prince. "Jack Currie lived down that way and asked whether we'd like to do it". The 1972 event, on Sunday 19 August, raised funds for both RAFA and the Johnnie Johnson Housing Trust, the organisation set up by the wartime fighter pilot to provide housing for elderly and disabled people.

"They were exciting times", Tim continues, "because we used the Air Tattoo contacts we'd made to get more participants, and having the likes of the Belgian Air Force F-104 team, the *Slivers*, doing opposition passes over a grass strip was a challenge. I remember they practised about four times, and on every one of those practices there were panic calls: 'Knock it off, knock it off!'" The *Slivers*, a two-ship of 350 Squadron F-104Gs, were unquestionably among the most exciting acts of the era, yet this was their only appearance at an Air Tattoo-organised show. Four more Starfighters came from the Canadian Forces, the CF-104s recalling the fact that 'Johnnie' Johnson had commanded No 127 (Canadian) Wing at Westhampnett during 1944. The *Red Arrows* headed the RAF line-up, Hawker Siddeley displayed second pre-production Harrier GR1 XV277, and the USAF sent a 20th TFW F-111E from Upper Heyford — there was plenty of heavy military metal over the historic aerodrome. The Battle of Britain Flight Lancaster, Hurricane and Spitfire IIa, and Adrian Swire's Spitfire IX, supplied the wartime element.

For the Air Tattoo volunteers involved, Goodwood was something different. "That was fun", Tim reflects, "with Lord March, and all the volunteers living in the stable lads' quarters where the beds were too short. I have fond memories of the AOC [air officer commanding] of 38 Group arriving in his Devon and me clearing him to do a land-after the Harvard ahead of him — I was still doing air traffic at that time, to help keep the team small — and the Harvard decided to stop, so the Devon burst its nosewheel tyre."

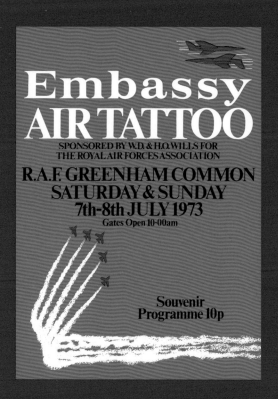

73

GREENHAM COMMON
7 & 8 JULY

The first two years at North Weald had been fun. They had certainly been pioneering. But the move to RAF Greenham Common and the expansion to a two-day format truly allowed the Air Tattoo — now, formally, the Embassy Air Tattoo, thanks to the continued sponsorship from W. D & H. O. Wills — to develop into the event we know today. Indeed, by being staged on a vast US Air Force base with acres of hardstanding on which to park aircraft, it set the pattern that has remained virtually the same ever since.

Tim Prince says the team realised it had "struck gold" at Greenham Common. "There was a very small team of people keeping the base going on a care and maintenance basis, but they were all characters, from the base commander, Col Blanton, to the comms squadron. The essential trust came very quickly, even though they didn't know us. To me, it was just like being given Boscombe Down. I was used to being a long-haired air traffic controller at Boscombe with loads of people above me in the chain, and somehow Paul, myself, [administration director] Frank Windle and others were running an airfield just like that for a week of the year. It was a feeling of awesome power, I suppose — but feeling slightly guilty about it at the same time."

But the 'can-do' enthusiasm of the volunteers would be required in quantity. From an operational standpoint, the highly secretive Atomic Weapons Research Establishment at Aldermaston was an issue. It lay just five miles east, and could not be overflown, except by USAF B-52s on occasional exercise deployments. And while Greenham Common may have offered a long runway, good access and huge amounts of apron space, much of the empty on-base accommodation was being used until just a few weeks before the show as a resettlement camp for Ugandan Asians expelled by Idi Amin's regime. Air Tattoo participants had to be put up at Aldermaston and Lyneham and bussed in. When more personnel arrived with the aircraft than had been expected, and vehicles hired for aircrew transport broke down, a small logistical nightmare resulted, but as always the public went unaware. Wrote Peter March in *Aircraft Illustrated*, "come Saturday morning the sun shone, the ground display and static park were ready and thirty minutes ahead of time the gates had to be opened to let the already large crowd enter". Once in, it was a familiar story — all the difficulties kept firmly behind the scenes, and on with a great show.

The 1970s Air Tattoos at Greenham very much captured the spirit of the time. This was a gathering of NATO aviators enjoying themselves, their flying relatively unencumbered by restrictions. In the Canadian Forces' five-ship of CF-104s from 421 Squadron at Baden-Söllingen, West Germany, there was in 1973 perhaps the perfect expression of the new Greenham era, with loud, low passes by these quintessential Cold War jets. Paul Bowen, whose favourite aircraft was the Starfighter, must have loved it. After a very close call with a glider over the nearby Inkpen Ridge, one of the Canadian pilots perhaps didn't...

Another of the performers most associated with the early '70s events made its first appearance in the five-hour programme, namely a KC-97L from the 126th Air Refueling Squadron, Wisconsin Air National Guard. It was over in Europe for a 'Creek Party' deployment to Rhein-Main. The other American military rarity in the flying was a US Army helicopter set-piece, courtesy of elements stationed in West Germany. A CH-54A returned to show its truck-lifting capabilities, joined by a CH-47A Chinook, UH-1H Iroquois, AH-1G Cobra and OH-58A Kiowa.

New this time was the French Navy, with displays from an F-8E(FN) Crusader, Étendard IVP and SP-2H Neptune. Never exactly a common

> The move to RAF Greenham Common and the expansion to a two-day format truly allowed the Air Tattoo to develop into the event we know today.

"The next morning, the pilot came in to take the aeroplane home — I asked him to come in and sit down, gave him a cup of coffee and told him the story..."

sight, the pugnacious Vought carrier fighter, on this occasion supplied by Flottille 14F at Landivisiau, gave occasional sparkling performances for more than a quarter of a century. West German support was notably extensive, the Luftwaffe offering no fewer than four flying items — F-104G, Fiat G91R, RF-4E and T-33A, the latter, from Waffenschule 10 at Jever, very rare even then — and the Marineflieger two, namely Atlantic and F-104G. Winner of the Embassy Solo Jet Aerobatic Trophy was Flt Lt W. Tyndall flying a Jet Provost T5. Strong competition once more came from No 79 Squadron's Rod Dean, flying a 'clean' Hunter F6 for the only time in an effort to defend his crown.

Sadly, one aircraft wouldn't make it home. Tim says why: "We had a Territorial Army unit who wanted to come and show off their skills, so they were our security force. One night, some of these troops had seen what they thought was an intruder near a Sea King, and they drove at speed to get there. In so doing, they went in their Land Rover through some crowd barriers — we had no lighting on the ramp — and hit the wing of a beautiful Sea Vixen [FAW2 XJ572 from the Royal Naval Air Yard Sydenham Station Flight] and wrote it off. The next morning, which was the Monday, the pilot came in to take the aeroplane home — I asked him to come in and sit down, gave him a cup of coffee and told him the story..."

The Embassy Air Tattoo 73 raised some £13,000 for RAFA, showing that the move from Essex to Berkshire, and thus the change to the show's audience catchment area, had worked. More importantly, the relationship with the US Air Force was sealed. Together, it and the Air Tattoo made for excellent partners.

The 1970s Air Tattoos at Greenham very much captured the spirit of the time. This was a gathering of NATO aviators enjoying themselves, their flying relatively unencumbered by restrictions.

Left: Air Tattoo operations team (Paul Bowen pictured at left).

Goodwood Air Show 27 August 1973

The August Bank Holiday Monday was the date for the second Goodwood show put on by the Air Tattoo volunteers. The weather failed to smile on their endeavours, but 16,000 people watched a very diverse flying programme — its highlights included the return of a Canadian Forces CF-104 four-ship team from 421 Squadron, the very rare sight of an AV-8A Harrier being demonstrated by Hawker Siddeley before delivery to the US Marine Corps, and the two-seat Spitfire VIII Trainer G-AIDN, then owned by John Fairey and Tim Davies. However, this was the last such event at the West Sussex aerodrome; Bill Newby-Grant recounted that "fuel restrictions and the proximity to the Farnborough Air Show" were cited as the reasons it wasn't repeated in 1974.

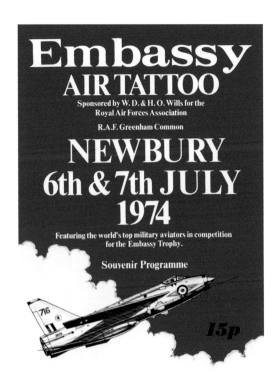

Embassy AIR TATTOO

Sponsored by W. D. & H. O. Wills for the
Royal Air Forces Association

R.A.F. Greenham Common

NEWBURY
6th & 7th JULY
1974

Featuring the world's top military aviators in competition
for the Embassy Trophy.

Souvenir Programme

15p

74

GREENHAM COMMON
6 & 7 JULY

The Cold War years were great times in which to put on a military airshow. Air displays were seen by NATO's air arms — far less budget-constrained, and far larger, than they are now — as a means of showing the Alliance's capabilities to the public while also sending out an important message regarding those capabilities to the Warsaw Pact. "The thing we adopted very early on when we went to Greenham Common was calling it a NATO gathering of military aviators, and that NATO 'hook' really made a huge difference", Tim Prince recalled.

Yet this didn't mean that the Air Tattoo's young organisers, not then going through official channels, were averse to inviting non-NATO air arms — even including their primary adversaries. Sponsors W. D. & H. O. Wills were, says long-time Air Tattoo team member Peter March, "very keen on competitions", and so the Embassy Trophy for best solo jet display was a prominent feature. In typically breathless tabloid fashion, this was how the *Daily Mail* described the diplomatic faux pas that came to light in April 1974:

"The Ministry of Defence has shot down a plan to allow Russia's famous MiG fighters to zoom over a top-secret nuclear weapons base. Other teams from Hungary, Czechoslovakia and Poland had otherwise been invited.

Mr Peter March, a spokesman from the association's Bristol office, said last night: 'It would have been the most sensational air display ever seen in this country and the first time anyone here had seen MiGs in action, but we were called in to a top-level meeting with RAF chiefs and told we couldn't go ahead. Now we are having to write and tell all the Iron Curtain countries the invitations are withdrawn. It's very embarrassing. We certainly reckon we will have lost about £12,000 as a result of this decision'."

THE TIMES WEDNESDAY APRIL 10 1974

Communists barred from jet contest

By Henry Stanhope
Defence Correspondent

Plans to invite communist countries to take part in the first World Jet Aerobatics Championships in Britain this summer have had to be dropped after objections by the Ministry of Defence.

The venue for the championships is to be RAF Greenham Common, a few miles from the top-secret Atomic Weapons Research Establishment (AWRE) at Aldermaston, Berkshire.

Airmen from Germany, Austria, The Netherlands, Denmark and the United States have said they will take part in the championships, which are organized by the Royal Air Force Association and sponsored by the Embassy cigarettes division of W. D. and H. O. Wills.

The RAFA will have to tell the authorities in Hungary, Czechoslovakia, Poland and the Soviet Union that invitations to them have had to be withdrawn.

The event, previously known as the Embassy Jet Aerobatics Championships was held at Greenham Common for the first time last year. No objections were raised because only

Nato and Commonwealth air forces took part.

Embassy said: "The RAFA then made £12,000 for RAFA charities and by making it a worldwide event open to all-comers, was hoping to double that figure this year.

"We were under the impression that Aldermaston was not a restricted flying area. But the Ministry of Defence objected as soon as it heard about it and as we rely so much upon the Services for support for the event we cannot argue about it."

The event will go ahead on the lines of that held last year.

The invite had been to take part in the World Jet Aerobatic Competition, a planned event on the first day of the 1974 show that, it was hoped, would build upon the trophy awarded in previous years. Tim Prince says, "We wrote direct to the Soviet Air Force and they said they were coming. However, when we mentioned it to the Ministry of Defence, they said, 'You can't do that!', and there was lots of diplomatic shuffling to see that they were un-invited. The Soviets were pretty reasonable about it, I have to say."

Less publicly, big changes were afoot within the Air Tattoo organisation. The first occurred when Jack Currie left the team just prior to the 1974 show, replaced by RAFA — "without warning", according to Bill Newby-Grant — with one Harry Adams. "After a hiatus in the organising team, consultation took place at the

Greater regulation wasn't far off, but in the early 1970s the Air Tattoo team exploited the freedoms still at their disposal to the full. So, it wasn't a problem for several of the organisers to fly in KC-97L 52-2630 of the Ohio Air National Guard's 145th Air Refueling Squadron during its display. Bill Newby-Grant was one.

In his book *Air Tattoo*, he described how he "lay prone in the tinted-glass cabin normally occupied by the boom-operator at the tail of the aircraft... once the 'boomer' had taken over, a low and slow demonstration pass was made while the boom was lowered. It was inadvertently let down too far, however, and touched the runway, sending up clouds of sparks". The pilot, Capt Floyd Nelson, reminisced in 2011 of how his unit commander had a gentle word when he got back to base: "Somehow I did not get the message I wasn't supposed to do a flight display".

Air Tattoo Memories: Malcolm Gault

Malcolm Gault has been on the team since 1974 and is one of our longest-serving volunteers. Originally an operations officer, Malcolm joined RIAT's follow-me team in 2001.

In one of his earliest IAT recollections, Malcolm remembers a KC-97 that arrived in the overhead about 07.30, having picked up a strong tailwind crossing the Atlantic. "We were all strolling to the chow hall for breakfast," Malcolm recalls. "So Tim Prince shot off to the tower to give him landing clearance and I think Andy Walton followed Tim, saying he would marshal him in. The aircraft was duly parked and about 15 minutes after landing, the crew joined us all in the queue for breakfast."

THE ROYAL AIR FORCES ASSOCIATION

(Incorporated by Royal Charter)   *(Registered under the War Charities Act, 1940 and the Charities Act, 1960)*

Please quote in reply   RAFA/A1/3050/AD/74

P.A. Bowen Esq
2 The Cleeves
Barford St. Martin
Salisbury
Wilts.

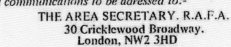

All communications to be adressed to:-
THE AREA SECRETARY. R.A.F.A.
30 Cricklewood Broadway.
London, NW2 3HD

Telephones and Telegrams: 01 - 452 4202

21st October 1974

Dear Paul,

I refer to your letter of the 13th October 1974 to Mr Collins concerning an Air Display at Greenham Common in 1975 and the report you forwarded on this subject for the consideration of the Air Display Committee.

The above matter was discussed at length at a meeting of the Air Display Committee held on the 19th October and the Committee wish me to thank you for your comprehensive and useful report. As a result of their deliberations the Committee recommended that an Air Display should not be mounted at Greenham Common in 1975. The concensus of opinion was that an Air Display on this scale would involve too great a risk with charity funds. This recommendation was agreed by the South Eastern Area Council at its 250th meeting held later the same day.

Yours sincerely
Gary Redwood

E.F. Redwood
<u>AREA SECRETARY</u>

...fumes from a fuel leak were entering the cockpit, yet still the crew pressed on with their low flypast en route to Lyneham.

highest level and the decision was taken to carry on with the show, since well over £30,000 had already been invested."

This was a year of surprises, and memorable appearances by classic 'heavies'. Aviation journalist Mark Ashley recalled that his earliest Air Tattoo recollection was of a Super Constellation "cruising majestically across Watership Down to the south [of Greenham Common]". No ordinary 'Connie', this, but C-121C 54-0157 from the 193rd Tactical Electronic Warfare Squadron, Pennsylvania ANG, often described in previous accounts as having served with Air America, though no confirmation of any use by the CIA-linked company has been forthcoming. A C-124 Globemaster II had been due to attend but couldn't because of a fleet-wide grounding, so the Air National Guard Bureau diverted the C-121 from a flight across California with an ANG band aboard and sent it to Greenham. As Bill Newby-Grant wrote, the bandsmen had been expecting to disembark in Sacramento, and found that "their lightweight summer blues were not the ideal clothes to have with them" upon arriving in the UK that Saturday lunchtime. Nevertheless, they played in the arena and provided the music at the post-show reception. The C-121 is still airworthy with the Historical Aircraft Restoration Society at Illawarra Regional Airport, New South Wales.

Today's authorities would probably have been none too pleased about the end-of-show appearance, no matter how brief, by ex-Indian Air Force B-24L Liberator KN751/HE807 on delivery for the RAF Museum. It was near the conclusion of a long day's flight from Rome, and fumes from a fuel leak were entering the cockpit, yet still the crew pressed on with their low flypast en route to Lyneham. Another memorable cameo in the Air Tattoo's 50-year history.

From the RAF, No 226 Operational Conversion Unit instructor Flt Lt Pete Chapman opened the display in a Lightning F3, a performance which earned him the year's Embassy Trophy. Somewhat surprisingly, this was the first time the *Red Arrows* had ever appeared at the Air Tattoo, the nine Gnat T1s being under the leadership of Sqn Ldr Ian Dick. The Austrian Air Force participated in the flying display with an S-65 and Saab 105, as did the Belgian Air Force with the *Swallows* team of SF260s and a Mirage V. The French Navy gave a 'buddy-buddy' in-flight refuelling demonstration with an Étendard IVP and Crusader, while another very rare two-ship performance was a duo of Royal Danish Air Force two-seat Starfighters, a CF-104D and TF-104G from Eskadrille 726 that flew a number of fast formation and opposition passes. Former Royal Canadian Air Force pilot Ormond Haydon-Baillie brought both his then charges, his famed CT-133 Silver Star *The Black Knight* and Sea Fury T20 WH589. He demonstrated the Silver Star with his characteristic flair, but also showed some entrepreneurial zeal. Selling raffle tickets to win a ride in the jet, he reportedly earned thousands of pounds...

A crowd of around 50,000 attended in 1974, generating a profit in excess of £15,000. It was good going in the face of increased costs. However, difficult times lay ahead. Jack Currie's departure was part of that; so too was the withdrawal of title sponsorship by W.D. & H.O. Wills, not to mention the international fuel crisis. Above all, RAFA was getting cold feet. As Tim describes, "The Royal Air Forces Association decided it

no longer wanted to be in this 'risk' business. Probably, they had seen more than we had that there were areas of risk involved where money was up front. Thinking back, I can't remember us working to a budget of any note, other than an exercise book with a few lines of figures in it. But RAFA saw that there was a risk to the charity's money. They also saw the wider risk of staging a dynamic air display. So, they decided to stand down from running airshows. We had become a bunch of airshow organisers with an airfield, but with no-one who wanted us to run an airshow. In 1975, we didn't run a show at all, but it gave us time to look around and see whether anybody else might want us."

During the winter of 1974-75, a group of leading Air Tattoo volunteers met in The Red Lion pub in the Somerset village of Rode to discuss the future. Paul Bowen brought good news, for he had made a very useful contact. Tim Prince explains: "We'd come across the Royal Air Force Benevolent Fund, with AM Sir Denis Crowley-Milling as the controller, who welcomed us with open arms even though we were an unusual mix of people. He agreed to talk about it — he obviously liked aeroplanes and missed them, having been 'flying a desk' for several years.

"He and his appeals secretary, Air Cdre John McKelvey, remembered that they had this trust" — the Development Trust — "which had been set up by the Air Force Board in 1950 following the very successful RAF Display that year at Farnborough. The proceeds from it were given to the Benevolent Fund in the form of a trust. It had been sitting dormant ever since, and it was there to support the welfare of the RAF 'family', but the other important charitable aim was to promote recruitment and efficiency in the Royal Air Force, which effectively meant PR. 'The Crow', as he was affectionately known, took us under the banner of the Development Trust, and so the Air Tattoo was started up again in 1976 with, at the recommendation of 'The Crow', his old World War Two chum Gp Capt Sir Douglas Bader as its president."

Sir Denis Crowley-Milling, Paul Bowen and Sir Douglas Bader (at left) with Tim Prince (second from right) and Air Cdre John McKelvey (third from right), meeting in 1974.

Air Commodore J. W. McKelvey CB, MBE, RAF (Ret'd)

THE ROYAL AIR FORCE BENEVOLENT FUND

REGISTERED UNDER THE WAR CHARITIES ACT 1940 AND THE CHARITIES ACT 1960

"The Royal Air Force Benevolent Fund is part of the conscience of the British Nation. A Nation without a conscience is a Nation without a soul. A Nation without a soul is a Nation that cannot live."

(The Rt Hon Winston Churchill, 1951)

TELEPHONE: 01-636 2654

Your Ref:-

Our Ref:- RAFBF/550/1/AP

SECRETARY (APPEALS)
67 PORTLAND PLACE
LONDON W1N 4AR

4th June 1975

P. A. Bowen, Esq.,
2 The Cleeves,
Barford St. Martin,
Wilton,
Wilts.

Dear Mr Bowen,

Air Tattoo 1976

The Finance and General Purposes Committee have agreed in principle to the Fund's involvement in the proposed 1976 Air Tattoo and the Royal Air Forces Association have confirmed that only financial considerations prompted their withdrawal from this event.

The Controller has now authorised me to continue negotiations with your team and to assess the full extent of the Fund's involvement and the implications. For example, we are not sure what is meant by para 6 of Annex 'C'. However, these are small matters.

In these circumstances you may now wish to contact the potential sponsors and perhaps arrange a preliminary meeting of your Directors with myself in attendance. If we are to go ahead then I believe a decision is necessary by late July and I should certainly like to sound the reactions of M.O.D. (Air) before the Controller retires next August.

As you may know one of our side lines here is the production of the Royal Air Force Yearbook and I enclose a copy of the 1975 edition which came off the presses on 30th May. These books are

/sold at

PATRON: HER MAJESTY THE QUEEN

of Kent

Chairman of Council: Sir Harald Peake

76

GREENHAM COMMON
31 JULY & 1 AUGUST

INTERNATIONAL AIR TATTOO 76

31st July & 1st August 1976 – RAF Greenham Common

IN AID OF

The Royal Air Force Benevolent Fund

50p

With the growth of the show and the new International Air Tattoo (IAT) title came the need to take a more focused approach. Thus was born the idea of holding themed gatherings of aircraft. The first was at IAT 76, marking the 25th anniversary of the Hawker Hunter's maiden flight. First prototype and world air speed record-breaker WB188 took pride of place as the centrepiece of the 26-Hunter line-up. But as Tim Prince says, its presence was nearly a disaster.

"We wanted WB188 as a centrepiece. It was at St Athan, and after a few 'phone calls from John McKelvey, who used to be the CO of St Athan, they said, 'Yes, you can borrow it'. On this lovely summer's day, we were all at Greenham Common when a Queen Mary drove in with this pretty red Hunter. A crane arrived, and the St Athan 'crash and smash' team, the Aircraft Recovery and Transportation Flight, got together with the driver and started to unload the aeroplane. Sadly, when the fuselage had just been lifted off the Queen Mary and the cradles it had been sitting on, the little pawl within a ratchet device that held the crane

Embassy Trophy winner
Flt Lt David Webb, RAF.

Air Tattoo staff and volunteers 1976.

mechanism together broke, and the fuselage came sailing down at speed onto these cradles, puncturing the fuselage quite severely. "Everyone went rushing around, back to those network contacts and friends, and we had an American airframe repair expert come along in a hurry [from Spain] the next day, together with a USAF paint specialist from Iceland and an engineer to fix the crane. Some fantastic work was done to repair the damage, and it went on display". It wasn't quite enough to scoop the Hunter concours d'elegance competition prize, though; judged by former Hawker test pilots Bill Bedford and Neville Duke, that honour went to T7 XF321 from the Royal Aircraft Establishment at Farnborough.

Slowly but surely, looking at these 1970s Greenham shows you can see the Air Tattoo of today taking shape. Military display teams had been a feature since 1971, of course, but this time there were eight on the bill. The Royal Navy's *Blue Herons* provided four of the aforementioned Hunters, civilian contractor-flown GA11s from the Fleet Requirements and Air Direction Unit, led by Derek Morter. Tim adds, "The *Blue Herons'* sponsor that year was Ind Coope, promoting its Arctic Lite low carbohydrate beer. Its marketing boss was Alan Smith who, as a true aviation enthusiast, went on to join the Air Tattoo volunteer team, and is now its company's non-executive chairman". From the RAF came the *Gazelles* helicopter team and the *Red Arrows*, the Belgian Air Force sent the *Diables Rouges* on six CM170 Magisters, the French Air Force's *Patrouille de France* brought nine further Magisters, the Italian Air Force *Frecce Tricolori* displayed nine Fiat G91PANs, the Austrian Air Force *Karo As* was equipped with four Saab 105OEs, and the Canadian Forces' *Tiger Romeos* was formed of four CF-104s from 439 Squadron. Equally as polished was the civilian *Rothmans Aerobatic Team* flying Pitts S-2A Specials, under the leadership of Colin Woods for 1976.

The US military, appropriately enough in the American bicentennial year, made its biggest showing yet. F-111Es of the USAF's 20th Tactical Fighter Wing were

resident at Greenham during runway resurfacing at their Upper Heyford base, one of them bearing special bicentennial colours. One of the IAT volunteers, technical services manager Bob Basing, had his Triumph GT6 done up to match — or, rather, it was done up for him. Bill Newby-Grant recalled how it was "appropriated and returned a day or two later with a beautifully finished if rather unorthodox spray coat". A rather older USAF type on static display was another KC-97L, this time from the 181st ARS, Texas ANG. This was the veteran type's final Air Tattoo appearance. Its crew, Newby-Grant wrote, "were so intent on reaching Greenham that they made an unnotified departure from Gander where their aircraft had gone unserviceable."

Out in force too was the US Navy, a group of aircraft from Carrier Air Wing (CVW) 6 aboard the aircraft carrier USS *America*, then deployed to the Mediterranean, being among the stars of the show. An F-14A Tomcat operated by VF-142 gave this variable-geometry air superiority fighter's debut British display, a typically brutish demonstration of the jet's power and manoeuvrability. Also first-footing in the flying programme were a VA-15 A-7E Corsair II and a VA-176 A-6E Intruder, while the static park featured an S-3A Viking from VS-28 and an E-2C Hawkeye from VAW-124, as well as a second Tomcat. Flown in from Rota in Spain to join them, an EA-3B Skywarrior of VQ-2 was a rare highlight. Among the historic contingent, this was the first time B-17G Flying Fortress *Sally B*, then owned by Euroworld and captained by Don Bullock, attended the Air Tattoo. Another Duxford resident at the time, Varsity T1 WJ945, gave its debut displays in civilian hands. Newly returned to airworthiness by the Duxford Aviation Society, 'Piglet', as '945 became affectionately known, was in the hands of that organisation's much-missed lynchpin Don Selway.

A new award, the Shell (UK) Oil Trophy, was presented for the best overall flying demonstration excluding those by solo jets and display teams of more than six aircraft. Its recipient was Peter Phillips, flying a Britten-Norman Defender as only

Alan Smith (second from left) along with Jim Glover (left).

"The Blue Herons' sponsor was Ind Coope, whose marketing boss Alan Smith, a true aviation enthusiast, went on to join the Air Tattoo volunteer team and is now RAFCTE's non-executive chairman".

he could. The RAF again scooped the Embassy Trophy, Flt Lt David Webb's routine in a Jet Provost T5 judged to be the best individual jet performance against the very stiff international competition.

Some of the ground attractions were very much 'of their time'. British Leyland cars made a drive-past down the runway, the company having provided loan vehicles for the use of IAT's managers; Dunlop demonstrated its ultimately unsuccessful Denovo 'run-flat' tyre, and there was a roadshow with BBC Radio One DJ Emperor Rosko. The Air Tattoo has always, after all, sought to have broad family appeal. Bringing the weekend to a close, a sunset ceremony involving the Royal Marines Band was presided over by Maj Gen Evan W. Rosecrans, commander of the US Third Air Force. Rosecrans' support, enabling the show to be staged at one of 'his' airfields, was crucial.

By a long way, IAT 76 was the biggest Air Tattoo yet. Numbers of participating aircraft were way up, and the weekend crowd numbered more than 120,000. No wonder, as Newby-Grant wrote, "The traffic congestion was appalling this year despite well-laid and equally well-implemented traffic control, as holiday traffic mixed with the sheer volume of display cars." This was, indeed, the latest in the year an Air Tattoo has ever been staged, well into the holidays during that famously hot summer of '76. But the show was an outstanding success, contributing in excess of £35,000 to the RAF Benevolent Fund, and would only grow from here.

Air Tattoo Memories: Mike McEvoy   Manager of air traffic services from 1976 to 1981.

"In 1976, we had a number of aerobatic teams present and, of course, there was no over-competitiveness. However, the *Frecce Tricolori* in their Fiat G91s always displayed con brio, and the finale of their act was when all their aircraft – 10, I think – having performed their break, then converged on airfield centre from all points of the compass. They were marginally separated vertically, but within a very small space of time, before turning downwind to land. I have a feeling that this manoeuvre was known as 'King's Cross'! The team had already rehearsed on a pre-display day but, on the Saturday, Sir Denis Crowley-Milling visited the tower coincident with the *Frecce's* display and, following the cross, produced a very thin smile, thanked us courteously and left. On the Sunday, the Italians' display was unexpectedly seven minutes shorter, taking us totally by surprise but, coincidentally, rescuing us from a potentially nasty overrun; and, in 1977, we had the flying control committee. Lovely man, Sir Denis; always got what he wanted with charm and tact and, as far as I could see, without ever raising his voice."

NATO TIGER MEET '77
INTERNATIONAL AIR TATTOO

Silver Jubilee
International
Air Tattoo 77
MRCA-Tornado
Newbury
Berks
Saturday and Sunday
25-26 June
Nationwide Building Society

It was the year of HM The Queen's Silver Jubilee, and, for the Air Tattoo, of the Tiger Meet. In fact, this was the first occasion on which the NATO Tiger Association's gathering of aircraft from units with a tiger in their emblem had been staged by anyone other than a member unit.

77
GREENHAM COMMON
25 & 26 JUNE

The 1977 meet had been due to take place at Upper Heyford under the auspices of the USAF's 79th Tactical Fighter Squadron, with IAT providing advice. Then the headquarters of US Air Forces in Europe forced the plug to be pulled, expressing concerns about commercial involvement being sought as a means of making the meet financially self-sufficient. In the end, 12 Tiger Association units took part including a couple of honorary members: the RAF's Puma HC1-equipped No 230 Squadron, later to become a full association member, and the Royal Australian Navy's 816 Squadron with an S-2E Tracker from HMAS *Melbourne*. The most spectacular tiger liveries were those on the French Air Force Super Mystère B2 from EC 1/12 and the CF-104 from 439 Squadron, Canadian Forces, the latter unit winning the Mappin & Webb Silver Tiger Trophy for 'Spirit of the Meet'.

The Royal Australian Navy was a one-time Air Tattoo participant, HMAS *Melbourne* having sailed to Portsmouth for the Silver Jubilee Fleet Review at Spithead, which took place on the Tuesday after IAT 77. To Greenham Common it sent not just the Tracker but also a Sea King Mk50 and two A-4G Skyhawks, one of the latter, operated by 805 Squadron, giving the type's sole British airshow flying display to date. Its pilot, the late Lt Dave Ramsay, later returned to the UK as an exchange pilot on the Royal Navy's Sea Harriers. He said, "We decided that a clean A-4 still couldn't compete in a high-performance show against the F-14s and '15s that would be there so we went for the biggest things we could load [it] with". These included the centreline-mounted 'buddy' refuelling pod.

US Navy carrier aircraft came this time from the USS *John F. Kennedy*, and in greater strength. No fewer than four were flying items: a VF-14 F-14A, a VA-72 A-7B, a VS-32 S-3A and a VAQ-133 EA-6B Prowler, the latter two types for the only time at an Air Tattoo. The Tomcat's display on the second day, however, had to be curtailed. "He exceeded the wheels-down power setting", says Tim Prince," and the doors shut around one of the undercarriage legs and severed the hydraulics. He did a roll, and one wheel came in and then out again! After a lot of consternation from air traffic, he stopped his display, used the pressurised emergency system to blow the undercarriage down and landed."

If there's one aircraft most indelibly associated with Greenham shows of the period, it's the F-104. Canadian Forces CF-104 teams gave some of the most memorable formation performances of the era.

Several of the US Air Force assets present in 1977 hadn't been seen at the show before. Presaging the attack aircraft's permanent deployment to Europe, an A-10A Thunderbolt II from the 355th Tactical Fighter Wing at Davis-Monthan AFB, Arizona, followed up its visits to the Mildenhall and Paris shows by giving a very effective illustration of its low-level prowess. The agility of the Bitburg, West Germany-based 36th TFW TF-15A Eagle was impressive, but all who saw it most recall its landing roll, scraping its tail along much of the runway. Dominating the static park was a 436th Military Airlift

Wing C-5A Galaxy, while a 2nd Bomb Wing B-52G Stratofortress brought the type back to Greenham for the first time since occasional Strategic Air Command training deployments in the 1960s.

For its contribution to the jubilee celebrations, the Portuguese Air Force went as far as forming the *Asas de Portugal* (Wings of Portugal) team of Cessna T-37Cs to help celebrate the occasion. In preparation, it sought advice from IAT. "They came over in advance and said that they wanted to form the team if we'd have them", Tim recounts. "Duncan Simpson [chief test pilot for Hawker Siddeley at Dunsfold] sat with us and we talked them through what we'd expect of them, in terms of the rules and how to run a team. They then went and spent a bit of time with the *Red Arrows* and, fully prepared, came to the 1977 show". The six-ship formation duly put on smooth, professional displays.

Papers held by the UK's National Archives in Kew reveal that other visitors from the Iberian peninsula proved more controversial. At the time, Spain was still going through its transition to democracy following the Franco dictatorship, and elections took place just a fortnight prior to IAT 77. When the UK Ministry of Defence heard that the Spanish Air Force was sending two CASA C-212 Aviocar twin-turboprop transports to participate, it wasn't best pleased. A memo sent two weeks before the Air Tattoo to the then Secretary of State for Defence, Fred Mulley, said the RAF Benevolent Fund "did not consult the MoD about the people they proposed to invite to take part in the programme. We have only very recently heard of this invitation... which had it been the subject of an official MoD programme would have been discussed with the FCO [Foreign and Commonwealth Office] and, if necessary, cleared with ministers, since HMG [Her Majesty's Government]'s current policy on Anglo-Spanish military relations requires us to avoid any contact which is likely to attract publicity."

Mulley was advised that, at such a late stage and in the immediate aftermath of the Spanish election, "it would be more damaging to cancel than to continue". Nevertheless, the MoD sent Sir Denis Crowley-Milling a friendly but firm letter, stating, "You fully understand, I know, the need to avoid embarrassment to the RAF by not inviting the Warsaw Pact countries to participate in your Air Tattoos; but you might not have appreciated that there could be other foreign powers whose presence

Silver Jubilee International Air Tattoo 77
Flying Programme

Subject to weather and aircraft availability

Item	DISPLAY
1	AGUSTA-BELL UH1B 7 Sqn. Royal Netherlands Navy 'de Kooy' WESTLAND WASP HAS1 860 Sqn. Royal Netherlands Navy 'de Kooy'
2	MESSERSCHMITT BF 108B TAIFUN Mr. L. Walton, Sutton Bridge
3	THE VINTAGE PAIR – GLOSTER METEOR T7 and DE HAVILLAND VAMPIRE T11 Central Flying School, Royal Air Force, Cranwell
4	NORTH AMERICAN P-51D MUSTANG Mr. O. A. Haydon Baillie, London
5	HAWKER SEA FURY and FAIREY SWORDFISH FAA Historic Aircraft Flight, Royal Naval Air Station Yeovilton
6 (Sat)	SAAB 105 ÖE Austrian Air Force, Hörsching
(Sun)	THE FALCONS RAF Parachute Display Team, Royal Air Force, Brize Norton
7 (Sat)	HSA NIMROD 1 42 Sqn. Royal Air Force, St Mawgan
(Sun)	SAAB 105 ÖE Austrian Air Force, Hörsching
8	WESTLAND LYNX AH1 Army Air Corps, HQ AAC Centre, Middle Wallop
9	BRITTEN-NORMAN BN2A-21 DEFENDER and TRISLANDER Fairey Britten Norman Ltd., Bembridge
10	THE ROYAL AIR FORCE 'BRABYN' TROPHY WINNER – BAC JET PROVOST T5 Central Flying School, Royal Air Force, Cranwell
11	FAIRCHILD A10 355th Tactical Fighter Wing, Davis-Monthan AFB, Arizona, USA
12	HSA HARRIER GR3 233 OCU, Royal Air Force, Wittering
13	LOCKHEED F104G STARFIGHTER 312 Sqn. Royal Netherlands Air Force, Volkel
14	GRUMMAN EA6B PROWLER USS John F Kennedy, United States Navy
15 (Sat)	THE RED ARROWS – 9 HSA GNAT T1 Central Flying School, Royal Air Force, Kemble

Item	DISPLAY
(Sun)	'THE WINGS OF PORTUGAL' – 6 CESSNA T37C Portuguese Air Force, Sintra
16	BAC JAGUAR GR1 226 OCU., Royal Air Force, Lossiemouth
17	CASA 212 AVIOCAR Spanish Air Force
18	LOCKHEED S3A VIKING USS John F Kennedy, United States Navy
19	AEROSPATIALE SUPER FRELON 32F Flotille, French Navy, Lanveoc-Poulmic
20	'THE KARO-AS' – 4 SAAB 105ÖE Austrian Air Force, Zeltweg
21	4 McDONNELL DOUGLAS RF4C PHANTOM 10th TRW United States Air Force, Alconbury
22	VOUGHT A7E CORSAIR II USS John F Kennedy, United States Navy
23	'COTY' PITTS S1 SPECIAL "MISS SMITTY" Mr. P. Meeson, London
24	'THE TIGER ROMEOS' – 4 CF104G STARFIGHTERS 439 (F) Sqn., Canadian Armed Forces, Soellingen
25	3 F104G STARFIGHTER 31 Sqn., Belgian Air Force, Kleine-Brogel
26	3 GENERAL DYNAMICS F111E 20th TFW,, United States Air Force, Upper Heyford
27	AEROSPATIALE WESTLAND PUMA HC1 230 Sqn., Royal Air Force, Odiham
28	'FLYING JOKERS' – 3 NORTHROP F5A 336 Sqn., Royal Norwegian Air Force, Rygge
29	3 SUPER MYSTERE B2 ESC1/12 French Air Force, Cambrai
30	3 LOCKHEED F104S STARFIGHTER 21 Gruppo Italian Air Force, Novara
31	McDONNELL DOUGLAS F15A EAGLE 53rd TFS, United States Air Force, Bitburg
32	SIKORSKY CH53G, and MBB BO105 German Army, Rheine Bentlage

Item	DISPLAY
33	4 NORTHROP F5E TIGER II 527th TFS., United States Air Force, Alconbury
34	HSA HAWK T1 Central Flying School, Royal Air Force, Valley
35	HAWKER HURRICANE IIC Battle of Britain Memorial Flight, Royal Air Force, Coningsby
36	SUPERMARINE SPITFIRE Battle of Britain Memorial Flight, Royal Air Force, Coningsby
37	AVRO LANCASTER Battle of Britain Memorial Flight, Royal Air Force, Coningsby
38	HSA BUCCANEER S2 809 Sqn., Royal Navy, Honington
39	CANADAIR NF5A 316 Sqn., Royal Netherlands Air Force, Gilze-Rijen
40	GRUMMAN F14A TOMCAT USS John F Kennedy, United States Navy
41	'THE BLUE HERONS' – 4 HSA HUNTER GA11 Fleet Requirement and Direction Unit, Royal Naval Air Station, Yeovilton
42	THE ROYAL AIR FORCE 'WRIGHT JUBILEE' TROPHY WINNER – BAC JET PROVOST T5 6FTS Royal Air Force, Finningley
43	HSA VULCAN B2 44 Sqn., Royal Air Force, Waddington
44	'THE VIPERS' – 2 BELL OH58A KIOWA 444 TAC Hel. Sqn., Canadian Armed Forces, Lahr
45	SUPER MYSTERE B2 ESC 1/12 French Air Force, Cambrai
46	McDONNELL DOUGLAS A4G SKYHAWK II VF805, HMAS Melbourne, Royal Australian Navy
47	BAC LIGHTNING F3 11 Sqn., Royal Air Force, Binbrook
48	DASSAULT ETENDARD IVP 16F Flotille, French Navy Landivisiau
49 (Sat)	'THE WINGS OF PORTUGAL' – 6 CESSNA T37C Portuguese Air Force Sintra
(Sun)	'THE RED ARROWS' – 9 HSA GNAT T1 Central Flying School Royal Air Force, Kemble

might be equally embarrassing". Sir Denis was reminded of the need to "seek the advice of the Ministry of Defence before issuing any invitations for participation by foreign air forces". The Aviocars duly showed up, one each for static and flying.

If there's one aircraft most indelibly associated with Greenham shows of the period, it's the F-104. There were no fewer than 22 present in 1977, and the Canadian Forces CF-104 teams gave some of the most memorable formation performances of the era. That year's outfit was still known as the *Tiger Romeos*, hailing from 439 Squadron, and opened a segment of the flying programme given over to displays and flypasts by assets from NATO Tiger Association units. '104s' were just as spectacular on departure day, as John Dunnell, an Air Tattoo volunteer for more than 30 years, recalls: "The lowest of the low was a Dutch Starfighter. After retracting the undercarriage, no height was gained at all. The aircraft accelerated with the pilot leaning forward to see over the nose. Too low to rotate, he gently nudged the aircraft up until finally, as the airfield boundary approached, he was able to rotate and hurtle up in a near-vertical climb."

One of the great Air Tattoo legends made his debut at the 1977 show. Oberleutnant Karl 'Charly' Zimmermann of the Federal German Army gave an outstanding aerobatic display in an MBB Bo 105M helicopter and was the inaugural recipient of the Nationwide Building Society International Display Sword for the best demonstration by an overseas participant. RAF domination of the Embassy Trophy continued, Flt Lt Derek Fitzsimmons of the Central Flying School winning in an almost brand-new Hawk T1. Derek Morter led the Royal Navy *Blue Herons* Hunter team to the well-deserved award of the Shell (UK) Oil Trophy.

This was an event full of notable performances. On the Sunday, the *Red Arrows* completed their 1,000th public display, concluding with a 'Jubilee Break'. Other teams taking part were the *Flying Jokers* comprising three F-5As from the Royal Norwegian Air Force, the Canadian Forces' short-lived *Vipers* duo of CH-136 Kiowa helicopters, and the Austrian Air Force *Karo As*. Opening the programme was a Royal Netherlands Navy rotary duet of a Wasp HAS1 and UH-1B, while a French Navy SA321 Super Frelon made this maritime helicopter's sole Air Tattoo flying display showing. The Royal Navy displayed a Buccaneer S2 from 809 Naval Air Squadron, nearing the end of its service with the Fleet Air Arm. Industry involvement was on the up, bringing about the Air Tattoo's first sight of a Tornado, in the form of development aircraft P08 (serial XX950) from BAC Warton. The second day witnessed the arrival on the scene of a new warbird, not that the term would have been heard in Britain back then, when Ormond Haydon-Baillie brought in his recently acquired Cavalier Mustang, I-BILL. The following weekend it crashed at Mainz-Finthen, killing Haydon-Baillie and a young passenger.

By now the IAT team had realised it had to tighten up its act where safety was concerned. Duncan Simpson was the driving force. As Tim remembers, "[he] said to us, 'Look, this is a great event, but I've just watched on two occasions F-104s and F-5s do barrel rolls, and I've seen the nose drop. Do you know what that means?' We said, 'No!' He said, 'That means the guy isn't actually

Frank Windle with Paul Bowen and Tim Prince.

Many look back on the Greenham Common IATs as having rekindled something of the spirit of Farnborough's golden age.

flying that well. At Farnborough, I'm part of the flying control committee there, and we stand between the pilots and the air traffic controllers, we're independent from the organisers, and we just make sure that everybody understands what the rules are and that they abide by them. You need a flying control committee here'... 'The Crow' asked Duncan to take on the mantle of chairman of the flying control committee and form it". IAT 77 was the first show under its jurisdiction. "In those days we had Roy Moxom, test pilot at Westland; Brian Trubshaw, which for me was marvellous as I'd always wanted to meet him; and Roland Beamont, all of whom volunteered. From that day on, we became a safer place. Thank goodness we'd survived up until that point, because we might have had to close down if there had been an aircraft accident. We'd got away with it, and those good people set up shop not with a big stick but on a respect basis, and managed the safety of the show. That's been there ever since."

What did change after 1977 was the frequency of the Air Tattoo. "By that time, I was in the 'it's got to get bigger' mode as well", says Tim. "Paul was very strong on that front, but I'd got into the swing of it and enjoyed the fun of it being bigger and better each time". That enjoyment of IAT's expansion wasn't shared by the

then Society of British Aircraft Constructors (SBAC), however. From the outset of the Greenham era, it felt having IAT take place in the same year as its Farnborough show was harmful to Farnborough in terms of crowd figures, and objected to the Air Tattoo being an annual event. For this reason, it became biennial after 1977.

Tim recalls the 'gentleman's agreement' between IAT and the SBAC, which existed until the early 1990s. "They had an air marshal running their organisation, we had an air marshal running our organisation. There is such a thing as an 'air marshals' club', and they had made an agreement and we would stick to it. It was very difficult for us, because you lost the continuity and you could lose the volunteers. Deep down, both Paul and I felt it was an unreasonable situation, because there were plenty of people in the south of England to go round — or, at least, there were in our minds."

It probably had nothing to do with the SBAC's objections, but many look back on the Greenham Common IATs as having rekindled something of the spirit of Farnborough's golden age. Even then, the opinion was being voiced that the SBAC show was becoming a shadow of its former self. IAT was a very different affair, of course, making the SBAC's worries all the more perplexing, but it had certainly replaced Farnborough as the place to see the most dynamic flying by the pilots of the day.

Air Tattoo Memories: Geoff Brindle

Geoff Brindle is another of the Air Tattoo's long-serving volunteers, and also a man who has worn many different hats. This former RAF Lightning pilot served with distinction, initially as the chairman of IAT's flying control committee, then flying display director, prior to bowing out recently after hosting RIAT's hugely successful 1st Class Lounge enclosure. In recalling memories of his time with the Air Tattoo, it's the occasions when Geoff performed his IAT flying displays that he most remembers:

"In looking up IAT 76 in my logbook, I noted that the transit was on 29 July 1976 in Lightning F3 XP695. Later the same day I flew XP737 for a press preview. It was on that trip that a Victor tanker flew through the circuit working the approach frequency, while I was on local. I had just pulled up into a loop and air traffic control quickly told me to hold off, as the tanker was coming through. So I held upside-down at the top of the loop while he passed underneath and then completed the loop and the rest of the sequence. The show at the weekend went well, and I flew XR720 back to RAF Leconfield and then down to RAF St Mawgan for their show on 3-4 August. I appear to have flown three different aircraft during the course of that show." Geoff also displayed in a Lightning at the Silver Jubilee-themed IAT at Greenham Common in June 1977. "That went off OK too!" said Geoff.

On the Sunday, the Red Arrows completed their 1,000th public display with a 'Jubilee Break'.

The USAF appreciated having the show to host at what had been a rather run-down airfield. Col Jim Salminen was the base commander by the time of the next Air Tattoo, and later recalled, "The former commander warned me that the [IAT] staff, who had an office on the base, would be a thorn in my side as they made demands annually for their air show. In fact, their interest in having things neat and tidy for the airshow got us support from the Royal Air Force and Army. By the end of June, the flightline looked great, as nice as any active base around... it was the IAT event that helped us repair and dress up many areas and buildings on the base."

But why was Greenham so special? "What was happening was that the participants very quickly rubbed shoulders with our volunteer team who wanted to do what they were doing", enthuses Tim. "It wasn't like going to a military base where they were told to stand there and park cars or take money or refuel the aeroplanes. All the people who came to run the Air Tattoo wanted to be there, and there was a buzz. "That buzz rubbed off onto the participants. You'd get a solo display pilot who would come one year, have a damn good time — fly well, play hard — and then later get into a position of influence, because many display pilots went on to become chiefs. They would say that the Air Tattoo is a good place to go, not just because it gets big crowds and it's supporting an RAF charity, but also because they knew the crews would have a good time there with like-minded people and share ideas and experiences. So, it started growing of its own accord."

That 'buzz' also attracted a new volunteer to the team in the name of Fred Crawley. At the time, he was a regional manager of Lloyds Bank, later to become the bank's deputy chief executive. Having been afforded a behind-the-scenes tour of the airshow, Fred went on to become a volunteer, finishing as non-executive chairman of the Air Tattoo's company.

Bassingbourn Anglo-American Air Festival 27 & 28 May 1978

With no Air Tattoo in 1978, an approach to assist in running a one-off show at Bassingbourn, Cambridgeshire, was met with interest. It was made by Lt Col Hugh Lohan, commanding officer of the Queen's Division depot, which was resident at the former RAF station. The intention of the British Army and the East Anglian Aviation Society was to stage an international air display as the climax to a week-long series of events mounted for veterans of the US Eighth Air Force's 91st Bomb Group, Bassingbourn's occupants between 1942-45. In this, IAT was ideally placed to help. Quite apart from anything else, its expertise in reactivating dormant airfields would come in handy — Bassingbourn had been handed over from the RAF to the army back in 1969.

The result was the Anglo-American Air Festival, held on 27-28 May 1978. Its most appropriate flying item was Euroworld's B-17G *Sally B*, remembering the Flying Fortresses of the wartime 91st BG, but upstaging the four-engined bomber was the same operator's A-26C Invader, a 'surprise item' on the programme and making one of its first appearances since being imported from the USA. Bolstering the vintage flavour, an international meet of North American T-6s/Harvards celebrated the famous trainer's 40th anniversary, with aircraft from the UK, France, the Netherlands, Sweden and West Germany present in a 14-strong gathering. A Harvard IIb, FT229, owned by Anthony Hutton won the concours d'elegance, while wartime Air Transport Auxiliary pilot and Air Tattoo volunteer Annette Hill was given the chance to reacquaint herself with the type during an hour-long sortie. Not long returned from their epic flight from England to Australia, Flt Lt David Cyster and Tiger Moth G-ANRF made for a popular attraction, the then RAF Gnat instructor's mastery of the biplane trainer — which continues to this day — apparent from his aerobatics.

There was excellent modern military involvement, a special feature being a spectacular battle demonstration involving elements of the home-based Queen's Division supported by No 72 Squadron Wessex HC2s and a No 237 OCU Buccaneer S2B. The Canadian Forces *Tiger Romeos* team mustered a pair of CF-104s, the Royal Danish Navy put in a float-equipped Alouette III, and the USAF provided a number of items — F-15A, RF-4C, F-5E and OV-10A — as its own salute to the wartime American presence.

By any standards, the Anglo-American Air Festival was a major success. More than 63,000 people attended, an exceptional result for a new show, and the RAF Benevolent Fund, Army Benevolent Fund and Ex-Services Mental Welfare Society benefited significantly. So did the Air Tattoo, as several army personnel who were involved at Bassingbourn joined the IAT team, Hugh Lohan remaining a stalwart for many years.

Air Tattoo People

Over 50 years, the Air Tattoo's army of volunteers and supporters may have changed, but their significant support and enthusiasm has never wavered. A small snapshot of some of these incredible people — to whom a huge debt of gratitude and thanks is owed — appears on these pages.

INTERNATIONAL AIR TATTOO
1979
LOCKHEED 25 YEARS HERCULES

International Air Tattoo 1979
RAF Greenham Common, Newbury, Berks Saturday 23 and Sunday 24 June
In aid of the Royal Air Force Benevolent Fund and in association with Nationwide Building Society

GREENHAM COMMON
23 & 24 JUNE

This was, with hindsight, a hugely important year for the now biennial Air Tattoo. The theme was the 25th anniversary of the C-130 Hercules, and, as Tim Prince recounts, it couldn't have proved a better choice. "Paul Bowen and a team went over to Atlanta and basically asked Lockheed, 'If we line up 25 Hercules, will you give us $25,000?' They chuckled, but we did it.

"They saw very early on that we were delivering on getting countries coming together, and they saw that opportunity to have the customers there with their aeroplanes. Lockheed with its Hercules Industry Team partners, including amongst others Marshall of Cambridge, became our first aerospace industry sponsors at that stage". With that came the need to provide facilities suitable for the hosting of VIP guests, not just from industry, but also the chiefs of air arms. Thus, the show would play a role in what became known as defence diplomacy, but for the moment the organisers were more concerned with just bringing together an interesting assembly of aircraft, and not fully aware of the need to do so through the proper channels.

Perhaps that explains why the potential existed for tension at IAT 79, when in the middle of the Hercules line were aircraft from both Israel and Saudi Arabia — countries that had not enjoyed the best of relations. "That was the first occasion for me", says Tim, "when we realised that perhaps we had overstepped the mark."

By that time, both Paul and Tim were working full-time on the Air Tattoo, having left their respective jobs. During the arrivals days, Tim was "sitting in our little office at the back of the control tower at Greenham Common — Paul and I always shared an office, probably to keep an eye on each other", when in walked the assistant chief constable of Thames Valley Police, "to see what was going on... We'd talked about security, and we hadn't mentioned which countries were coming because we didn't think about it then". When he became aware that Israeli and Saudi C-130s would be there together, the senior policeman became, as Tim phrases it, "quite upset... I said, 'Look, let's jump in the car, and let's go out and see'. We went down there, and the crews were talking, smiling and getting on famously with each other. For me, that was what the Air Tattoo is all about."

The Hercules line was headed by the first C-130A delivered to the USAF in 1956, 55-0023 *City of Ardmore* from the 185th Tactical Airlift Squadron, Oklahoma ANG. A Hercules Industries Team, led by the Lockheed-Georgia company, sponsored an operators' symposium and looked after the social needs of the C-130 crews. They arrived from far and wide — the concours d'elegance was won by a C-130H of No 40 Squadron, Royal New Zealand Air Force, while the Argentinian, Brazilian, Israeli, Saudi and Venezuelan examples brought to Greenham air arms that had never contributed to the show before. Among the unusual derivatives were the RAF Meteorological Research Flight's Hercules W2 XV208, and from the USAF a ski-equipped C-130D of the 139th TAS, New York ANG.

A Royal New Zealand Air Force C-130H – winner of the Concours d'Elegance Trophy, awarded by Lockheed at the Hercules 25th Anniversary Meet in 1979.

Other anniversaries marked in 1979 were the 60th anniversary of the first non-stop trans-Atlantic crossing by Alcock and Brown in a Vickers Vimy in 1919 and the 30th anniversary of NATO. Sponsored by Rolls-Royce, two RAF Phantom FGR2s from No 56 Squadron were specially painted to mark both of these events in colours designed by artist Wilf Hardy, by then established as the painter of the show's poster and programme artworks. One of them was to be flown non-stop across the Atlantic, arriving at Greenham Common during the IAT 79 press preview. The pilot was Sqn Ldr Tony Alcock, a nephew of Capt John Alcock who made the first historic crossing. An RAF Phantom navigator called Brown could not be found, so the role was filled by Flt Lt Norman Browne, drawn from the Buccaneer force — he had previously been on Phantoms. The primary aircraft was XV424, which duly made the trip from Goose Bay, Labrador, in five hours 40 minutes. It involved five air-to-air refuellings from Victor K2 tankers. On board with Alcock and Browne was Twinkletoes, the original toy black cat mascot that had been carried on the Vimy during the 1919 flight.

The crew of the specially liveried 'Alcock and Brown' RAF Phantom after landing at IAT 79, greeted by Sir Douglas Bader and Sir Denis Crowley-Milling.

The primary aircraft was XV424, which made the trip from Goose Bay, Labrador, in five hours 40 minutes. On board with Alcock and Browne was Twinkletoes, the original toy black cat mascot that had been carried on the Vimy during the 1919 flight.

Tim remembers, "During our press call, we were in the old building to the rear of the control tower at Greenham when 'The Crow' was briefing the press on the show generally. We had a big old-fashioned Bakelite telephone next to the podium where he was standing, linked up to a prehistoric amplification system in the building there. It rang, and it was Alcock reporting in over the peat bog in Ireland [where the Vimy had landed in 1919], saying, 'We'll be with you in 15 minutes'. We marched all the press out — it was a pouring wet day, couldn't have been worse, so thank goodness we had the radar there — and, sure enough, they appeared in front of us". Even with the unique presence of a Spanish Air Force F-4C from Ala 12, XV424 was the show's star Phantom.

Lockheed aside, other new associations were forged in 1979. The appearance of two Pitts S-2 Specials in the colours of the Jordanian state airline Alia, flying as the *Royal Jordanian Falcons*, heralded the start of a long connection between the Air Tattoo and Jordan, which was to culminate in HM King Hussein becoming patron of IAT. The Swiss Air Force attended for the first time, making the UK debut of its *Patrouille Suisse* aerobatic team with six Hunter F58s. Led by Hptm Hans-Rudolf Beck, the elegant, well-practised formations that have always been a *Patrouille Suisse* hallmark were absolutely in evidence.

The Hunters would soldier on for many years, but the Swiss Air Force's Venoms were due for retirement. One of them, FB54 serial J-1704, was flown to Greenham for formal presentation to the RAF Museum. On the Sunday of the show

the aeroplane was handed over to Sir Douglas Bader, IAT's president, looking rather different to how it did on arrival — the long nose fitted by the Swiss as part of an avionics upgrade had been replaced by a standard Venom nose. Initially J-1704 was stored at Greenham, "pending a decision on its future", in the museum's words. For a time it was thought to keep the Venom flying and add it to the Meteor T7 and Vampire T11 of the RAF's *Vintage Pair* team. Eventually, though, in March 1980 the airframe was taken by road to Cosford for museum display, and there it has stayed ever since.

This was a good show for classic British types. A Venezuelan Air Force Canberra B(I)82 joined the static park in that type's 30th anniversary year. It had been to the British Aerospace plant at Warton for a major upgrade. Making its sole Air Tattoo visit was Sea Vixen FAW2 XJ608, from the Royal Aircraft Establishment but still in the old grey and white Fleet Air Arm colours.

Perhaps 1979's flying programme didn't quite hit the heights of 1977's, but it still featured some noteworthy items. One was, surprisingly, the Air Tattoo's only ever Mirage III display, by a French Air Force IIIE model from Escadron de Chasse 4. The German Navy F-104G duo, dubbed the *Vikings*, was short-lived at this stage — August's fatal accident to a Marineflieger Starfighter at the Yeovilton Air Day put paid to further outings. However, the *Vikings* would return.

An IAT 79 one-off was a battlefield demonstration by four AH-1S Cobras operated by the US Army's Hanau-based 503rd Aviation Battalion, part of a large-scale exercise deployment to Greenham that also took in CH-47s, OH-58s and UH-1s. "They had come into the country to do exercises on Salisbury Plain", explains Tim. "I remember their arrival at Greenham very well — I was in our little office in Building 91, where Rear Admiral Nick Goodhart was building his Kremer Trophy man-powered aeroplane in the other end. In fact, Paul and I ended up as adjudicators for his man-powered flight. There was some work to do, I'd just made a cup of coffee, and a whole bunch of Americans turned up. I'd heard the noise. They had mistaken our building for the headquarters building, and these guys literally just wanted to know where the accommodation was, where to get fuel, and where to get maps of Salisbury Plain. We helped them out a bit, and before we knew it, they'd agreed to take part in the show. We had no runway sweepers that particular year, and I went up in their Chinook with no headset on and a hand-portable radio; Paul was in a car driving around the airfield looking for foreign object damage (FOD), and we then just blew it away with the Chinook, together with a whole pile of wooden folding tables, if I remember rightly!"

The *Patrouille Suisse* went home from their first IAT with the Shell (UK) Oil Trophy, as overseas air arms took all the flying display awards. Oblt Erich Wolf of the Austrian Air Force became the first non-RAF winner of the Embassy Solo Jet Aerobatic Trophy for his Saab 105OE routine. The Nationwide Display Sword was presented to Maj G. E. C. 'Boy' Soons from 334 Squadron, Royal Netherlands Air Force, who gave a breathtaking exhibition of near-aerobatics in the F27-300M Troopship.

Since the previous event at Greenham, Friends of the International Air Tattoo (FIAT) had been established to cater for the enthusiast, and IAT 79 was the first to feature a crowd-line enclosure and facilities for FIAT members. Those facilities were especially welcome on the Sunday morning, when a torrential storm turned the static park into a lake. More than 1,000 people were estimated to have taken shelter in, or beneath, the USAF C-5A. But with an attendance of 160,000 generating £125,000 for the Benevolent Fund, the event was a great success — and Lockheed, today Lockheed Martin, and Marshall of Cambridge still support the Air Tattoo more than 40 years on.

Duncan Simpson and Mike McEvoy at a Greenham Common briefing.

GREENHAM COMMON   R/W 29
CAUTION - MINOR DAMAGE TO RIGHT HAND
SOUTHERN TAXIWAY AT 29 END OF AIRFIELD

Nº1 WEATHER DIVERSION   CRASH DIVERSION
MANSTON R/W 11 , FULLY 'S'   BRIZE NORTON
Nº2 WEATHER DIVERSION   R/W 26 , 'S'
UPPER   R/W 27 'S   (TACAN UNCALIBRATED)
HEYFORD (ILS U/S)

Embassy Solo Jet Aerobatic Trophy winner
Oblt Erich Wolf of the Austrian Air Force.

Wilkinson Match Safety & Protection · International Air Tattoo 79 - R.A.F. Greenham Common

NATO 30
THIRTIETH
ANNIVERSARY
1949-1979

TATTOO OPERATIONS

PHOTO: PAUL FILMER

PHOTO: PAUL FILMER

PHOTO: PAUL FILMER

Newbury Air Festival 31 May & 1 June 1980

The history of airshows run by the Air Tattoo team records that it staged the Newbury Air Festival at Greenham Common on 31 May–1 June 1980 — but that doesn't tell anything like the full story. Tim Prince takes it up: "The mayor-elect of Bristol had been to our show at Greenham Common, and decided that he would like one at Lulsgate Airport because he wanted to put it on the map [and to mark the 50th anniversary of the opening of the municipal airport at Whitchurch on 31 May 1930], and we spent a lot of time planning, working, securing sponsorship. With about two months of planning done, and with it going quite well, we then realised that the CAA regulations for a commercial airport there, due to the way it was built, would preclude us from running it with a big enough crowd. It was a hugely embarrassing moment when we found that out — we should have realised it earlier, in truth, but we didn't.

"So we went to Filton, and asked BAe if we could do it there. They said, 'Brilliant idea, we'd love it'. They gave us some offices, they gave us the key to the management diner, and we started planning again. We got a long way into it, and then, for my sins — and I don't know why this came about, but I've always ended up doing the insurances for the shows — I was having a meeting with BAe and Rolls-Royce about the risks, and they obviously wanted assurance that we would cover any event that caused damage to their factories. When I said, 'OK, but in order to do that I need to know how much they're worth', we very quickly realised that there was no way to put a value on it. It was open-ended and given that we were a small charitable trust, there was no way we could afford to take that risk on. With only two months to go, if that — we'd had the posters done for Bristol, we'd had the T-shirts made, and so on and so forth — it had to be cancelled.

"Luckily, we had some cancellation insurance, which paid for the Filton event to be called off, and we had to go cap in hand to the base commander at Greenham to say, 'If we can get approval from the SBAC, could we run a show here?' He said yes, so we went to SBAC and explained that we were in a hell of a pickle, we're committed, the cancellation insurance didn't cover all our costs, we've got aeroplanes coming, and can we tell them to turn 50° right and land at Greenham instead? SBAC were supportive, and said yes, but they added that we mustn't promote it outside, I think, a 25-mile radius of Greenham Common and that it mustn't be called IAT, because they were again worried about their crowd size. We ran the event, but it was probably the only time we'd made a loss, even with the cancellation insurance."

The Bristol International Air Festival would have celebrated 70 years of Bristol aircraft. The Newbury Air Festival marked 70 years of de Havilland aeroplanes, since Geoffrey de Havilland made his first flight from nearby Seven Barrows in September 1910. A static display of types from the Shuttleworth Collection's DH51 to a recently delivered Canadian Forces CC-132 Dash 7, with RAE Farnborough's Comet 4 XV814 as the centrepiece, looked impressive.

Not helped by dreadful weather on the opening morning, the show cannot be described as a roaring success, despite strong international involvement. It should have featured the UK debut of the Royal Netherlands Air Force's helicopter team, the *Grasshoppers*, in their four Alouette IIIs, but a disagreement with the flying control committee about minimum altitudes kept them on the ground. From the 'home team', this was the first time an Air Tattoo-organised event had seen the *Red Arrows* in their new Hawks, or a Royal Navy Sea Harrier FRS1 display. The *Blue Herons*, meanwhile, were at Greenham for the last time, though their Hunters had many years still to serve — and the *Rothmans Aerobatic Team* Pitts S-2s were on their way out as well, when 1980's season concluded.

GREENHAM COMMON
27 & 28 JUNE

Even for the Air Tattoo, it was going a bit far. "With the 'Hercs' at IAT 79, we had a symposium and a Hercules Industry Team", Tim Prince says, "but in 1981 we went a stage further and had a flying competition as part of SeaSearch". This first operational theme for the show brought together the maritime aviation community: patrol, strike, search and rescue, and more. It resulted in almost a full week of activity from the first arrival to the last departure, since the flying exercise elements took place on the Wednesday prior.

"For the fixed-wing competition", wrote Bill Newby-Grant, "maritime patrol aircraft were tasked to fly a four-hour sortie which included a visit to five search areas where they had to locate a small target and pass information to the Rescue Services, photograph a target and send an actual weather report, locate a dinghy and then locate and carry out a simulated attack upon a subsurface target. This was

linked with a recognition contest. For helicopters a specified route had to be flown with pre-selected targets photographed leading to a wet-winching competition on the lake and lawns at Bowood House in Wiltshire, the home of Lord Shelburne who had kindly consented to such unusual activities taking place."

Surprise winner of the fixed-wing contest against strong military competition was the BAe 748 Multi-Role demonstrator, virtually the variant's only notable achievement, while an RAF Wessex HC2 from No 22 Squadron took the rotary-wing prize. The Air Tattoo would never stage anything like it again, though. Tim says the flying competition "stretched us to the limit. We were effectively running an operational military exercise. It was great fun, and it worked, but logistically we got through by the skin of our teeth, and financially it was hugely expensive with the extra day's arrangements for the exercise participants. We were stretching our volunteer team members, and their annual leave allowances, by opening the airfield a day earlier on the Tuesday."

SEA SEARCH '81
INTERNATIONAL AIR TATTOO
ROYAL AIR FORCE GREENHAM COMMON
27~28 JUNE 1981

BAe(HS) NIMROD   10p
WESTLAND SEA KING   15p
DASSAULT-BREGUET ATLANTIC   20p
LOCKHEED CP-140 AURORA   30p

№ 09589   Issued on behalf of the Royal Air Force Benevolent Fund

INTERNATIONAL AIR TATTOO
SEA SEARCH 81
LOCKHEED

International Air Tattoo

Also being marked this year was the 40th anniversary of the maiden flight of a British jet-powered aircraft, the Gloster E28/39. Three examples of the first in-service British jet, the Meteor, were featured in the static line — No 79 Squadron's much-loved F8 VZ467, known as 'Winston', T7 WA662 from RAE Llanbedr and RAE Bedford's NF11 WD790 — with a fourth, the Vintage Pair's T7 WF791, in the flying. Bringing the theme up to date, BAe Warton demonstrated the new Tornado F2 air defence variant in prototype form. On the first day, BAe also supplied Nimrod AEW3 XZ286 for what turned out to be the disastrous airborne early warning derivative's sole IAT appearance, and British Airways sent Concorde G-BOAC for the supersonic airliner's long-awaited Air Tattoo debut.

More than usually, IAT 81 was an extremely varied affair. The Leisure Sport fleet of replica historic aircraft had one of its biggest single outings, pitching a Sopwith Camel and SPAD XIII against a Fokker Dr.I, D.VII and D.VIII in a First World War dogfight, and flying the Supermarine S5 racer reproduction over from Thorpe Park. Among the aerobatic teams, the French Air Force's *Patrouille de France* had new equipment since its previous IAT outing, the Magisters having given way to Alpha Jets. The days of Canadian Forces CF-104 formations were coming to an end, and 441 Squadron's *Starfighters* team took a final Air Tattoo bow. It was part of strong Canadian representation, 424 Squadron displaying a CC-115 Buffalo and 412 Squadron a CC-132 Dash 7. A French Navy F-8E(FN) was back in the flying, and very welcome too, but eclipsed on this occasion by the Étendard IVP and new Super Étendard showing off the 'buddy-buddy' aerial refuelling technique. The Royal Jordanian Air Force's 9 Squadron provided a singleton F-5E Tiger II, and 332 Skvadron of the Royal Norwegian Air Force flew an F-16A, the first Fighting Falcon display at IAT. Not seen before at Greenham, an MC-130E Combat Talon version of the Hercules from the USAF's 7th Special Operations Squadron demonstrated the mildly terrifying Fulton STARS (surface-to-air recovery system) kit, which raised an eyebrow or two within the flying control committee when the recovered 'pilot' was whisked into the sky over the top of the spectators' enclosure.

More than 50 items were featured in each day's eight-hour flying programme, as tightly packed as the schedule would ever get. There was a lot to fit in, but individual slots were all considerably shorter in those days. IAT's flying display manager, former RAF Lightning display pilot Wg Cdr Geoff Brindle, imposed a strict seven or eight-minute limit for solos, including take-off and landing. Today it is not uncommon for a singleton fast jet display to last upwards of 12 minutes, as long as some team routines used to be. From everything on the IAT 81 bill, some acts inevitably stood out, and the Royal Netherlands Air Force achieved something unique in Air Tattoo history when it swept the board at the awards presentation. Shortly before his retirement — he was then 62 — F27 pilot Maj 'Boy' Soons went home again with the Nationwide Display Sword, 315 Squadron's Capt Hans Hemmelder won the Embassy Solo Jet Aerobatic Trophy for his NF-5A demo, and the previous year's issues at the Newbury Air Festival had clearly been forgotten as the *Grasshoppers* scooped the Shell (UK) Oil Trophy.

It had been an outstanding weekend, and a fitting note for Sir Denis Crowley-Milling to retire on as IAT's chairman. It was not known at the time, of course, but 1981 was also the last Air Tattoo attended by its president, Sir Douglas Bader. Still, the influence of both men would continue to loom large.

Air Tattoo Memories: Bob Archer

One of the show's longest serving volunteers, Bob Archer is a member of the aircrew transport team.

"My first Tattoo was in 1981 at the huge American base at Greenham Common. I was a minibus driver, collecting the aircrew as the aircraft arrived. I quickly got the 'IAT family' bug and I've worked at every Air Tattoo since.

"Volunteering for me means 'The answer is yes, what was the question?'; working quite long hours and in all weathers; being part of a team and returning home exhausted but totally satisfied at having helped produce the greatest airshow in the world.

"My most memorable moments? Too numerous to recall all of them, but one that immediately comes to mind was supporting the groundcrew of a USAF B-1B in 1989 whose jet began to sink into the concrete because it had been over-fuelled. Defueling was very time-consuming and we eventually delivered the tired personnel to their hotel at 1am. Job done, and another group of satisfied personnel. That's the RIAT way!"

Army Air 82 Middle Wallop 23-25 July

Finding an event to occupy both the full-time Air Tattoo team and the volunteers in the years between biennial IAT shows was important. Otherwise, says Tim Prince, "you lost the continuity and you could easily lose the volunteers". During IAT 81 the director of the Army Air Corps, Maj Gen Bill Withall, asked Paul Bowen whether the Air Tattoo could organise an airshow at Middle Wallop the following year to mark the 25th anniversary of the corps. The enthusiastic response led to a formal approach, and so was born Army Air 82.

The AAC had staged regular Army Air Days at Middle Wallop before. This was a different kettle of fish, a much-expanded 'mini-IAT' on the big grass airfield in Hampshire, held from 23-25 July 1982. Part of it was Heli-Meet International, with associated flying and ground competitions, a symposium and social activities, and an International Military Helicopter and Equipment Exhibition, IAT's first industry trade fair. Both went extremely well, Heli-Meet — staged on 20 July — attracting no fewer than 40 participating rotorcraft. Their flying contest, Bill Newby-Grant recorded, "consisted of navigation, air to ground photography and low level reconnaissance tests over a timed route which took them from Middle Wallop via Upavon and Keevil to Broadlands, the stately home of the late Lord Louis Mountbatten and now the home of Lord Romsey. The house provided an ideal setting for the precision hovering and manoeuvring competition which was watched by several thousand spectators who were admitted to the grounds. All the competitors successfully found their way from Middle Wallop to Broadlands, even if for one of the larger aircraft the route had been via Bristol!" Sqn Ldr Mike Chapple and his Gazelle HT3 crew from the RAF's Central Flying School (Helicopters) were crowned overall champions.

The Army Air 82 flying display was first-rate. While it reprised popular elements from Middle Wallop shows past, particularly the massed approach by close on 100 helicopters rising above the horizon, much else was new. There was nothing newer than Hughes' YAH-64 Apache attack helicopter prototype, its European debut affording the crowd — and the Duke of Edinburgh, who sat in it before it flew — a first chance to see what would become one of the most significant items of military aviation hardware. It almost goes without saying that IAT attracted some high-quality overseas military acts, the stars being an Italian Army A109A and the Swiss Air Force displays of two Pilatus products, a PC-6 Turbo Porter and PC-7 Turbo Trainer. Royal Navy Hunter GA11s supported a Royal Marines ground assault, AAC Beaver AL1s made a supply drop from underwing canisters, and the spectacle of an RAF Harrier GR3 and Hercules C1 operating off the grass impressed.

The demands of the Falklands conflict, Newby-Grant wrote, lost the show "not only participation but also some other desirable items for air show organisers such as tents, stores, medical support and engineers to build bridges from the car parks to the public enclosures". Neither for the first nor the last time, the organisers made up for the shortfall through help, contacts and ingenuity. The attendance was three times as good as any previous Army Air Day, but still not as high as IAT had hoped. Still, with agreement to run a 1984 show at Middle Wallop, there would be time to improve on that.

Group Captain Sir Douglas Bader and the Air Tattoo

At each Air Tattoo, one display item walks away with a fine item of silverware called the Sir Douglas Bader Trophy for the best overall flying demonstration. But this is much more than a famous name being given to an award. It is one of the ways in which the show pays lasting tribute to a man whose involvement with the fledgling International Air Tattoo during the late 1970s and early '80s was truly close. In fact, Tim Prince feels, it's no coincidence that the event's growth at Greenham Common into the world's largest display of military aircraft occurred in exactly the period during which Sir Douglas was at the helm. Tim naturally got to know him well, and his affection for the man remains clear.

"The first encounter came through Air Marshal Sir Denis Crowley-Milling", Tim says. "When the Royal Air Forces Association decided to no longer be involved with airshows [after the Embassy Air Tattoo 74] and we went to the Royal Air Force Benevolent Fund, Sir Denis was the boss there. 'The Crow', of course, flew with Bader in his 'Big Wing', and when the Benevolent Fund took on the Air Tattoo he thought that we ought to develop the structure of it, and that it would be good to have a well-known personality as the head man. He asked Sir Douglas, who was a very good friend, if he would be our president. Sir Douglas lived just north of Newbury with his wife Lady Joan Bader, and he very quickly said yes. Sir Denis then really showed us what you do when you've got a president, in terms of how you use him.

"The personality was so well-known with the world's air arms that he was of great assistance in boosting our credibility. He helped us a lot in terms of getting overseas participation, over and above having Sir Denis Crowley-Milling. So he lent his name to it, but come show time he was a very significant person there, 'pressing the flesh' and making certain that everybody at all levels knew that he was grateful for what they were doing, whether it was an air force for sending aeroplanes or the guy who was driving the runway sweeper as a volunteer. He got involved, and he was terrific. It was interesting the way that our sponsors took a shine to us because Sir Douglas was there. It gave people the opportunity to meet the great man, this icon.

"He was a challenge at times — he wanted things to be right, but he didn't need to be looked after. If you tried to help him, he could get a bit hacked-off; he liked to do his own thing. His stamina was incredible, because he would spend all day in the president's enclosure as the senior host there, and then come our final function on the Sunday night, which in those days was at the manor house at Greenham Common, he would stand and receive each detachment commander and every volunteer manager of the organisation, shake hands and hand over one of our Air Tattoo plaques. You could tell that he was getting uncomfortable, standing on his two artificial legs, but he always saw it through. Quite incredible... He gave our organisation a boost, certainly. What stood out to me was his ability to inspire and motivate people."

As two of Tim's other anecdotes confirm, when Bader was committed to something like IAT, he really was committed to it. "I think it was the second show he did for us when he found there was a total clash, because quite a close family member of his was getting married over the show days. Knowing what's involved in a wedding, we thought, 'Oh, gosh, we've lost our president for the weekend'. But he told us, 'Just get me a helicopter — I'll do the wedding and I'll do the airshow'.

And he did. That was pretty impressive. I don't think Lady Joan was that pleased about it, but she knew she'd married a man who would always find a way.

"There was another occasion when we'd asked him to do the tailpiece for the Air Tattoo video, which entailed him coming to Greenham Common. We had a helicopter there with a camera crew in — the aim was that he would start talking about how good the event was, and as he came to the end of his bit the helicopter would climb up, leaving this little dot on great big Greenham Common. It was an awful day, it was pouring with rain, and foolishly we spent all our attention on the camera crew rather than going to the gate and waiting for Sir Douglas to arrive. He got to Greenham Common — he was driving a Mini, I think, at the time — was administered by the, even in those days, fairly secure US military system and got given directions to where we were, but he basically got totally lost. So, it was raining,

"Where Sir Douglas was often to be found was in a corner quietly talking to aircrew. He'd do all the things that had to be done, like meeting Royalty and other important guests, but what he really enjoyed was to meet the participants."

he was half an hour late, he'd gone on his own tour of the airfield twice, and he was just a little bit grumpy. But as soon as we were on to filming, it was superb. He did take after take in the rain. The man knew how to cope with adversity really well."

Interviewed by *Aircraft Illustrated*'s Mark Ashley, Paul Bowen said, "Where Sir Douglas was often to be found was in a corner quietly talking to aircrew. He wanted to learn what things were like in each air force today. He was very much of the people. He'd do all the things that had to be done, like meeting Royalty and other important guests, but what he really enjoyed was to meet the participants. When the Israelis brought a C-130 to Greenham in 1979, they had just taken part in the Entebbe Raid. I can remember Sir Douglas talking with the aircraft commander for many hours. He wanted to know about the entire mission. The rest of the airshow just went on around him."

Alas, as Tim Prince remembers, the association was ended by Bader's

passing. "On 5 September 1982, after a dinner honouring Marshal of the Royal Air Force Sir Arthur 'Bomber' Harris at the Guildhall, at which he spoke, Bader died of a heart attack while being driven home. That was desperately sad, and of course for the 1983 show we put on our special tribute at Greenham Common. It was a tricky time for us, because of course it was when the cruise missile site was being built and there were lots of changes to the airfield, and it threw us a bit, but fortunately for us, Lord Shackleton agreed to take on the role.

In thinking about what Sir Douglas had done for us — and over those years he really had helped us in achieving a great reputation — we wanted to do something special to recognise this. There were all sorts of ideas, like stained glass windows in churches and so on, but our view was that he was such a dynamic man, so inspiring, that it had to be something fitting, and as a consequence the Air Tattoo Flying Scholarships for the Disabled were born."

GREENHAM COMMON
23 & 24 JULY

Come the early 1980s, Greenham Common meant only one thing to most people. In 1980, it had been confirmed that it was to become the first US cruise missile base in the UK, housing 100 ground-launched cruise missiles (GLCMs). Not only would this lead to major construction work at the airfield, but it soon became clear that there would be significant opposition to the presence of the missiles on UK soil, headed by CND, the Campaign for Nuclear Disarmament. IAT 81 was unaffected, but IAT 83 would be an entirely different matter.

"The USAF people at Greenham confided in us", Tim Prince recalls, "because we'd been there several years whereas they rotate in and out every two years, so continuity of knowledge was with us. We knew quite a long time in advance". Not only that, but the people at the top of IAT were privy to high-level discussions, both politically and militarily, regarding the issue.

"We had to look very long and hard at things", he continues. "We were nervous about it for the obvious reasons. We knew the plan was to dig up the taxiway at the western end of the airfield in order to get the GLCM site built — sacrilege as far as we were concerned, because an airfield is for aeroplanes. All the empty barrack blocks that our volunteer team slept in would have had people living in them from the 501st Tactical Missile Wing. We were energetically assessing what we might do. Could we go elsewhere?

"But we were under significant pressure from the British government to stay. They wanted to show normality — that these cruise missiles were things that weren't going to be a problem day to day when they were stored there and when the USAF was doing its operational exercises. We conceded and we did stay there for the first year."

That year was 1983, by which time the peace camp had been set up outside the fence at Greenham. Founded in September 1981, it soon became a cause célèbre,

a reported 250,000 people marching through London the following month in support of CND's stance. April 1983 saw a 14-mile-long 'human chain' being formed between the Greenham peace camp, Aldermaston and the Royal Ordnance Factory in Burghfield which carried out weapons production for the Atomic Weapons Research Establishment (AWRE). Clearly, the atmosphere was going to be highly charged when Greenham hosted the world's largest military airshow that summer. Indeed, the STAR — Strike, Attack and Reconnaissance — operational theme was downplayed somewhat because of its nuclear connotation. It had already been scaled back, plans for a SeaSearch-style flying competition element being

Greenham military to fete Chile pilots

By CHRIS MYANT

SOON after the first Cruise missile equipment is landed at Greenham Common, the base will also be host to pilots and planes from Chile's fascist junta.

The Chileans are coming as part of the International Air Tattoo in July, run by the RAF Benevolent Fund.

Disclosure that permission for Chileans to take part has been granted yesterday took the glitter off claims by Defence Secretary Michael Heseltine that the Easter peace demonstrators

were undermining all his efforts to defend "freedom."

Acting up to his role as the government's official stunt man, Mr. Heseltine has taken himself off to be filmed standing in front of the Berlin Wall as the gates at Greenham Common were being blockaded by hundreds of women.

MILITARY THEME

The July tattoo goes under the acronym STAR—83 standing for "strike attack and reconnaissance." It will be accompanied by a major exhibition of the most up-to-date aerial military hardware from around the Western world.

The co-ordinator of the event, retired Wing Commander John Patterson, is telling potentially interested firms that the military theme will continue to be promoted in the specialist press, the armed forces and industry.

"However, the publicity aimed at the general public has been changed completely," he says in private letters now being circulated to the industrial and military customers.

For the "general public" the big theme will appear to be a tribute to the past president of the benevolent fund, Sir Douglas Bader, the Battle of Britain ace who died last year.

The chairman of the organis-

ing committee, Air Chief Marshal Sir Alastair Steedman, however, was worried that firms interested only in the military content might be discouraged by such a cover, he says.

JEOPARDISED

He "is most anxious to have your support and would not wish this to be jeopardised by external influences.

"He wishes you to know therefore that the STAR theme activities will continue as planned.

The "external influences" are the Greenham women's peace camp.

Wing Commander Patterson

had been "in constant and close touch with all those concerned in security matters. The threat has been considered at a very high level in the Ministry of Defence.

"It is assessed that any attempt at disruption at a public event of this type and magnitude, aimed at raising funds for the relief of distress, could only be counter-productive to the aims of CND."

So Mr. Heseltine joined in a cynical move to exploit Sir Douglas Bader's popularity as a cover for a military display and a ploy to turn public opinion against the Greenham women.

"I went to Berlin because the demonstrators are trying to turn Easter into a high visual weekend, and I felt it was necessary to give our point of view," he told reporters at Heathrow just before yesterday's peace chain was formed.

In another stunt to set off the peace activities, the government ordered the expulsion of a Soviet journalist and two diplomats.

New Times correspondent Igor Titov was told he had "engaged in unacceptable activities." Only a few days ago the Home Office had given him permission to stay for another year.

PEACE AT EASTER **Weapons factory** **Travelling, searching, waiting and**

Fregattenkapitän Witte and his crew flying Atlantic 61+13 of the Federal German Navy's Marinefliegergeschwader 3 had a fraught time. Having completed a display rehearsal on Thursday, all four of the maritime patrol aircraft's mainwheel tyres burst on landing.

deemed a bridge too far, while an accompanying exhibition was called off due to lack of support.

"Of course, we had tremendous consideration of the peace movement", Tim adds. "It was a situation that I found difficult personally, because some of those around the fence were my friends, and friends of my family. We had to strike a balance. Could we keep the show running logistically and, at the same time, would our sponsors want to be involved with it? Inevitably, one or two of them pulled out.

"Lady Bader came into play, because she lived just north of the airfield and was obviously still a good friend. On one occasion, she went and met with the protestors and asked that they be sympathetic, especially given that the show was to pay tribute to her husband, but also promoting what we did as actually being valuable, bringing these air forces together in a spirit of friendship. The peace women were very good as we let them have a space to protest inside, and all went off very peacefully. We had established a good working arrangement with them. It was a great relief."

Held in late July due to the need to accommodate crews in hotels and at Reading University, IAT 83 proved a tough one in all sorts of ways. There was the arrival incident involving the *Asas de Portugal*, when the lead pilot in the final pair of T-37s slammed his brakes on to avoid running over the temporary runway arrester gear too fast and was rammed by the aircraft behind. Both were written off, but two more 'Tweets' were brought in, and their show went on. When the 416th Bomb Wing B-52G (callsign 'Bowen 13' as a nod to Paul Bowen) got close to Greenham, its pilot declared he had no confirmation that the undercarriage was locked down. "I knew that the logical thing was to have him divert", says Tim Prince, "because though the pilot was fairly confident that it was OK, what we didn't want was a B-52 spread on the runway. In the end, we decided to let it land, and it was great."

Fregattenkapitän Witte and his crew flying Atlantic 61+13 of the Federal German Navy's Marinefliegergeschwader 3 had a fraught time. Having completed a display rehearsal on Thursday, all four of the maritime patrol aircraft's mainwheel tyres burst on landing. So as not to block the runway, Witte taxied clear, but the aircraft thus required new wheels. They were flown in from Nordholz aboard another Atlantic and fitted in time for Saturday's show. However, during its routine, a bird-strike on 'unlucky 61+13' caused an engine shutdown, forcing the Atlantic out of the rest of the event. At the Sunday night prizegiving, Witte was presented with two special awards: a trophy for Best Hard Luck Story and the volunteer British Airways stewardesses' award for the Most Outstanding Landing.

It wasn't all hard going. Dedicated to the memory of Sir Douglas Bader, IAT 83 not only launched the Air Tattoo's Flying Scholarships for the Disabled scheme, but also featured what was at the time the largest assembly of Hurricanes and Spitfires seen together at a British airshow. The Battle of Britain Memorial Flight provided both of its Hurricanes (then the only examples airworthy in the country) as well as its Spitfire IIa P7350, V AB910 and XIX PM631, joined by Rolls-Royce's Spitfire XIV RM689, Patrick Lindsay's Ia AR213, Classic Aircraft Displays' XIV G-FIRE and Mike Connor's recently-restored XIV NH749, which sadly went 'tech' after John Allison had flown it in the rehearsal and couldn't participate any further. Yet the sight of the static line-up was suitably impressive, and the flying — in front of Lady Bader — even more so. The five camouflaged Spitfires passed by together, before the red G-FIRE and a single Hurricane each performed solo aerobatics. The final salute saw all six Spitfires in formation and a 'missing man' tribute. Just like today, seeing a combination of RAF and civilian warbirds was rare indeed. First and foremost, though, it was a genuinely moving tribute.

Combined with the STAR 83 meet was a celebration of the F-4 Phantom's 25th anniversary. No fewer than 27 were amassed, the line headed by pre-production Phantom FG1 XT597 from the Aeroplane and Armament Experimental Establishment at Boscombe Down. As for 1979's Alcock and Brown commemoration, Wilf Hardy came up with a special livery, based around the 'raspberry ripple' scheme recently applied to XT597 at St Athan. It was produced in decal form and applied on the ground at Greenham. The massed rank alongside took in Phantoms from every RAF squadron then operating the type — No 111 Squadron FG1 XT863 winning the concours d'elegance — along with 11 examples from West Germany's Luftwaffe and seven belonging to European-based USAF units, the

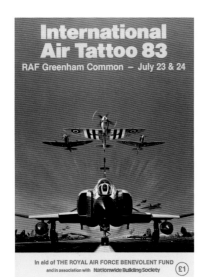

Air Tattoo Memories: Graham Finch

Graham has been the designer of the Air Tattoo souvenir programme since 1989 and a volunteer since 1981.

"As a member of the photo team at the 1983 Air Tattoo, I was tasked with photographing the 25th anniversary Phantom line-up from the on-site 'cherry picker'. Having climbed into the basket, it wasn't until we reached the full height of the extended arm that I realised how different conditions were up there. The basket, which had little in the way of safety features (and I wasn't attached to anything), was swaying in the wind and this unnerving instability influenced my rapid decision to hunker down on the floor and shoot from there... Thankfully I got the pictures I wanted, although I'm sure the chap in the basket with me wasn't sharing my sense of impending doom as he stood nonchalantly puffing on his cigarette. Never have I been more glad to set foot on solid ground!"

83

When the 416th Bomb Wing B-52G got close to Greenham, its pilot declared he had no confirmation that the undercarriage was locked down.

greatest rarity being the F-4E operated by the 57th Fighter Interceptor Squadron at Keflavík, Iceland.

Framing the F-4s, the USAF put a 17th Reconnaissance Wing TR-1A and 9th Strategic Reconnaissance Wing SR-71A on show at the Air Tattoo for the first time. On arrival from Mildenhall, its home with Detachment 4 of the Beale AFB, California-based wing, 'Blackbird' pilot Lt Col Bredette 'BC' Thomas put on a spectacular series of overshoots and low, fast passes. This was, in every way, the individual aircraft highlight of IAT 83.

Many others played their part, of course. Static newcomers included an RAF BAe 146 C1, Chilean Air Force C-130H, Italian Air Force PD808GE, NATO E-3A Sentry and Royal New Zealand Air Force Boeing 727. Among a fine collection of MoD test and trials aircraft, the ex-Argentinean IA-58 Pucará captured after the Falklands War and under evaluation by the A&AEE, and the sole Short SC9 from RAE Bedford, were particularly noteworthy. In the air, the Italian Air Force *Frecce Tricolori* made a first UK visit flying their 10 new Aermacchi MB339As, the Royal Jordanian Air Force Mirage F1EJ was a debutant, and two regular items from several Air Tattoos, the Austrian Air Force *Karo As* team and the Goodyear airship *Europa*, bowed out.

Against stiff opposition from Dutch and Norwegian F-16s in particular, the RAF Lightning F3 flown by Flt Lt Mike Thompson from the Lightning Training Flight won the renamed Superkings Trophy for the best solo jet demonstration. Thompson lost his life a month later in an accident while carrying out an unauthorised display at Scarborough seafront. Hauptmann 'Charly' Zimmermann of the Federal German Army was even more successful than he had been at IAT 77, being awarded the International Display Sword and the Sir Douglas Bader Trophy for his aerobatics in the Bo 105M.

Even after proceedings closed, there was a sting in the tail. It involved the SR-71. Tim takes up the story. "We had to move the SR-71 south-side at the end of play on Sunday in order to prep it for its flight home the next day. Its KC-135Q tanker was with it, because at that time they would fuel the SR-71 from the tanker on the ground, it being 'special' fuel. Whilst it was over there, guarded, a breakaway group from the peace ladies had decided it was a good target

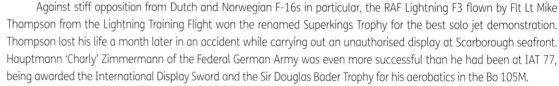

Wilfred Hardy

On arrival from Mildenhall, 'Blackbird' pilot Lt Col Bredette 'BC' Thomas put on a spectacular series of overshoots and low, fast passes – the individual aircraft highlight of IAT 83.

and found a way to get over the fence at an appropriate time, countered the guards by going this way and that, and threw paint.

"The big worry was whether the paint was going to affect the surface on the 'Blackbird'. We spent a very worried few hours there, with all sorts of significant members of parliament and senior UK and US air force officers worried that we'd lost control — which, of course, in a small way we had. But, didn't that crew depart in style when they left? It was the most outstanding flypast down the runway, followed by another flypast which just happened to be just slightly south of the runway over the top of the peace camp."

SR-71 pilot Maj Jim Jiggens gave IAT 83 a fine sign-off, but this incident showed why the show had to leave. As when North Weald became unsuitable as a venue, the team went on a search for somewhere new, but this time with more in the way of high-level support. "When we decided that we had to leave Greenham Common, we were very worried about moving to a new location", Tim says. "We'd established some fantastic friendships around the Newbury area, with some great people who helped 'grow it', in the community who accepted it, and who also became part of our strong team.

"We looked at many airfields, as we had been told to leave no stone unturned. We went to Odiham, we went to Manston, and a good possibility was Bedford, but when we got there we found that there had been so many experiments there over the years with bits of metalwork bolted to the ground, ski ramps and so on that it was actually an impractical site to clean up to be safe for the public. So we ended up with Fairford, and the USAF was incredibly receptive. We'd got used to working on an American base, without doubt, and we fitted in with them very, very well, so it seemed appropriate that we'd find another stand-by base that the Americans were running. They tended to have very long runways, and obviously the longer the runway the more interesting aeroplanes you can get in. Fairford fitted that mould well."

In fact, Tim and Paul Bowen already knew the Gloucestershire airfield. "Of course, at one stage in the 1970s there were going to be KC-135s based at Greenham, which made me come over to Fairford to see if we could relocate here even then. In fact, there was a plan at that stage to refurbish the runway at Fairford, which would have precluded us coming here. That runway refurbishment programme was delayed until 2000-01..."

Volunteers who run the Tattoo

Some of the local volunteers helping at the Tattoo. Left to right — Bryan Philpott the Press centre manager, Mrs Annette Hill the information officer, Mr Nigel Dennis, Mr Tony Sangwine and Mr Mike Jarratt. All are members of the International Air Tattoo committee.

Tattoo job six years

Mr Mike Jarratt, a partner in the local firm of solicitors Ward Bowie, was responsible for the enclosures at the Tattoo — a job he has done for the last six years.

"We started off with two or three enclosures," he said on Sunday." "We have 15 this year." He had been working on the necessary arrangements since September last year, and took four days holiday so that he could devote his time to the Tattoo.

Mr Jarratt, who lives in Northcroft Park, ran all the enclosures, including those for various firms and the Hospitality Suite. The job involved planning the facilities which would be offered in the enclosures, preparing promotional literature and supervising the actual building of the enclosures themselves.

Information officer loves her work

MRS ANNETTE Hill from the Glade, Newbury, has been involved with the Tattoo for about 10 years and is at present information officer and group travel manager, a job she "absolutely loves."

During the last war Mrs Hill flew a variety of aircraft, delivering them to operational stations. She served with the Air Transport Auxiliary, which she joined in 1943, and among the aircraft she delivered was the Barrracuda torpedo-bomber.

She was stationed at Prestwick, and most of the planes she delivered were for the Fleet Air Arm. She continued with the Auxiliary until just after the war.

Some years ago she had the opportunity to fly a Havard, one of the aircraft she had delivered during the war. During the war she also flew Hurricanes.

Mrs Annete Hill, the Tattoo's information officer.

She is responsible for the information centre at the Tattoo, and also helps with arrangements for the Press. "I think it has put Newbury on the map," she said of the Tattoo.

Former Mayor's second tattoo

THIS is the second year that Bryan Philpott, from Cheviot Close, has been press centre manager at the Tattoo, although he was interested in it before he took on the role.

A former Mayor of Newbury, Mr Philpott said that he became involved in the Tattoo because of his aviation writing. He has written more than 20 books, mainly about military aircraft, the first of which was published in 1971.

Mr Philpott went to Park House school and spent three years in the RAF. After leaving the forces he joined the Royal Air Force Volunteer Reserve and was commissioned in 1957. He was then adjutant to 211 (Newbury) Squadron of the Air Training Corps, and became its commanding officer in 1961.

He has lived in Newbury all his life and is sales manager with UK Solenoid, a firm he has been with for 26 years.

As press centre manager he has been responsible for writing press releases on a variety of subjects and organising tickets for the national, local and specialist press.

"As soon as this show is over we start to think about the next one," he said, adding that he had been working for this Tattoo since the end of last year.

He took a week's holiday from his job in order to concentrate on the Tattoo.

International Air Show 84 Middle Wallop 7 & 8 July

Having taken on the Army Air Corps' main airshow at Middle Wallop in 1982, some changes were implemented for the next show in what became a biennial series. It was given a new name, and the public days became a two- rather than three-day affair, on 7-8 July 1984. In other ways, however, this first International Air Show followed the same pattern: six hours of diverse flying, the massed helicopter approach as its unique showstopper, and the accent very much — but not exclusively — on helicopters, with participants in the Heli-Meet taking up a good proportion of the static display and the International Military Helicopter and Equipment Exhibition being repeated.

Heli-Meet guaranteed the attendance of some rare birds. This time a pair of Swedish Army Hkp 3Cs (AB204s), a Swedish Navy Hkp 4B (BV-107-II), a soon-to-be-retired Belgian Navy HSS-1 and a French Navy Alouette III were the choicest visitors. In the 40th anniversary year of the D-Day and Arnhem landings, the flying mixed a mass Parachute Regiment descent, RAF Hercules tactical demo and a multi-service battlefield display featuring helicopters and a Harrier GR3 with the 1944 nostalgia of Aces High's Duxford-based C-47A Skytrain and regular Air Tattoo supporter Jim Buckingham in his invasion-striped Miles Messenger, depicting the example used to transport Gen Montgomery. Pilatus Britten-Norman looked to the future with the debut of the CASTOR (Corps Airborne Stand-Off Radar) Islander testbed G-DLRA, its platypus-esque nose containing a Ferranti multi-mode radar.

TVS Air Show South Bournemouth 18 & 19 August 1984

Aside from the Middle Wallop shows, IAT took on another event in the 'off years' between Air Tattoos. The opportunity came courtesy of TVS (Television South), the local ITV franchise company for the south and south-east of England. According to Tim Prince, "The head of TVS had been to our show, liked it a lot, and asked us to run one. He wanted it run alongside his offices in Southampton, so we went down there and Paul and I recced Southampton Airport. With all that Supermarine history there, what better place? But we quickly realised that with the commercial operations and the limitations and the infrastructure around, we couldn't do it there. So we went to Bournemouth, where both Paul and I had trained as air traffic controllers. We were warmly welcomed by the director there, who said he'd love it to happen."

Happen it did, beginning with the first TVS Air Show South on 18-19 August 1984. Perhaps the biggest attractions were some of Bournemouth's unusual based aircraft: classic jet operator Hunter One flew its Meteor NF11, WM167, with red Hunters G-HUNT and G-BOOM, while the static park contained Flight Systems' F-100F Super Sabre N417FS, then looked after by FR Aviation. And it was, notes Tim, "interesting mixing the commercial traffic with flying displays". But the weekend presented more than its fair share of difficulties. Having starred in the opening ceremony of the Los Angeles Olympics and been Sean Connery's James Bond stunt double, jet pack-equipped 'rocket man' Bill Suitor's appearance cost several thousand pounds for just a few seconds of flight. More precisely, Tim says, it was "£14,000 for a roughly 14-second burst". Even that might have been cut short, but for Suitor just avoiding getting his legs caught on the control tower balcony railing. Worse was to come. During a pairs departure by two RAF Phantom FG1s on the Sunday morning, one of them, XV569, experienced what was described as a nosewheel steering malfunction. As the aircraft veered off course, onto the grass to one side of the runway, the navigator ejected, sustaining quite serious back injuries. The pilot got things under control, climbed away and went on to make an emergency landing at Lyneham. All things considered, a lucky escape.

85

RAF FAIRFORD
13 & 14 JULY

From the outset, RAF Fairford felt right for the Air Tattoo. Being there perpetuated the link with the US Air Force built over 10 years at Greenham Common, which was a very good thing. It also had all the attributes needed to host the world's largest display of military aircraft. But there was still a risk attached, and both Paul Bowen and Tim Prince, as co-directors, knew it.

As Tim puts it, "We were moving house, moving our families, and we were trying to establish relationships with all of those local people and agencies on whom we were going to rely very heavily, or on whose lives the show was going to have an impact. Obviously we'd built gradually at Greenham, and people had grown with us. Here we were going to move to a whole new set of Lions Clubs and Rotary Clubs selling programmes and parking cars, highways departments, a new police force — or even three new police forces, Gloucestershire, Oxfordshire and Wiltshire — and the base itself, because it was operational with KC-135s.

"I think the fact it was an operational base was exciting, but there were lots more considerations there. Every day you went on the airfield, unlike Greenham where you just went out, here you had to check with the airfield manager and air traffic and follow the rules, which was no bad thing."

Those KC-135s were detached from units in the USA. With NATO's increasing need for air-to-air refuelling support in the European theatre, it had proved necessary to augment the Stratotankers on temporary duty at Mildenhall with a complement at a second base. The choice fell on Fairford, and in mid-November 1978 the USAF established the 11th Strategic Group

With Danish and Canadian F-104s appearing for the final time, accompanied by Italian and West German jets, the classic Lockheed fighter was having its last major Air Tattoo showing, with no fewer than 16 on Fairford's tarmac.

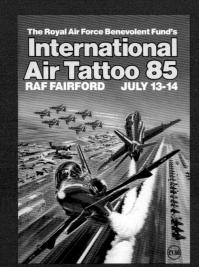

The Royal Air Force Benevolent Fund's
International Air Tattoo 85
RAF FAIRFORD   JULY 13-14

£1.50

to oversee operations. KC-135s began to arrive during September 1979, the 7020th Air Base Group having been set up as Fairford's 'host unit'.

"It was nice moving here — we had the support of all the volunteer team because they were determined that the show should continue — and when we got here, we found it was bigger; there was more 'depth' to the airfield", Tim comments. "There were more taxiways, and there wasn't a cruise missile bunker site at the end of the runway! It gave us lots of opportunities to 'grow' the event, but I think the other reason it felt right was because there were operational aeroplanes here. When you're on a disused or stand-by airfield, you tend to get more rules and regulations than when you're on an operational base. When you're on an operational base, you get a realistic approach to challenges by the aircrew running it. Col Pittman, commander of the 7020th ABG and Col Lunt, commander of the 11th SG made us very welcome, and yes, it felt really good."

Given Fairford's day-to-day role, it was very appropriate for IAT 85 — staged over the same July weekend as the Live Aid concert — to take aerial refuelling as its operational theme. The result was the SkyTanker meet, by far the biggest assembly of different tanker platforms ever seen at a single event, even if they hailed from just four countries. Of course, KC-135s dominated the static line, no fewer than 12 being on hand. The concours d'elegance winner was KC-135E 56-3611 of the 145th ARS, Ohio ANG, the same squadron that had provided the outstanding low-level KC-97 display at Greenham 11 years earlier. But there were also debuts from a newly delivered RAF VC10 K3, a French Air Force Transall C-160NG with a hose-and-drogue set-up, and a Federal German Navy Tornado 'buddy-tanker'.

Unlike some of the other Air Tattoo operational meets, there was a substantial SkyTanker element to the flying as well. Two KC-135As, both 509th Bomb Wing examples on detachment to Fairford, opened the show. It was closed by an EC-135H command post from the 10th Airborne Command and Control Squadron at Mildenhall flying through with three 20th TFW F-111Es, one of them actually hooked up to the boom. In between, the RAF impressed with a stream flypast by a Hercules C1K, Victor K2, VC10 K2 and the first Tristar K1 conversion, flown for the first time from Marshall of Cambridge — an IAT sponsor since 1979 — only a few days before. The French Navy again contributed a 'buddy-buddy' refuelling demo with an Étendard IVP leading a Super Étendard.

More international than the SkyTanker gathering was the Douglas DC-3/C-47 50th anniversary contingent. Ten of these classic machines were seen at Fairford, the preceding Thursday witnessing the mass arrival of five from Eindhoven where the Dutch Dakota Association had staged a week-long DC-3 half-century celebration. Two of them, Col Tom Thomas' DC-3 N53ST and the Confederate Air Force's R4D-6 N151ZE, had flown over from the USA. Joining them for the trip from the Netherlands were the DDA's own PH-DDA, Air Atlantique's G-AMSV and the Aces High C-47A G-DAKS. They taxied in to park with RAE Farnborough's Dakota III ZA947, which — like the Phantoms in 1979 and 1983 — wore special anniversary markings designed by Wilf Hardy. The Hibernian Dakota Flight's Dublin-based N4565L had been held up at Eindhoven by a technical snag, but it followed a little while later, as did the Italian Air Force EC-47A, used for airfield navigation aid calibration work by the 14° Stormo at Pratica di Mare. While G-AMSV had to leave temporarily, F-GDPP from Transvalair at Caen-Carpiquet made up the eight-aircraft line. Over the weekend, Air Atlantique brought G-AMRA and 'AMSV in with passengers from Bristol and Norwich respectively. Only the Aces High machine represented the 'Dak' in the IAT 85 flying display, with the Dutch example winning the DC-3 concours d'elegance.

This was, for various reasons, not the best Air Tattoo flying programme ever put on. Particularly apparent was the almost complete lack of overseas military display teams. Not only did the *Patrouille de France* and *Frecce Tricolori* have commitments at home, but Austria had disbanded the *Karo As* and the *Asas de Portugal* were temporarily in abeyance. The *Patrouille Suisse* didn't come as, Peter March wrote in *Aircraft Illustrated*, "the Swiss were not happy about the loss of the RAF's order for the new trainer", the Pilatus PC-9 having lost out to the Shorts Tucano as a Jet Provost successor. Only the Dutch *Grasshoppers* and the Federal German Navy's *Vikings* were left, the latter joined in the show by a four-ship of Luftwaffe F-104Gs operated by Luftwaffenversorgungsregiment 1 at Erding, West Germany's last Starfighter pilot training unit. With Danish and Canadian examples appearing in the static display for the final time, accompanied by Italian and further West German jets, the classic Lockheed fighter was having its last major Air Tattoo showing, with no fewer than 16 on Fairford's tarmac. Under Sunday's low cloud, the *Vikings* gave a truly scorching show, Kapitänleutnants Axel Ostermann and Siggi Schmidt on superb form in their two Marinefliegergeschwader 2 mounts.

RAF participation was also limited due to fuel shortages. However, the *Red Arrows* were of course present, performing a flypast with a British Airways Concorde — under the command of Capt David Leney — for the first time in public. With the number of military acts down, civilian performers took a greater share of the programme than usual. Two other wartime American types celebrating their 50th anniversaries were Plane Sailing's recently arrived PBY-5A Catalina and B-17 Preservation's much-loved B-17G Flying Fortress *Sally B*. Rather different from the Air Tattoo norm were the Unipart-backed Fournier RF4 motorgliders flown by Brendan O'Brien and John Taylor, and the late Yves Duval's pair of tiny twin-engined Colomban Cri-Cris sponsored by Brittany Ferries, but both were featured strongly in BBC1's post-event coverage, a new feature in 1985.

Some major plans for IAT 85 unfortunately didn't come off. Discussions were had with the Confederate Air Force about bringing some of its warbird fleet to Britain aboard an aircraft carrier, but failed to come to fruition. A contingent of Air National Guard fighters — including what would have been the F-106 Delta Dart's only Air Tattoo appearance — was scheduled to come but, Peter March wrote, "it was found that funds could not be made available for the ANG to fly them across the Atlantic specially to take part in the Tattoo". But, despite these and other disappointments, the show still proved a success. More importantly, Fairford had proved itself as IAT's new home.

PHOTO: KEV SLADE

PHOTO: PAUL NELHAMS

TVS Air Show South Bournemouth 31 May & 1 June 1986

Back to Bournemouth, this time on 31 May-1 June, the sun largely failed to shine on the south coast. In fact, Saturday's flying programme was all but wiped out by the atrocious weather conditions. But this was still an excellent show, extremely international and with a dash of nostalgia. With eight aircraft across the flying and static displays, the French Navy made one of its biggest showings yet; the Spanish Air Force returned after quite a long absence, with a C-101 Aviojet and C-212 Aviocar in the static park. Again the based historic jets were present in force, among them the FR-operated Sea Vixen D3, XS587. And when Sunday's weather allowed, notable items included the last display at an IAT show by the Federal German Navy *Vikings*, the 2,000th public performance by the *Red Arrows* and the début of IAT's own ex-Argentinian Air Force Bell UH-1H G-HUEY, restored by Rob Tierney.

International Air Show 86 Middle Wallop 12 & 13 July

As a wartime RAF fighter station, home to the Spitfire-equipped No 609 Squadron during the Battle of Britain, Middle Wallop lent itself to celebrating the Supermarine fighter's 50th anniversary.

On 12 and 13 July, the 1986 International Air Show did so with 10 examples, more than had been brought together at a British airshow for a long time. The Battle of Britain Memorial Flight brought its MkIIa P7350, MkV AB910 and PRXIX PM631; on the civilian front, Shuttleworth sent its MkV, AR501; MkVIII MT719 came from Italian owner Franco Actis; the Old Flying Machine Company and The Fighter Collection supplied their MkIXs, MH434 and ML417; two-seat MkIXT ML407 was provided by Nick Grace; PRXI PL983 was owned by French collector Roland Fraissinet; and Rolls-Royce's familiar MkXIV RM689 was on hand too. Linking wartime and present-day Middle Wallop, BBMF commanding officer Sqn Ldr Paul Day flew the MkXIX with the Army Air Corps' *Eagles* helicopter team of Lynx AH1s.

The Heli-Meet line-up was superb, too. Sweden's contingent was remarkable: army Hkp 3Cs (AB204s), Hkp 6B (AB206) and Hkp 9 (Bo 105), plus Hkp 4s from the navy and air force. The Italian Army was a significant supporter too, with A109, AB212 and CH-47C, while the US military helicopter contingent ran into double figures, two new US Army UH-60A Black Hawks among it. In the air, the massed approach once more presented a remarkable spectacle. Many would consider IAS 86 the best of the Middle Wallop shows, and it's hard to disagree.

World Festival of Aerobatics Airshow

South Cerney 16 August 1986

Right: Paul Bowen, Jeff Bullen and Sir Alasdair Steedman.

Only a few miles away from its home, IAT was brought in to arrange the World Festival of Aerobatics Airshow as part of the 13th World Aerobatic Championships, staged at South Cerney — just up the road from Fairford. Stars of the display on 16 August were three Sukhoi Su-26Ms of the Soviet national team, following their victory in the championships, which performed an exhilarating celebration routine. Other competition machines in the programme included new French CAP 230s, Czechoslovak and Hungarian Zlin 50s and aircraft from the US team. Other items from the RAF — *Red Arrows* among them — and USAF, Czechoslovak support Antonov An-2 and a British Airways Concorde made this a diverse and entertaining airshow.

Sir Alasdair Steedman with G-HUEY.

87

RAF FAIRFORD
18 & 19 JULY

The Royal Air Force Benevolent Fund's
International Air Tattoo 87

RAF FAIRFORD 18-19 JULY

Lessons had been learned from that first Air Tattoo at Fairford. Holding the show at an airfield so deep in the countryside, further from the major road network than Greenham Common, proved a challenge in traffic and accommodation terms, and integrating the event into the activities of an operational US Air Force KC-135 base brought its own issues. Moving on to IAT 87, the organising team had taken the change of venue in its stride. All the greater a shame, then, that the weather conspired to affect things so severely. It was bad throughout, reaching a nadir with a three-hour downpour on Sunday that disrupted the flying display and turned parts of Fairford into a quagmire. But, as always, the Air Tattoo team rose to the occasion.

IAT 87 was still an excellent show, its content well up on the previous Air Tattoo. This was typified by the SkyLift meet, a gathering of transport aircraft that in itself produced a more than mile-long static line of airlifters and one of the Air Tattoo's finest ever flypasts: the massed formation of 15 Lyneham-based Hercules C1/C3s, marking 20 years since the C-130K's entry into RAF service. In fact, a third of the total Lyneham Transport Wing fleet participated in some form over the weekend, other flying appearances including a refuelling flypast from C1K and C1P variants, and a famine relief food drop demonstration as performed during Operation 'Bushel' in Ethiopia. Tim Prince says, "It was rekindling that early Farnborough spirit, where the sky goes dark because of the number of aeroplanes, and I think that's what airshows are all about. Since 1979 when we did the Hercules meet we'd established a very strong rapport with Lyneham — a lot of our volunteers came from there, and the 'truckies' are always keen to push the boundaries a bit."

Also pushing the boundaries was the most spirited Hercules display seen in the UK at that time, by a Swedish Air Force Tp 84 (C-130E). Somewhat surprisingly, Sweden had never before contributed to the Air Tattoo in any form — the Flygvapnet was not then a regular part of the wider European display scene. Its Hercules solo set a new standard, featuring vertiginous wingovers and, in its rehearsal, a double outboard engine shut-down during one of them. "Surprisingly", Peter March's *Aircraft Illustrated* report recorded, "this was frowned upon by the IAT Flying Control Committee, although it did not break the very precise display regulations, a fact which was pointed out by the crew, but to no avail."

The USAF's support was ever more apparent. Again the Ohio ANG's 145th ARS was the concours d'elegance victor, KC-135E 55-3146 beating the SkyLift competition. A-7D and A-7K Corsair IIs from the Pennsylvania and New Mexico ANGs were present during UK deployments, but Strategic Air Command's 509th BW flew in two FB-111As just to appear at Fairford, only the second time the variant had been to a British show. A first for IAT 87 was the presence of two different EC-130 Hercules variants: an EC-130E of the 193rd SOS, Pennsylvania ANG and a 43rd Electronic Combat Squadron EC-130H based at Sembach, West Germany.

Display teams were much better-represented this time, nine in total taking a major slice of the programme. All first-footing in Britain, the Spanish Air Force *Patrulla Aguila* with its CASA C-101 Aviojets, the *Halcones* of the Chilean Air Force flying Pitts S-2s and the two CAP 10s of the Royal Moroccan Air Force *Marche Verte* were imbued with a certain degree of innovation, the *Aguila*'s close-formation landing and the tied-together aerobatics of the *Marche Verte* being especially notable. The French Air Force provided the exceptional *Phénix* parachute team, jumping for the first time in the UK and doing so from an Armée de l'Air type new to the show, a DHC-6 Twin Otter.

The times were a-changing as far as fast jet fleets were concerned. A section of the programme dubbed SkyShield, celebrating 75

International
Air Tattoo 87
RAF FAIRFORD 18-19 JULY
CIRENCESTER, GLOS
in association with
Nationwide
Building Society

International
Air Tattoo 87

RAF FAIRFORD
CIRENCESTER, GLOS
18-19 JULY

in association with

Lloyds
Bank

IAT

International
Air Tattoo 87

RAF FAIRFORD 18-19 JULY

"The Aviation Event of the Year"

IN ASSOCIATION WITH

Nationwide Building Society

years of UK air defence, saw both the last IAT display by an RAF Lightning, an F3 version from No 5 Squadron, and the first from a Tornado F3, an award-winning effort by No 229 OCU's Flt Lt Paul Brown. This was the first Air Tattoo since 1972 not to feature a Starfighter demonstration of some sort, a sole F-104G from West German military test unit WTD 61 being the only example in the static park. But the French Navy's F-8E(FN) Crusaders were soldiering on, and Flottille 12F returned to the IAT flying with a scintillating display of this great carrier-borne fighter.

The Royal Jordanian Air Force's solo Mirage F1EJ and the *Royal Jordanian Falcons* Pitts trio were watched enthusiastically on the Sunday by King Hussein, patron of the Air Tattoo. He had earlier made his own flypast on arrival in the Royal Flight TriStar, JY-HKJ. Understandably, Tim Prince recalls him with great affection. "Having Sir Douglas Bader as our president in our early days was really special. Then, when His Majesty King Hussein took over as patron, that was another wonderful situation for us. The man loved aviation, he loved people, and it did us a lot of good. Having him fly in in his TriStar was outstanding."

This was an event of uncommon depth. Australian national airline Qantas bolstered the civil side of the SkyLift theme by sending Boeing 747-338 VH-EBX

> "Having Sir Douglas Bader as our president in our early days was really special. Then, when His Majesty King Hussein took over as patron, that was another wonderful situation for us. The man loved aviation, he loved people, and it did us a lot of good."

TVS Air Show South 88 Bournemouth International Airport 4 & 5 June

It was possible to reflect themes at the Bournemouth show, too. Unusually, the 1988 event on 4-5 June celebrated a civil aeroplane: the 25th anniversary of the BAC One-Eleven. Hurn had, after all, been the main production and flight-testing site for the type. In the end, three came together: one from the Sultan of Oman's Air Force, XX919 from the Empire Test Pilots' School, and EI-BVI, on delivery to a small Irish airline called Ryanair. Elsewhere, a very rare static showing of an Alconbury-based TR-1A away from a USAF base, the last-minute attendance of an Oklahoma Air National Guard A-7D and a very sizeable clutch of US Army fixed- and rotary-wing assets affirmed the event's international credentials. But this was IAT's last Bournemouth display, for it and sponsor TVS ended up with bigger plans for 1990.

to fly past on Sunday. There all weekend in the visiting and charter aircraft park was the extraordinary Hurel-Dubois HD34 F-BHOO. The ultra-high aspect ratio, twin Wright Cyclone-powered machine had been one of eight used as survey platforms by France's Institut Géographique National, but was sold in 1986 to the Association des Mécaniciens-Pilotes d'Aéronefs Anciens at Melun-Villaroche, and flew a group of French enthusiasts to Fairford. While moving Short SC1 XG900 from storage at Hayes to Wroughton, the Science Museum took the opportunity to exhibit this example of the experimental vertical take-off and landing jet in public after 15 years out of view. A sad reminder of 'what might have been' was the wreckage of Graham Warner's first Blenheim restoration, which would have been seen in the air had it not crashed at Denham the month before. A more enduring act in its debut season was that great showman Vic Norman's Stearman wingwalking display, John Adams flying the Yugo Cars-backed biplane with Lesley Gale strutting her stuff on its upper surfaces.

The weather might have prevented an attendance record from being set, but if 1985 had been a little light on content, IAT 87 was anything but. The scene was set for a vintage period.

International Air Show 88

Middle Wallop 16 & 17 July

The 1980s Middle Wallop shows all had their own special character. This one saw a mass, multi-national gathering of T-6 Texan/Harvard variants to salute the 50th anniversary of the type entering RAF service, including a 14-strong line-up. The Army Air Corps' Eagles team, combining historic and modern fixed- and rotary-wing aircraft, included an Alouette II for the first time. Having missed out on flying in the 1986 show following a landing mishap, the Museum of Army Flying's Sopwith Pup N5195/G-ABOX was able to take to the air this time. Industry representation brought two S-70 Blackhawk variants, the Westland-built WS-70 demonstrator and Rolls-Royce's RTM322 engine testbed. In the static park, the Royal New Zealand Air Force was a Wallop newcomer, bringing a UH-1H for the Heli-Meet contest aboard a C-130H, while a US Navy SH-3H operated by HS-3 — and flown in from the destroyer USS *Hayler* — rivalled it for rarity. But this was the last IAS staged in full collaboration with the Air Tattoo team, the Army Air Corps deciding to go it alone from 1990 onwards.

US Air Force Col Tom LaPolt (second from left) at a show briefing with Paul Bowen and Tim Prince.

89

RAF FAIRFORD
22 & 23 JULY

A great deal of attention was focused on UK airshows in 1989, and not for positive reasons. The appalling accident involving the *Frecce Tricolori* at Ramstein, West Germany during August 1988 caused the loss of 70 lives and many other injuries, and provoked much debate as to whether the price of display flying had become too high. It went as far as the Prime Minister, Margaret Thatcher, who reportedly declared that airshows should continue in Britain so long as such a disaster could not happen here. "When that tragedy happened", says Tim Prince, "it sent a shockwave through the world of airshows."

The result, come 1989, was a raft of new regulations on the part of both the civilian and military authorities. Events held earlier in the season bore the brunt of their impact, but IAT was not unaffected. "Since taking Duncan Simpson's advice in the earlier years we'd had a flying control committee", Tim continues, "so we were always seen by participants as a place where they behaved according to the regulations. The *Frecce* had been with us in 1987, and when they displayed with us they undertook the same manoeuvres but they were absolutely fine. We stopped and thought about it, we worked with our government, and believed that our rules on the flying side of things were robust; that so long as we maintained that approach we could continue. What we did learn from it was that we needed to enhance our emergency safety plans to be able to cope with a disaster. We spent a lot of time with the people from Ramstein, the medical personnel, the emergency services, to learn the lessons. All of them were very helpful and wanted to share, and as a consequence we enhanced the robustness of our safety plans quite considerably.

"With the Air Tattoo everybody involved in the organisation, whether volunteers or permanent staff, has done it before, bar any newcomers. We were well-practised in the art of running airshows — it was our business — whereas what can happen at military-run airshows is, 'We're having an airshow, who's available to run it?' You don't necessarily have quite the understanding or experience levels that we enjoy, so we're very lucky in that respect."

IAT 89's particular slice of good fortune was the weather. Record-breaking temperatures reached 94°F, and unbeaten hours of scorching sunshine saw to it that Fairford welcomed the highest-ever Air Tattoo attendance, exceeding 250,000. From first arrival to last departure, the show had never quite seen anything like it, though the heat did mean the weekend's jet noise was accompanied by the regular sound of sirens as ambulances dealt with the effects of heat exhaustion within the spectators, participants and the IAT team.

In NATO's 40th anniversary year, it was fitting that the Alliance's 'big stick', US Air Force Strategic Air Command, so dominated the flying display. A sequence dubbed 'SAC Attack' saw a stream take-off by one of the home-based 11th SG's KC-135Rs, an FB-111A of the 380th BW, a 319th BW B-1B, and a B-52G from the 2nd BW, followed by individual flybys from each. Of the three bombers, only the Stratofortress had ever appeared in an IAT flying display before. Never had such a concentrated display of SAC air power been witnessed at a British show — no wonder Tim says, "I think the USAF was extremely pleased with how we presented their capabilities".

> # Record-breaking temperatures reached 94°F, and unbeaten hours of scorching sunshine saw to it that Fairford welcomed the highest-ever Air Tattoo attendance, exceeding 250,000.

In NATO's 40th anniversary year, it was fitting that the Alliance's 'big stick', US Air Force Strategic Air Command, so dominated the flying display. Never had such a concentrated display of SAC air power been witnessed at a British show.

More was to come, as SR-71A 61-7967 made the 'Blackbird's' Air Tattoo flying debut, and its last ever UK show appearance, when it displayed on departure during Sunday afternoon.

On an exercise deployment to Leck, West Germany, dubbed 'Coronet Rock', two A-10As of Tactical Air Command's 23rd TFW from England AFB, Louisiana, were n unexpected addition to the static park. The pair of A-7Ds provided by the 112th Tactical Fighter Group, Pennsylvania ANG crossed the Atlantic just for IAT, their immaculate finish contrasting with the decidedly weathered look of the Hellenic Air Force A-7H and TA-7H from 345 Mira, making up a fine gathering of Corsair IIs. Perhaps surprisingly after so many years, this marked Greece's debut at the show, adding another country to the long list of NATO partners — and others — brought together by the Air Tattoo. Among 19 aircraft sent by different branches of the Ministry of Defence (Procurement Executive), a highly uncommon outing by RAE Llanbedr's Meteor D16 WH453 was the star.

SeaSearch was the operational meet for the second time, the concours d'elegance falling to the No 37 Squadron, Royal Australian Air Force C-130E. Another Hercules, a US Coast Guard HC-130H based at Borinquen, Puerto Rico, carried an HH-65A Dauphin in its hold. The colourful rescue helicopter was among several 'firsts' for a UK show, such as a Portuguese Air Force SA330C Puma and a Swedish Coast Guard C-212. The long journey from Comox, British Columbia, by a bright yellow Canadian Forces CC-115 Buffalo from 442 Squadron was especially appreciated. While the Kinloss Wing was unable to make such a big flypast commitment as had Lyneham two years earlier, its three-ship Nimrod MR2 flypasts were still unusual.

In honour of the *Red Arrows*' 25th display season, one of their Hawks was briefly parked with aircraft from the other participating teams — the *Halcones, Royal Jordanian Falcons, Marche Verte, Asas de Portugal, Aguila* and *Patrouille Martini* — for a photocall. Less cause for celebration, sadly, was the RAF Canberra PR9 display. On the circuit for the 40th anniversary of the English Electric twin-jet, it had already made several successful showings elsewhere. At Fairford, though, what *Aircraft Illustrated* called "a contretemps with the IAT Flying Control Committee" after Saturday's performance led to the No 1 Photographic Reconnaissance Unit aeroplane taking no further part in proceedings, save for its early departure that afternoon.

But there is an argument for saying the single most significant attendee at IAT 89 was an unassuming civilian biplane. Hungarian Air Service took crop-spraying Antonov An-2 HA-MEV to several western displays that summer, its visit to Fairford being the first time an active aircraft from eastern Europe had come to the Air Tattoo. Many more would follow. In fact, with détente between east and west developing, records show that preliminary discussions about the possible participation of Soviet military aircraft had taken place in the lead-up to the 1989 event. Following the historic MiG-29 visit to Farnborough in 1988, the door had been opened in political terms by the Soviet withdrawal from Afghanistan. In the event, it took a few more years to become reality. But the political upheaval that swept through the Warsaw Pact states as 1989 drew to a close, and the resulting renewal of old alliances in the post-Cold War world, would change the character of the Air Tattoo forever.

Representative aircraft from the aerobatic teams participating at IAT 89 gathered together in honour of the *Red Arrows*' 25th display season.

Opposite page top right: Michael Bentine, Sir Peter Masefield and Sir Denis Crowley-Milling chatting to Prince Feisal in 1990.

Opposite page middle right: Fred Crawley (left) and AVM Freddie Hurrell (right) – RAFBF director of appeals in 1990.

TVS Battle of Britain Air Show

A&AEE Boscombe Down 9 & 10 June 1990

With continued backing from TVS, the aim of the Battle of Britain Air Show was to assemble the year's biggest gathering of 1940-era warbirds for a large-scale set-piece.

It came as quite a surprise: a full international airshow, an Air Tattoo by any other name, at the Aeroplane and Armament Experimental Establishment (A&AEE) Boscombe Down. The famed test and evaluation airfield in Wiltshire had effectively been off-limits to the public for years, but that changed as the 1990s dawned. Tim Prince recalls, "We'd got to a state where the relationship with the SBAC and Farnborough was such that they'd accepted that there perhaps wasn't the level of concern about our show and theirs running in the same year, and we felt we needed to 'ratchet it up' in the 'even years' from the level of the Bournemouth and Middle Wallop shows to something closer to the level of the Air Tattoo.

"The feeling was that we should take an intermediate step, and both Paul and I had worked at Boscombe Down as civilian air traffic controllers. We thought, you know, there's a nice long runway, there should be friendly people there, we knew the airspace and all the danger areas, and we thought we'd give it a try. I remember going there and being told each time, 'You can't, because of...' this or that. We said, 'Why don't we do it this way, then?' Slowly, we persuaded the commandant that it would actually be a good thing to host a show. Air Cdre David Bywater, the commandant at Boscombe at the time, was so receptive to the vision that we had... It would have been easy for him to say 'no'." The 50th anniversary of the Battle of Britain helped smooth the way. The RAF Benevolent Fund aimed to mark the occasion by raising some £20 million, and where better to hold an airshow in aid of the 'Reach for the Sky' appeal than a Fighter Command station from the battle itself?

With continued backing from TVS, the aim of the Battle of Britain Air Show was to assemble the year's biggest gathering of 1940-era warbirds for a large-scale set-piece. If only the weather had played ball. Saturday's crosswind kept the 12 Spitfires and two Hurricanes ground-bound. Co-ordinating the aerial action was Dave Southwood, then a test pilot with the A&AEE, who put the scenario together alongside commentator Seán Maffett and flew Carolyn Grace's two-seat Spitfire IXT ML407 that weekend. "On the Saturday", says Dave, "there was a fair bit of crosswind on the main runway, and we decided we couldn't land back on. We said we could launch part of the scenario, land at Bournemouth where the wind was within limits, and recover on the Sunday morning. They didn't want that because there was a big layout of all the aeroplanes on one of the pans, and they wanted them there on Sunday morning. But the Messerschmitts" — actually a pair of HA-1112 Buchóns depicting Bf 109s, and a Nord 1002 playing a Bf 108 — "weren't involved, so we just launched the three of them. A lot of Battle of Britain veterans there were pretty hot under the collar about having the Messerschmitts whizzing around with no Spitfires or Hurricanes!

"For Sunday the wind was coming down, but everybody had got a bit 'ground-happy' by then and become really circumspect about the weather. There was a slot about half-way through the day when something had cancelled, so we agreed that Stephen Grey in his Hurricane and me in Carolyn's Spitfire would fly that slot together, just to get two of the aeroplanes airborne to show everybody else that it was fine to fly. Stephen and I did this, and then we had the whole scenario right at the end. It worked out extremely well."

Making an uncommon appearance, Warbirds of Great Britain's Spitfire IX NH238 and PRXI PL983 simulated the instruction in fighter combat of a newly fledged pilot. Fittingly, NH238 was in the hands of a man performing his debut Spitfire displays, Rod Dean — his first of many. Then the scene switched to the German airfield attack, a pair of Buchóns, provided by Charles Church Displays and Hans Dittes and flown by Reg Hallam and the very enduring Walter Eichhorn, joined by probably the 'most shot-down man' in the British airshow annals, Lindsey Walton with his Nord 1002. The civilian Spitfires and Hurricane scrambled after them, and a vigorous tailchase ensued.

One element was almost too realistic. Following a successful RAF 'attack', the Nord was to disappear below the horizon, whereupon a pyrotechnic explosion simulated its

Air Commodore Mike Stanton

AIR COMMODORE MIKE STANTON, who has died aged 67, flew many operational sorties as a Lancaster bomber pilot during the Second World War and later underwent some alarming experiences as British Air Attaché in Saigon during the Tet Offensive.

In retirement he served for some 10 years as a most successful appeals director of the RAF Benevolent Fund. A key figure behind the Fund's biennial International Air Tattoo, Stanton was driving out of RAF Boscombe Down, scene of the recent Battle of Britain 50th Anniversary Air Show, when he was killed in a collision.

A few hours earlier, as crosswinds curtailed a dogfight display by a Me 109, Hurricane and Spitfire fighters, he had commented on the perils of flying the "old ladies" under such conditions.

Tall and elegant, with a deceptively languid air, Stanton charmed contributors to the fund with much the same insouciance as he had, during his time as air attaché, kicked hand-grenades out of his Saigon garden.

A naval commander's son, Michael Peter Stanton was born at Hastings on Jan 25, 1923, and educated at the Imperial Service College and Skinners' School, where he was a sergeant-major in the OTC.

He earned his wings in Canada, where he spent a year as an instructor at the RCAF's Central Flying School. Stanton then served in Transport Command and was seconded to BOAC until 1945, when he took part in the bomber offensive against Germany in 149 and 138 Lancaster Squadrons.

In 1946 he commanded No 70, a Lancaster squadron in the Middle East, where he later took over No 216, a Dakota communications squadron. After a series of desk appointments Stanton flew Canberra jets in the late 1950s and had a spell as a flight commander in No 9 Squadron. He then held various Intelligence posts at the Air Ministry until 1966, when he was sent to Vietnam as Air Attaché.

Provided with a De Havilland Devon, Stanton took part in the rescue of British families from a rubber plantation; he also built a rapport with American diplomats.

On his return from Vietnam in 1969 he was appointed to the command of RAF Fylingdales, the nerve-centre of Britain's early warning system, and three years later his Far East experience made him an ideal choice as Air Commander in Hong Kong.

His final appointment was to RAF Halton, renowned as a centre of excellence for technical training, where he was Commandant from 1975 to 1978.

The next year he joined the RAF Benevolent Fund, and when he retired from that two years ago he joined the team running the current Battle of Britain 50th Anniversary "Reach for the Sky" appeal.

Stanton was appointed CBE in 1969. He is survived by his wife, Peggy, and a son.

Left in the photo above is the director of the *Patrouille de France* Col Pierre-Alain Antoine, Mike Stanton centre, with Derek Morter on the right. Derek led the *Blue Herons* and then became the Air Tattoo's aero teams liaison man.

the RAAF pilots who flew with Fighter Command in 1940, it was back. No 1 Squadron deployed two F-111Cs the long distance from Amberley, Queensland, transiting through the Marshall Islands and into the USA before crossing the Atlantic and arriving at Upper Heyford a week before the Boscombe show. The intervening days were spent, in part, using the opportunity to fly operational training missions including low-level work. While a lack of time prior to leaving Australia prevented Sqn Ldr Mark Skidmore from working up a full aerobatic display, the 'dump and burn' still lit up the grey Wiltshire skies.

Although it had become a regular performer elsewhere, this was the first time the much-acclaimed French Air Force Mirage 2000 demonstration had been at an Air Tattoo event, EC 2/2's Cne Laurent Fournier doing the honours. The Canadian Forces put in a four-ship formation of 439 Squadron CF-188s as a further Battle of Britain salute. Following nine years' absence, the Hunters of the *Patrouille Suisse* made a return.

No other show could hope to boast the line-up of British test and trials aircraft the Boscombe static park was able to muster, with Royal Aircraft Establishment (RAE) aircraft from Bedford, Farnborough and Llanbedr joining the home-based fleets of the A&AEE and Empire Test Pilots' School (ETPS). Eleven years after it had gifted the Venom at Greenham, the Swiss Air Force gave another classic de Havilland jet to the RAF Benevolent Fund. This time it was a newly retired Vampire T55, U-1215, intended as a replacement for the *Vintage Pair's* Vampire T11 which had been lost at Mildenhall in 1986. In the event it ended up with the Royal Jordanian Air Force Historic Flight. The Portuguese Air Force provided a selection of aircraft the like of which it had never sent to a UK show: two T-38A Talons from Esquadra 102 were making the Northrop jet trainer's British airshow debut, the Esquadra 502 C-212ECM was a variant of the Aviocar hitherto not seen here, and the pair of Esquadra 302 A-7Ps were welcome as always. Rather than Corsairs, the Hellenic Air Force this time brought a Mirage 2000BG from 332 Mira for a first-time visit.

Even away from Fairford, the USAF took a big portion of the static park. A quartet of 33rd TFW F-15C/Ds, normally based at Eglin AFB, Florida, came over from Soesterberg in the Netherlands where they were on a deployment dubbed 'Coronet Trigger'. Similarly, the 112th TFG, Pennsylvania ANG A-7Ds flew in from their Exercise 'Cold Fire' detachment to Spangdahlem, West Germany. A very scarce catch indeed was a CT-39A from the 375th Aeromedical Airlift Wing's 1467th Facility Checking Squadron, normally home-based at Scott AFB, Virginia, but temporarily stationed at Rhein-Main for navigation aid checking around Europe. Never again would a Sabreliner attend an Air Tattoo event. A US Coast Guard HU-25A Guardian was a newcomer, and the US Navy contingent was the best for some time. An A-6E, S-3B, F-14A+ and F/A-18A Hornet came from the USS *Dwight D. Eisenhower*, and a CH-53E flew in from NAS Sigonella, Sicily, its base with helicopter transport squadron HC-4.

Inevitably there were some drop-outs from the intended line-up. Canadair CL-215 and Conair Firecat fire-bombers from France's Sécurité Civile fell by the wayside, as did plans to have a Royal New Zealand Air Force Boeing 727 and some of the A&AEE's aircraft in the flying display. But the TVS Battle of Britain Air Show was still a great success, as well as an historical turning-point in the IAT story. East European participation was here to stay, and would only become more exciting.

downfall. Fine in principle, but some of the emergency services didn't know it was just an act... This, incidentally, was the much-missed Walton's last Air Tattoo before the genial Lincolnshire potato farmer retired from airshow flying a few years later. He had regularly brought his aeroplanes to Greenham Common and Fairford since the earliest days.

The finale was another nice bit of choreography. Four of 1990's air defenders, Phantom FGR2s from No 56 Squadron, performed their own scramble while most of the warbirds formed up for a mass flypast. 56 had itself been stationed at Boscombe half a century earlier. One of the Phantom crews was made up of a Luftwaffe exchange pilot and navigator, very much in the spirit of reconciliation the whole tribute sought to engender.

That went for Czechoslovakia's pioneering involvement, too. "Paul and I had always been determined to get Eastern Bloc countries to the show because it was aviation we celebrated, not air forces in particular", Tim Prince says. "We liked to bring the world together. So, we'd been beavering away at the embassies on every possible opportunity. We've always — since we found out — had to go through the Foreign Office and the appropriate MoD departments, and there was an easing. It was just continuous approaches direct to their chiefs and to their air attachés, and eventually we struck a chord with the Czechoslovaks. In fact, we struck that chord with them because their air attaché in London saw great benefits in what the RAF Benevolent Fund was doing, and they saw an opportunity to start up their own Benevolent Fund. When we got the breakthrough for that first show at Boscombe Down, luckily David Bywater had the foresight and the courage to say it was a good thing, because going into a place like Boscombe was of course a very interesting step to take."

At one stage a Czechoslovak display team of three L-39 Albatros jet trainers was foreseen as attending. In the event, a single L-39C and an L-410UVP Turbolet twin-turboprop light transport made the trip, provided by manufacturers Aero Vodochody and Let. It was a useful way in for the east European nations. "We showed 'the system' that we could do it", Tim went on, "and we could manage it well, and that opened the door and they trusted us. I think the government had seen the benefits of the east Europeans coming to this sort of event."

Not since 1977, and the Silver Jubilee Review of the RAF at Finningley, had the Royal Australian Air Force given its famous F-111 'torching' flyby at a British show. Now, recalling

★ ★ ★ THE DAILY TELEGRAPH, TUESDAY, MAY 22, 1990   7

NEWS

Pictures TONY PRIME

No wings and a prayer: A rebuilt 1909 Bleriot due to help launch the RAF benevolent fund's Battle of Britain appeal in the entrance of Phillips yesterday. The aircraft will be auctioned at RAF Bentley Priory at Stanmore Middx. in September.

Volunteer engineering services manager Bob Basing delivering the RAF Benevolent Fund's Bleriot to Phillips Auctioneers for the Fund's £20m Battle of Britain Appeal in 1990.

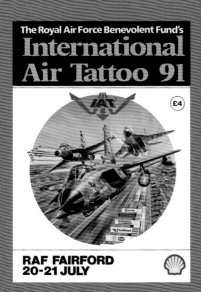

91

RAF FAIRFORD
20 & 21 JULY

What a difference a few years make. Back at Fairford for IAT 91, the Czechoslovak Air Force made British airshow history. Yes, Soviet firms Mikoyan and Sukhoi had exhibited their fighters at the last two Farnborough shows, but these were manufacturers' aircraft, not front-line examples. The Czechoslovak contingent was very much operational, forming part of a first-class show.

"We struck up an extremely good relationship with the Czechoslovaks", Tim Prince says. "That Battle of Britain show [in 1990] was a draw for them, such that in consequence we got very close to them... that relationship really grew, and there was a strong thread running through it in that these countries saw the opportunity to get close to NATO, to find out how it works, because obviously they saw the benefits of being able to join NATO."

This was an early opportunity for the Czechoslovaks to get close to NATO, and they grasped it with both hands. In this, the Air Tattoo played its part in the later expansion of the alliance.

IAT 91 welcomed seven aircraft from the Czechoslovak Air Force, most notably two MiG-29s — one flying, in the hands of Col Václav Vašek, one static — and a MiG-23ML for the static park. An L-39ZA gave a solo display, while An-12BP and Tu-134A transports, both exhibited statically, supported the contingent. The only disappointment was the technical problem that curtailed the MiG-29's flying appearance on the second day, especially since this rendered it ineligible for any of the trophies. At this point, these were judged solely on the basis of Sunday's programme. Vašek's performance was a stylish account of the agile fighter, showing well the excellent slow-speed handling characteristics that had already become its hallmarks. His two tailslides were nicely executed, if rather more limited than those the Mikoyan test pilots had demonstrated.

A small but potent sign of the times was the way in which the 11. SLP, the unit that provided the 'Fulcrums', aligned itself with the NATO Tiger Association as part of the Tiger Meet staged at the show. It even painted small tiger stripes on the fins of its aircraft. This was an early opportunity for the Czechoslovaks to get close to NATO, and they grasped it with both hands. In this, the Air Tattoo played its part in the later expansion of the alliance.

It was a doubly auspicious occasion, being the Tiger Meet's 30th anniversary, and a very colourful static display ensued. The Portuguese Air Force Fiat G91R from Esquadra 301, the Mirage F1C and CM170 Magister of French Air Force unit EC 1/12,

the CF-188 belonging to the Canadian Forces' 439 Squadron, the Belgian Air Force F-16A from 31 Squadron and the Italian Air Force F-104S of the 53° Stormo were especially outstanding. Perhaps it was a little surprising to see the Upper Heyford-based 79th TFS F-111E winning the concours d'elegance with just a tiger-striped fin, but this USAFE squadron was one of the founder members of the Tiger Association. Another of them, the RAF's No 74 Squadron, put up a neat four-ship formation routine of Phantom FGR2s.

The two Ilyushin Il-18Ds from German operator B-Air that attended over the IAT 91 weekend even got into the Tiger Meet spirit. Both previously on the strength of East German state carrier Interflug, D-AOAO and D-AOAU had the now defunct airline's titles amended to read 'Tigerflug' on one side. They each brought a group of enthusiasts in from Berlin-Schönefeld and gave an hour-long pleasure flight during the flying programme. Out of B-Air, which had been formed by ex-Interflug staff members, was formed the short-lived Berline concern, which went under three years later. German unification also saw the Luftwaffe taking over certain East German military types, among them the An-26s of the air force's Transportstaffel 24, one of which came to the show.

Appearances at Fairford by such aeroplanes would not have been possible without the end of the Cold War. The strategic landscape had changed, and with it Fairford's own role. Since the previous Air Tattoo, on 7 August 1990 the USAF had

Team meeting 1991.

Teresa Smith busily bed-plotting at IAT 91

TIGER MEET

INTERNATIONAL
AIR TATTOO
91
RAF FAIRFORD · 20-21 JULY

It was a doubly auspicious occasion, being the Tiger Meet's 30th anniversary, and a very colourful static display ensued.

disbanded the 11th Strategic Group, making KC-135 detachments a thing of the past. It reverted to being a Strategic Air Command stand-by base just days after Iraqi forces invaded Kuwait, as coalition forces began massing in the Persian Gulf. The consequences would reach Gloucestershire, too. During Operation 'Desert Storm' from January-March 1991, B-52Gs from different units brought together under the 806th Bomb Wing (Provisional) flew 62 missions from Fairford, expending 1,158 tons of munitions.

A Gulf Salute became IAT 91's largest theme, involving more than 100 aircraft that had been engaged in efforts to liberate Kuwait. Often still sporting either their temporary 'desert pink' colour schemes, Gulf War nose art and mission symbols or both, the RAF's Tornado GR1s, Jaguar GR1As, Buccaneer S2B, Puma HC1, Tristar K1, Victor K2 and VC10 K2 attracted much attention in the static display. The highlights, though, came from US Navy squadron VQ-2 at Rota, Spain: an EA-3B Skywarrior and EP-3E Orion, the former on its last outing to a UK event prior to replacement by

TO BE RETAINED AT ENTRANCE GATE

This ticket is valid for one day and is not transferable. Ticket invalid if ENTRANCE GATE STUB is detached.
See conditions on reverse.

COMPLIMENTARY

**The Royal Air Force Benevolent Fund's
INTERNATIONAL AIR TATTOO**
RAF Fairford, Gloucestershire
20/21 JULY 1991
Sponsored by
Price £12
Admit ONE ADULT
IN ASSOCIATION WITH ALLIANCE ◆ LEICESTER

VALID FOR ONE DAY ONLY AND IF STUB IS ATTACHED

G223240

the converted P-3s. If the USAF had been able to send an F-117, it would have been the icing on the cake, but the 'stealth fighter's' British public debut would have to wait until Mildenhall the following May. At the time of IAT, the 37th TFW reportedly remained 'on call' for further Gulf operations.

A substantial chunk of the daily flying schedule was given over to Gulf Salute items, opening with the nose-down take-off of a 97th BW B-52G and closing — eventually, once a few snags had been resolved — with a 7th SOS MC-130E demonstrating the Fulton STARS system. The most esoteric element was Boeing 707-338C G-BDEA of Anglo Cargo, representing the civilian carriers that augmented the huge military airlift effort in the Gulf. Anglo itself had completed nearly 200 flights to and from the region, making 22 of its crew members eligible for the Gulf Medal. The 707's low opening pass in the hands of Capt Graeme Smith, in opposition to the backtracking B-52, created one of the show's unique vistas.

The list of flying display 'firsts' was especially long. An in-service Italian Air Force AMX from the Reparto Sperimentale Volo, a Spanish Air Force EF-18A Hornet and a duo of Swiss Air Force F-5Es — dubbed the *Tigers* both after the aircraft type and the fact that their operator, Flieger Staffel 11, was the Swiss Tiger Squadron — were all UK debutants. Nods to the Hunter's 40th anniversary came from a Royal Navy GA11, with long-time FRADU pilot Brian Grant at the controls, and the *Patrouille Suisse*, its F58s resplendent with new red and white national markings on their undersides.

In terms of all-round quality, IAT 91 was arguably the best Air Tattoo since the move to Fairford. It was announced that Boscombe Down would again host the 'even year' event in 1992, when the new-found friendships with east

PHOTO: ANTHONY NOBLE

In terms of all-round quality, IAT 91 was arguably the best Air Tattoo since the move to Fairford.

European air arms would bear still further fruit.

They were solidified when, in September 1991, Paul Bowen and Tim Prince went to Prague-Kbely for Czechoslovakia's inaugural international military airshow. The country's representatives had taken much away from their visits to Boscombe Down in 1990 and Fairford in 1991: as Tim describes, "They liked what they saw, they liked the fact that the public got close to the military which they hadn't been able to do there in the past under Soviet control, so we were able to offer a lot of support and

advice on how to do it. Obviously, after Ramstein, we wanted airshows to be run safely, so we were very happy to lend support with our procedures, our flying regulations and the like. We hopped backwards and forwards to Prague to help, and the quid pro quo for us was that we got more aeroplanes. That's the sort of approach that Paul and I used for many years. We'd go and help, so long as somebody paid for our air fare — and it was a wonderful experience to go to these places, which had long been 'closed shops' — and in return aeroplanes were sent". Some unforgettable years were in store.

Air Tattoo Memories: Mike Pomeroy

Mike's first show was TVS Air Show South in Bournemouth in 1984. Currently RIAT's site manager, he is one of our longest-serving volunteers.

"In our early years at RAF Fairford I looked after the water supply to the chalets and public. At that time the water was drawn from the original piped mains around the airfield. Unfortunately, whilst fit for drinking when tested by the environmental health officer, it came out with a rusty appearance in content because of lack of use of the mains and it didn't give a good impression. Prior to running IAT, I had this bright idea that if we ran the water through a hydrant overnight on a quiet part of the airfield it would clear the pipes. It got a popular vote with management so I duly turned on the hydrant before going home to bed (or the bar!). Unfortunately, and unbeknown to me, the water came from a tower holding tank on the base. At 4am an MoD policeman went to make a cup of tea to find there was no water in the pipes – it was all on the airfield. You can image the panic that I caused. I'm glad to say that it didn't take long for the tank to refill. Paul Bowen never ever allowed me to forget the incident — but actually, he was really understanding. I'm pleased to say that contractors now deal with the water supply from off-site."

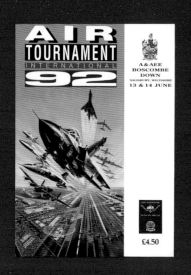

Air Cdre David Bywater chats with Tim and Paul in the hangar at Boscombe Down.

Air Tournament International 92
Boscombe Down 13 & 14 June

A front-line fighter from Russia's long-secret test and trials base, appearing at Britain's equivalent. It had been the stuff of dreams. It nearly turned into a nightmare. But it produced one of the most jaw-dropping moments in the half-century of the Air Tattoo. The aircraft was a Sukhoi Su-27P, serial 595, operated by the Gromov Flight Research Institute, or LII, at Zhukovsky near Moscow. Its pilot was Anatoly Kvochur, the man whose MiG-29 demonstrations had so wowed the west at Farnborough in 1988, and whose low-level ejection from his stricken 'Fulcrum' in Paris the following year made more headlines around the globe. The combination of Kvochur and the 'Flanker' was to create new legends in the world of airshows.

Tim Prince takes up the story. "We'd got the initial approval for Anatoly to bring his Su-27 from Zhukovsky, and we gave RAF Air Cdre Ray Dixon, a volunteer heading our air operations department, the task of making sure it all happened. There was all manner of things — we were trying to get the visas sorted out for the Russians, the fuel, the accommodation, the diplomatic clearances and so on — and, of course, there was a hiccup. We found there was a problem with that particular aeroplane leaving Russia, whereby their computerised flight planning system was not happy with it. There was a huge amount of work done — our man had been working day and night, and so had Anatoly — but it was so close to being cancelled.

"Eventually the approval came through, so he set off, and we knew he'd set off to arrive in the middle of the flying display on Saturday. Even though he'd missed his normal arrival day slot, we were determined that no matter what, we'd get him in. It was touch and go as to whether he was going to have to divert, because the *Patrouille de France* were displaying. The agreement was that he, in the single Su-27,

would arrive with a Tu-134 and that they would do a conventional landing. That was the arrangement, and that's what should have happened. Anatoly was obviously so pleased to be there after all the trials and tribulations that he gave the most fantastic performance, where he approached between the runway and the crowd with the Tu-134 as it was landing, came down to an extremely low level with wheels up, and then pulled into a three- or four-minute routine.

"Air traffic obviously made sure the airspace was clear — there was a bit of a language problem, even though there was a Russian speaker in the tower — and it happened. It shouldn't have happened, and our flying control committee were not happy about it because it was not briefed and Anatoly was potentially tired. He then, having got his magnificent aeroplane to the show, had to stand in front of the flying control committee and have a severe reprimand, which potentially could have meant he couldn't fly the next day. In so doing, he also missed meeting the Duke of Kent! But, after some humble pie was eaten, the committee agreed that he could fly the next day."

The delightful Boscombe Down venue, some fascinating aircraft, perfect weather — almost everything came together.

The Su-27 saga caught the attention of everyone in the organisation. Commercial director Caroline Rogers says, "I can remember the atmosphere at Boscombe for two days before he arrived, and it was quite electric — people sitting by 'phones, Ray Dixon who was project-managing this going from one drama to another, the situation moving forwards and backwards. When they appeared in the sky, it was really quite a moment!"

The 'Flanker' set the seal on what some would argue was the Air Tattoo team's finest show to date. The delightful Boscombe Down venue, some fascinating aircraft, perfect weather — almost everything came together. Why, though, the rather odd Air Tournament International title? It was, after all, basically an Air Tattoo. "That was part of the transition, for Farnborough to get used to us running an annual IAT, or an ATI as we

cheekily named it!", says Tim. "Boscombe Down did us proud in letting us have two years there, I have to say."

The Czechoslovak Air Force was back in real force, with two front-line types new to the UK. Aside from the returning MiG-29 and L-39, it flew a Su-25K operated by the 30. BILP, painted in a love-it-or-hate-it scheme. Reflecting both the aircraft's NATO reporting name 'Frogfoot' and its anti-armour role, the livery incorporated an artwork of a cartoon frog hammering a tank. On the flying programme it replaced the listed MiG-21, which stayed at home due to a fleet-wide grounding caused by a fatal accident. Shown statically, the other newcomer was a Su-22M4K from the 20. SBOLP, offering a western audience a first chance to see this hard-hitting strike jet. But it wasn't just in Czechoslovakia that close ties had been forged. They had with the Hungarian Air Force, too, the static attendance of a smart An-26 transport being an initial result.

An enormous contingent from the German military — nearly 30 aircraft — offered further evidence of these changing times. The ex-East German Navy Mi-8T, one of 15 taken on by the unified German Navy and now operated from its old Parow base by the Marinefliegerhubschraubergruppe, looked immaculate. It was the first Mil helicopter to attend an IAT show. Landing just before Saturday's flying programme and staying until Sunday afternoon, Tu-154M 11+01 was a former Interflug machine transferred to the Luftwaffe as a VIP transport, which function it fulfilled on its visit to Boscombe.

Part of a big contingent from the USS *Saratoga*, then on a Mediterranean cruise, a US Navy F-14B brought a taste of Tomcat action back to an Air Tattoo flying display after fully 15 years away. VF-74 commanding officer Cdr Chuck Wyatt's demo of the big carrier fighter was a charismatic and polished one, but not enough to win the Superkings Trophy. Not presented at the previous Boscombe show, this time it was, to Belgian Air Force Alpha Jet pilot Cdt Dany Payeur. There was no opportunity for any of the formation displays to win an award — had there been, the Swedish Air Force's *Team 60*, mounted on six Saab SK 60s and debuting in Britain, might have been in contention.

As at the previous Boscombe show, warbirds were a prominent feature, as ATI marked the 50th anniversary of the arrival in Britain of the US Eighth Air Force. This featured two of the event's biggest attractions: the Confederate Air Force's B-24A/LB-30B Liberator *Diamond Lil*, kicking off its summer tour after a troubled flight from Fort Worth, and The Fighter Collection's P-38J Lightning that had only just arrived at Ipswich Airport following restoration at Chino and its own shipborne trans-Atlantic voyage. The B-24 joined B-17G *Sally B*, TFC's B-25D Mitchell and BAe's freshly re-covered and repainted Mosquito in representing the 'heavies', while the still unpainted P-38 — in the hands of Stephen Grey — tailchased with its P-47D Thunderbolt stablemate, two Spitfires and two P-51D Mustangs, provided by TFC and Spencer Flack. The latter example was flown by Rod Dean, who designed the whole Eighth Air Force Salute.

Test aircraft were again out in force, in part to commemorate 50 years of test flying at Boscombe Down. Sadly, almost all the expected visitors from overseas establishments had to pull out, leaving just an Alpha Jet from German military test unit WTD 61, a Royal Netherlands Air Force F-16B operated by that air arm's Test Groep and a US Navy P-3C from VX-1 to join the static park — not forgetting the Su-27, of course. Nor did it prove possible, as planned, to put some Boscombe residents up for displays. But the addition to the static of Martin-Baker's modified Meteor T7 ejection seat testbed WL719, which seldom ventured out from Chalgrove, and BAe Warton's Lightning F6 XS904, more than made up for any disappointment.

To park the Lightning next to the Czech 'Fitter' typified the quality and the spirit of ATI 92. Unfortunately, 1992 was the last time the Air Tattoo team used Boscombe Down, the logistics of switching venues to another airfield away from IAT's home proving increasingly prohibitive. In any case, it was unnecessary, now the SBAC's objections to an annual Air Tattoo had been nullified. But no-one would have missed the two Boscombe years for anything.

And what of that red, white and blue 'Flanker'? Well, it and the Tu-134 left as they had arrived, in close formation, bound for Biggin Hill's International Air Fair. There should actually have been a pair of Sukhois, but clearance to bring the two-seat Su-30 could not be obtained in time. It was received just prior to the RAFA Woodford Air Show, which thus boasted the debut of the *Test Pilots* team. The 'Flanker' duo went on to thrill the European air display circuit for the rest of the 1990s, but never again came back to the Air Tattoo. No matter, though. Russia had much more to offer, and could even have done so in 1992. One of the early participation lists for Air Tournament International included a Tu-95 'Bear'. It couldn't really happen — could it?

Escorting the 'Flanker' Ian Black

Some weeks before IAT's Air Tournament International 92 at Boscombe Down, I was sitting in the operations room at RAF Leeming when a chance call from No 11 Group hinted that a pair of Russian Su-27s might be visiting the UK in the near future. Details were sparse, but the plan was that a pair of 'Flankers' were coming to the ATI via a refuelling stop in Poland, and they had no objections to being intercepted by the Royal Air Force. Simple!

It was agreed that No 11 Squadron would put up a pair of Tornado F3s to meet the Russians as they entered UK airspace. The plan was to launch three F3s, meet a tanker, then formate on the 'Flankers', do a photoshoot and head for Boscombe. We came alongside our VC10 and, as we began to take fuel, GCI told us the 'Flankers' were delayed. Plan B now came into force — we'd do some practice intercepts and then go back to the tanker to fill up again. Little did I know I'd be on plan X by the time I actually came alongside our elusive Russians. Back to the tanker we went, only to be informed that they had cancelled. So, on to plan C. I left the pair and headed to Boscombe to park myself in the static display and try and recover the situation.

Summer had arrived, and Saturday 13 June was basking in heat. The morning was spent trying to find a man who knew what was going on. I had a conversation with a Russian pilot who flew Tu-142 bombers and yes, he could help me! As far as he knew, it was going to be 14.00hrs local. With plan G now in force, my back-seater and I strapped in and prepared to launch. With 50,000-plus people watching, the temptation to leave the 'burners in and stick the Tornado on its tail was huge. The fact that the Chief of the Air Staff was in the audience was a good enough reason to keep it legal!

Blasting off into the blue, we were soon heading east out to the North Sea. The visibility was unlimited and the aircraft was performing well. What else could go wrong? Eastern Radar were looking after us, but soon our plan was about to change. Our controller passed us a message to say the 'Flanker' formation was delayed. With the best will in the world, even plan X wasn't going to work now. Our fuel was dropping fast and I was running out of ideas even faster. I asked if any tankers were airborne and the answer was no. As a last idea, I asked if Mildenhall was open and whether they would accept us for a rapid turn-round. To my eternal gratitude, the controller made a few calls and got us the OK.

With the clock ticking fast, we were marshalled into the hot refuel area. Our American friends understood our need for speed and quickly filled our empty tanks. We strapped in

quickly and started up, scramble-style. We lined up and pushed both RB199s into full reheat. Airborne, gear up, we thanked our hosts and called Eastern Radar. Still in full 'burner, the nose 30° above the horizon, our controller sounded tense, dispensing with any pleasantries and just saying, "your targets are on the nose, range 30, FL350". My back-seater raised the radar scanner and I kept pulling.

"Contact nose, 28 miles. Two targets in close formation". At a closing speed of 18 miles a minute, it would all be over in 90 seconds. My back-seater maintained contact and I kept pulling nose-high. At 18 miles, we both got visual on two Arctic-white contrails. Still in full reheat, our two targets moved through the green writing in the head-up display as we rolled, pulled and throttled back, all in one smoothly controlled manoeuvre as we rolled wings level, about a quarter of a mile behind the duo.

The first shock we got is that our two targets were not 'Flankers', as briefed. One was, but the other was a Tupolev Tu-134 transport in Aeroflot markings. As we came close to the 'Flanker', its pilot gave me a friendly wave and came in close to my wing. Sitting a few feet off my wingtip, in the blink of eye he rolled through a full 360° — impressive after a two-hour transit. As we cruised west, negotiating UK airspace, I could see the huge airfield at Boscombe Down crammed with cars and spectators. How ironic that Britain's super-secret test base was about to play host to Russia's latest high-tech fighter.

With a few minutes to run, I steered our formation towards the airfield and signalled to the Russians that they had the lead. I didn't want to steal their thunder. As I broke off and held to the south, I watched in amazement as the Tupolev configured to land but the 'Flanker' stayed on his wing, gear up. As the Tu-134 kissed the tarmac, the Su-27 kept low, very low, flying down the runway and pulling up into his display routine. I was glad I'd stayed clear!

With the Russians finally on the ground, and having parked my Tornado on the tarmac, we climbed out of our mount to meet our Russian counterparts. With helmet and mask off, the face

With helmet and mask off, the face of Anatoly Kvochur was instantly recognisable.

of Anatoly Kvochur was instantly recognisable. I'd seen him arrive in one of the first MiG-29s to visit Farnborough in 1988, and his spectacular ejection from a 'Fulcrum' in Paris the following year. He smiled and offered his hand. I reciprocated, and he gripped my hand with the force of a Siberian tiger. We spoke in broken English for some minutes before his minders moved him on.

A chance meeting indeed with one of aviation's greats and following one of the defining moments in airshow history. I was glad to have been a part of it.

Tim and Paul chat with HRH The Duke of Kent.

It was the year of the RAF, specifically its 75th anniversary year — but, above all, it was the year of the Russians. The menacing drone of four Kuznetsov NK-12M turboprops, sounding almost like a mighty modern Zeppelin, heralded the arrival of the Air Tattoo's most significant participant to date. On the Wednesday prior to IAT 93, a Russian Air Force Tupolev Tu-95MS 'Bear-H' settled onto Fairford's runway for a genuinely historic first appearance, making its presence felt in less hostile fashion than had long been the case during the Cold War years.

Recollections of that time flowed thick and fast when personnel from Russia's Long-Range Aviation made a preparatory visit. "We'd opened the door with the Russians, we'd worked hard on the embassy, and we'd effectively found a middle-man", Tim Prince remembers. "We also talked to the British air attaché in Moscow, and he saw that it was a great thing to try and do. He got the go-ahead, and we were quite delighted. We had a pre-recce, where a team of about eight from Long-Range Aviation came over to meet us and to talk about everything from whether we had the right couplings for the start units to whether the airfield was big enough for them. We took them out for an evening meal, and our air ops man Ray Dixon brought some photographs of when he was flying Phantoms and intercepting 'Bears'. An acquaintance was struck up there, because one of the guys in

the Russian party was on the 'Bear' being intercepted in one of the photos. They actually had some extremely good maps of Fairford — we didn't have to help them with that! One slight worry we had was that they weren't getting the flying hours in that their western counterparts were getting, but on the basis that it was going to be static, we were happy about it. There was a lot of concern about the financing of it, and in those days when we were so determined we did expend quite a lot of our budget on helping make it happen, but we felt it was worth it."

It was. Many times RAF fighters had shadowed 'Bears' and other Russian bombers as they probed the edges of British airspace, but never had they escorted one in to land. As it arrived in UK airspace on the Wednesday before the show, the Tu-95MS, from the 182nd Guards Heavy Bomber Air Regiment at Mozdok, duly met with two Tornado F3s. It was a high-powered delegation that came over on the 'Bear' and its supporting Il-78 'Midas' tanker, including Col

The menacing drone of four Kuznetsov NK-12M turboprops, sounding almost like a mighty modern Zeppelin, heralded the arrival of the Air Tattoo's most significant participant to date.

Gen Igor Kalugin, commander of Long-Range Aviation. While both aircraft were to be static exhibits over the weekend, it was agreed that a refuelling demo between 'Midas' and 'Bear' could be performed on the Thursday press day, treating those present to another great spectacle.

That, then, was the high of Russian involvement in IAT 93. The low — even lower than one of the senior Long-Range

The Tu-95MS, from the 182nd Guards Heavy Bomber Air Regiment at Mozdok, arrived in UK airspace on the Wednesday before the show. On the ground, the 'Bear' faced a USAF B-52H, two old warriors brought together in friendship. It exemplified the Air Tattoo's ambition.

"It was so pleasing that the USAF and RAF were on our side to make this happen" Tim Prince comments. "It was really quite special to have it an on operational USAF base."

PHOTO: MARTIN POLE

PHOTO: STEPHEN COOKE

The port wing of Beschastnov's aeroplane had sliced through the fuselage of Trevsvyatskiy's just aft of its cockpit. Both men ejected without serious injury, floating down beneath their parachutes as the two stricken MiG-29s fell to earth.

PHOTO: ROB SCHLEIFFERT

Aviation officers having his hat 'liberated' by an RAF counterpart — was Saturday's mid-air collision between the LII's two MiG-29s from Zhukovsky. "That wasn't so good", Tim reflects. "It was a beautiful display they brought with them. We were very pleased that they came, we were very pleased with their professionalism, they were good people, but sadly it went wrong."

They were test pilots Sergey Trevsvyatskiy and Alexandr Beschastnov, their mounts a pair of 'Fulcrums' liveried in the striking yellow, blue and black colours of the pre-revolutionary Tsar's Air Fleet. In the words of the RAF accident report, "The display was normal until the final manoeuvre which was simultaneous loops commenced from long line astern, prior to a break to land. The leader, who pulled up first, carried out a normal loop. The aircraft entered cloud at the top. The Number 2 commenced his loop with some lead on the first aircraft, executed a slightly tighter loop and experienced difficulties with the cloud. At some stage during the manoeuvre, both pilots lost visual contact with each other and called it. As a result of the Number 2's tighter loop, the leader was lower and not as far in front of the Number 2 as he expected. Although still unsighted, the lead pilot decided to carry out his break to downwind, believing it would take him out of the flight path of the other aircraft. Shortly after commencing his break, the left wing of the lead aircraft impacted the fuselage of the number 2 aircraft. Both aircraft immediately became uncontrollable."

The port wing of Beschastnov's aeroplane had sliced through the fuselage of Trevsvyatskiy's just aft of its cockpit. Both men ejected without serious injury, floating down beneath their parachutes as the two stricken MiG-29s fell to earth. One crashed outside the airfield, the other on the north-eastern boundary fence. There several bystanders had a very lucky escape, like the crew of a Belgian Air Force C-130H — captained by an RAF exchange officer — who had been relaxing in the sun on top of their aircraft, and jumped off it as one of the MiGs plunged towards them. It sliced off part of the Hercules' tailplane. Just as fortunate were two women who had been watching from atop a hay cart just outside the wire. Falling to the ground saved their lives, although they did suffer shock and some relatively minor injuries.

"When the two pilots came into the office with Paul and myself, they were expecting to be hiked off into confinement", Tim continues. "They really were so embarrassed to have spoiled this great international event, over and above being in shock from having been in an horrific accident, while of course being delighted to be alive. It was a very moving time for both Paul and me. We'd never had that sort of incident happen before. It took a time to ascertain whether anybody was badly injured or not — some people were injured, and some aeroplanes were

The Chilean Air Force Halcones had been on the list for the 1990 and 1992 Boscombe Down events in their new Extra EA300s, but took until 1993 to make it. The long haul from South America was worthwhile, as the team scooped the Sir Douglas Bader Trophy.

damaged. What was going through my mind at the time was, 'Is this the end of the Air Tattoo?' It was outstanding how our volunteer team acted so professionally, whether they were the air traffic controllers, the engineers, the emergency services or whoever. Everybody sprang into action and did what we'd planned they would do, and as a consequence we got quite a good 'tick in the box' when the inquiry happened, in that we'd done things right.

"My immediate role was to go to the air traffic control tower as 'top cover' and make decisions, and right after the accident the *Patrouille Suisse* were calling up for start-up. I had a very good relationship with the *Patrouille Suisse* going back to the early days, we knew each other well, and we asked if they would still be happy to display. I was most impressed that they felt they were well-enough together, not too shocked, to continue as planned."

What lessons were learned? "In fact, the decision about flying the *Patrouille Suisse* was one of them. What I hadn't realised was that when two MiGs collide with each other at that height, there are going to be bits of MiG all over the place. In hindsight, I shouldn't have allowed the Swiss to taxi out, because the Hunter engine is pretty good as a FOD [foreign object debris] collector. That was a big lesson. Other ones included the photobuses, which we had operating beneath the flying displays at the time. We had to reassess that. And, with the hazardous materials in modern aircraft that emit noxious fumes when they burn, we realised that we had to delve a little deeper as to how we handled such things."

The RAF anniversary was somewhat overshadowed. Most of the service's current types were on view in the static park, and a celebratory pageant occupied the final part of the flying schedule. Shuttleworth Collection types — Avro 504K, SE5a, Miles Magister, Hawker Hind and Gloster Gladiator — took the story from 1918 to World War Two, where it was picked up by the Battle of Britain Memorial Flight's Lancaster, Hurricane and Spitfire XIX, and a duo of twins comprising the Aircraft Restoration Company's newly restored Blenheim IV and BAe's Mosquito. On into the modern day, 20 Hawks from Valley's No 4 FTS, led by chief instructor Wg Cdr Martin Stoner, wrote '75' in the sky. Many of the RAF's solo display aircraft, and flypasts of tankers and Hercules, led in to the finale: Lancaster, Spitfire and Mosquito in line astern, followed by the *Red Arrows* with a Tornado F3, GR1A and Harrier GR5.

The biggest gap in the flying tribute concerned the earlier jets. For the second year running, displays from the A&AEE Comet and Hunter FGA9 were cancelled, the two aircraft going into the static instead; the RAF's solo Buccaneer pulled out, and none of the privately owned types then available — Meteor, Vampire, Venom, Gnat and so forth — were booked. Subsequent RAF anniversaries did better on that score. But as an international celebration, IAT 93 hit the spot.

The Hungarian Air Force's first British flying display could scarcely have been more impactful: a four-ship of MiG-21bis, known as the *Hungarian Sky Hussars*. Tim says, "Paul had gone to Hungary — they had invited him and a small Air Tattoo team over there to talk about airshows. Having seen the MiGs displaying Paul, in his inimitable way, said he'd really like them to come to Fairford. I think only one of the MiG pilots spoke English, so getting them here was going to be a challenge. They were sponsored by Camel, but for that particular occasion it was appropriate for them not to be because of our Imperial Tobacco sponsorship". The aircraft from the 31. 'Kapos' Harcászati Repülo Ezred (fighter aviation regiment) at Taszár included one in a yellow scheme, dubbed 'Cápeti' after a yellow cartoon shark, which usually carried the Camel backing. It played the 'bogey' in the *Sky Hussars'* sequence, taking on two of the other aircraft in an air combat scenario, interspersed by passes from a solo.

Brian Trubshaw with Paul Bowen.

100

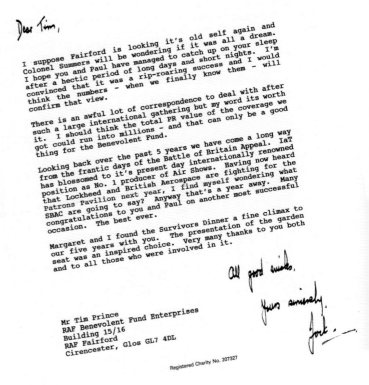

ACM Sir 'Jock' Kennedy (left), with HRH The Duke of Kent, receiving a cheque on behalf of the RAF Benevolent Fund.

That was one of IAT 93's new teams. In a very different vein, the Czech Air Force's *Szobi Kvartet* was another. The four L-410UVP-Ts, all with smoke generators, gave an excellent show considering the grotty weather in which they flew and the limitations of these light transports as display mounts, closed by an on-crowd bomb-burst. Szobi, by the way, was the surname of former leader-turned-team manager Lt Col Josef Szobi. The Czech Republic and Slovakia had split at the turn of the year, so the Slovak Air Force took its British bow with the *Biele Albatrosy* (White Albatrosses), flying six L-39Cs.

Grateful for British support in liberating its territory during 'Desert Storm', the Kuwait Air Force was especially keen to attend the RAF's anniversary. It did so by putting together a two-ship team of F/A-18C Hornets from 9 Squadron, which it called the *Red Hats*. They were backed up by a static F/A-18D and L-100-30 Hercules, together with a DC-9-32 in support. Alas, the *Red Hats* committed a display line breach during their Saturday appearance and did not fly on Sunday. This remains Kuwait's one and only UK show visit.

The first Swedish Air Force Viggen display in Britain for seven years, in a JA 37 fighter from F 4

wing, won for Maj Jan Fröjd the International Display Sword. Another comeback was made by the *Royal Jordanian Falcons*, now on three Extra EA300s. King Hussein was there to see them on the second day, making his own contribution when he gave a departure flypast in the Jordanian Royal Flight's DH104 Dove, JY-RJU — and it was a low one. We would never again see a Royal Australian Air Force F-111C 'torching' across British skies, and the rest of its display was a potent piece of airmanship by Sqn Ldrs David Coote and Rick Owen. Possibly the most surprising aspect was the complete lack of any USAF flying participation, the American military putting up only a US Army AH-64A Apache.

There was no lack of US support for the static park, though. Making its inaugural visit was an HH-60G Pave Hawk combat rescue helicopter from the USAF's 56th Rescue Squadron at Keflavík, Iceland, and a trio of US Navy carrier aircraft — A-6E, F-14A and F/A-18C — this time came from the USS *Theodore Roosevelt*. The Tomcat would have featured in the flying, had not its pilot run out of display currency owing to the time the 'TR' had been at sea. Elsewhere there were firsts, like the Israeli Defence Force/Air Force IAI 1124N SeaScan, but also lasts, such as Canberra B2 99+34 from Germany's WTD 61 trials fleet or the two Portuguese G91Rs, soon due for retirement. Yet more stalwarts were gradually on their way out.

The Air Tattoo team had come through the tribulations of 1993 and emerged to tell the tale. Graham Hurley's book *Airshow* later recorded how, in the wake of the MiG collision, some people got "excitable" at the 'survivors' dinner' — the traditional Monday night social function. "With all these things, shock affects people in different ways", Tim Prince says. "The team really did pull together very well indeed, but when the shock wore off and the adrenaline levels went down, emotions for some of the team ran a little high. An interesting time for Paul and me as we endeavoured to keep spirits up, as we still had an airfield to run and a board of inquiry to cope with; rather an exhausting time, I have to say. But the important thing when something like that happens is that you don't react immediately..."

IAT, though, had arguably never been in better health. At a time when western air arms were beginning to contract in size and concentrate on fewer types, the east European involvement was adding a new dimension to the show. Confirmation that Fairford would henceforth be its venue on an annual basis gave the Air Tattoo a fresh sense of optimism for what lay ahead.

INTERNATIONAL
AIR TATTOO

30 - 31 JULY 1994
RAF FAIRFORD

ALL EYES
WILL BE ON
THE SKIES!

MAKE SURE YOU'RE EN ROUTE
TO A MAJOR ATTRACTION —
THE MOST SPECTACULAR AIRSHOW
IN THE WORLD THIS YEAR!

LOCKHEED C-130 HERCULES
40TH ANNIVERSARY · IAT 94 RAF FAIRFORD 27-31 JULY
40
Lockheed

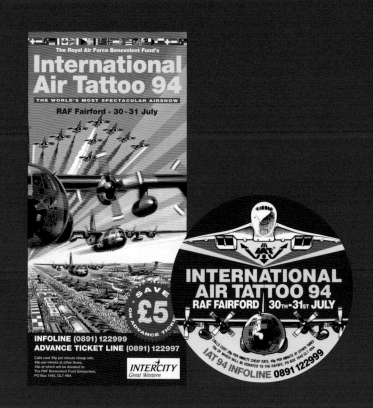

94

RAF FAIRFORD
30 & 31 JULY

After 17 years, IAT finally went annual again at Fairford in 1994. "It was a natural progression", says Tim Prince. "We'd satisfied the Society of British Aerospace Companies (SBAC) and Farnborough that the impact [on their crowd figure] wasn't that great. What it gained for us was continuity. Our local constabularies, our local agencies, our local organisations didn't have a year off, so didn't forget the lessons learned each year. It gave us an opportunity to build, it kept our volunteer team on side and enthusiastic, and it kept the income coming in to the Benevolent Fund."

The primary theme took the Air Tattoo back to familiar ground: a Hercules anniversary, this time the 40th. The aim, of course, was to line up 40 of the transports. Multi-national relief efforts in Rwanda, and US preparations for military action in Haiti, took some away, and the Turks pulled all their aircraft out — F-4s, F-5s and F-104s as well as a C-130 — due to financial constraints. Even so, 36 was good going. The figure was bolstered by a last-minute injection of RAF aeroplanes, but some of those had to return to Lyneham before the second day to go on stand-by for missions to Africa.

Heading them all was *First Lady*, AC-130A 53-3129 of the US Air Force Reserve's 711th SOS, which had started life in 1954 as the initial production C-130A. The concours d'elegance winner was ski-equipped LC-130H 83-0490 of the 139th Airlift Squadron, New York ANG. Those two were joined in the centrepiece of the line by the 2,000th Hercules built, C-130H 91-1231 from the Kentucky ANG's 165th AS, and the unmistakeable Hercules W2, XV208 — the meteorological research aircraft better-known as 'Snoopy' — provided by what was now the Defence Research Agency at Farnborough. Bringing another country to the show, the Royal Malaysian Air Force provided a smart, stretched C-130H-30. In the hold of the Rhode Island ANG C-130E was transported the first ever US Army National Guard asset to attend the Air Tattoo, a diminutive OH-6A Cayuse helicopter from the same state.

The Russians this time sent two 'Bears' — in the static, the Russian Navy made its début with a Tu-142M-3 'Bear-F' from its training centre at Ostrov, while the air force's Long-Range Aviation brought another Mozdok-based Tu-95MS, which gave a flypast on the Sunday. The Czech Air Force Mi-24D 'Hind' pair, one in a striking tiger livery, appeared in Britain for the first time and put on a very fine flare-firing show. With pairs of MiG-21MFs, L-39s, Su-25s and Su-22M4s, one of each appearing in the display, and the *Szobi Kvartet* of L-410s, this was an exceptional effort by the Czechs. Aside from the returning *Biele Albatrosy*, the Slovak Air

HRH Prince Michael of Kent and RAF Benevolent Fund controller Sir Roger Palin meet the *Patrouille Suisse* team.

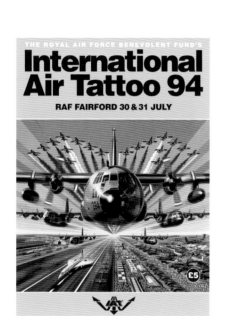

THE ROYAL AIR FORCE BENEVOLENT FUND'S
International Air Tattoo 94
RAF FAIRFORD 30 & 31 JULY

£5

IAT 94 aircrew briefing.

L: 02753
INTERNATIONAL AIR TATTOO 94
LUNCH MEAL
NOT VALID 29/30/31 JULY 199
NORTHSIDE O
SOUTHSIDE DI
RAF FAIR

LS: 0386
INTERNATIONAL AIR TATTOO 94
LUNCH MEAL
VALID 29 JULY 1994 ONLY
SOUTHSIDE DINER ONLY
RAF FAIRFORD

Above: Adrian Nind and Lesley O'Brien enjoying a break.

Force provided some of its combat aircraft, with MiG-29s and MiG-21MFs for static and flying. The static 'Fishbed' was gifted to the RAF Benevolent Fund, being handed over to HRH Prince Michael of Kent. After several years in storage at Boscombe Down, it ended up being sold to new owners in the USA, and is now displayed by the Florida Air Museum at Lakeland. Contrasting with such levels of east European input, this was the first ever Air Tattoo not to feature a single American military flying item.

Italy's Reparto Sperimentale Volo test pilots have always been relied upon to mount very fine aerial exhibitions, and the first Air Tattoo outing for its P180 Avanti was in a class of its own. A virtually aerobatic sequence, including a hammerhead stall, by a pusher-configured, twin-turboprop VIP transport with three lifting surfaces? Sounds unlikely, but that was what Maj Massimo Barocco flew in this astonishing Piaggio-built machine. His rehearsal had been fully aerobatic, but the flying control committee put paid to that.

The Aeronautica Militare's quartet of Starfighters — pairs of F-104S/ASAs and TF-104Gs, operated by the 5° and 4° Stormi respectively — were leading static attractions in what was a very good year for older jets. The French Air Force at last supplied a beautiful Mirage IVP, one of the last 18 reconnaissance examples in use by Escadron de Bombardement 1/91 at Mont-de-Marsan. Having spent the weekend on static display, a flat battery prevented its departure on Monday, a replacement being flown in the following day. When the Spanish Navy AV-8S and TAV-8S Matadors arrived, the single-seater suffered a multiple tyre burst, requiring it to miss Saturday's show. Replacements were sourced with the help of RNAS Yeovilton, and the 8a Escuadrilla's Lt Pedro Galiana Navarro was able to give the air arm's first British display on Sunday — the final time a first-generation Harrier would fly at an Air Tattoo. The Swedish Air Force's F 10 wing sent three J 35J Drakens, one being flown by Capt Ingemar Axelsson to victory in the Superkings Trophy solo jet contest, and an even rarer J 32E Lansen operated in the electronic countermeasures training role by F 16M.

Billed as farewell appearances by both, the demonstrations by the A&AEE's Comet 4C XS235 *Canopus* and Hunter FGA9 XE601 were marvellous to watch. In fact, both aeroplanes would soldier on for a little while longer, but this in no way dilutes memories of their flying. Sqn Ldr Dave Southwood gave a sparkling showing of the Hunter, while Flt Lt Mark Seymour, the senior multi-engine test pilot at Boscombe Down, put *Canopus* through its paces with real verve, taking it to the vertical during a closing wingover. The most enduring image

PRESENTED TO THE RAF BE...
INTERNATIONAL AIR TATTOO BY...

Slovakia

PHOTO: AIR CDRE PHIL WILKINSON

FORÇA AÉREA BRASIL

U.S. AIR FORCE

EMPIRE TEST ... SCHOOL

4307

The most enduring image of the Comet was its landing on Sunday, engulfed in spray after a downpour.

YOUR VOUCHER FOR SUPPER

DO NOT DETACH UNTIL HUNGRY 0268

YOUR VOUCHER FOR A DRINK

DO NOT DETACH UNTIL THIRSTY 0268

You are invited to the C-130 Hercules 40th Anniversary Party

Hangar 1200
Royal Air Force Fairford
Sunday 31st July 1994
1900 hrs - 2300 hrs (local)
DRESS FLYING SUIT

of the Comet was its landing on Sunday, engulfed in spray after a downpour. On Saturday's programme, in a neat juxtaposition, it had followed the departure of British Airways Concorde G-BOAC, performing one of several charter flights to honour the supersonic airliner's 25th anniversary.

The *Patrouille Suisse* took away the Sir Douglas Bader Trophy, as the Swiss Air Force prepared to say goodbye to its Hunters. By the next Air Tattoo, they would have been supplanted by F-5Es. Yet another example of the Hawker fighter should have been displayed by the newly established Royal Jordanian Air Force Historic Flight, based at Bournemouth under the auspices of RV Aviation, but its two-seat Hunter Mk53 — the well-known G-BOOM — made only a brief pre-show rehearsal appearance, suffering a ruptured wing tank while being readied to return to Fairford for the weekend. However, the flight's Vampire T55, the aircraft presented to the RAF Benevolent Fund at Boscombe Down in 1990, did manage to make it, on Sunday flying in front of His Majesty King Hussein.

Thankfully, after the previous year's near-disaster, a ground collision on the north-eastern taxiway loop between an RAF Nimrod MR2 and a runway sweeping vehicle was the only real incident of the IAT 94 weekend. It undeniably set a very high standard, despite such significant cancellations as a Russian Navy Beriev Be-12 'Mail' and, after its forced landing in the Sahara, the South African Air Force Museum's Shackleton. However, equally undeniable was the fact that crowds were down. Why was this? Never resting on their laurels, Paul Bowen, Tim Prince and the rest of the Air Tattoo management set about both considering the reasons, and addressing them. It resulted in an altogether different spectacle.

By 'Bear' to Britain Air Cdre Phil Wilkinson

I had been defence and air attaché in Moscow since January 1993, and was used to regular requests for information from the MoD and the rest of the UK base. In early 1994, when Paul Bowen 'phoned and asked if I could persuade the Russians to send a Tu-95 'Bear' (or two!) to International Air Tattoo 94, I knew I was in for long and complicated meetings, leading to an almost certain refusal. A supplementary call asked if I could also arrange for a Central TV team to film the whole excursion for a documentary. Unlikely was hardly the word.

My gast was absolutely flabbered when the basic request was given an almost immediate 'Da'. But the supplementary one got an equally emphatic 'Nyet'. I urged the Russians to think of the publicity value of such a film: the newly-opening links between Russia and the west would be underlined, the Russian TV audience would see how their air force was welcomed into the UK, and be reminded of the Cold War as the RAF came up to see the old adversary into UK airspace. Suddenly the game was on and I got another 'Da'.... but at a price!

I was told the 'Bear' (or 'Bears' — not yet fixed) would have to be accompanied by technicians and other 'representatives' of the Russian Air Force and Navy, travelling in an accompanying Il-76 'Candid'. Also necessary would be full fuel and accommodation for all aircraft and travelling personnel and a little assistance with entertainment and hosting of everybody involved. Altogether it amounted to 71 people. I don't think Paul was very amused.

Leaving him to think about it, I decided to capitalise on the apparent willingness of the Russians to let a British TV team fly on board and film the operational 'Bears'. I suggested it would be sensible to have me on board to act as airborne interpreter and explain the correct procedures as we entered UK airspace. More disbelief — a third 'Da' in a row. Things then moved very fast. The deal was for two 'Bears': a Russian Air Force Tu-95MS and a Naval Aviation Tu-142M3 would go, and the Il-76 would carry the slightly top-heavy 'delegation' (including eight generals, two colonels in the naval 'Bear' crew and one in the air force complement).

The Central TV team of two met me in Moscow and we went to the main transport hub near the capital, Tchakalovsky. We climbed aboard the 'Candid' and flew to the naval air station in Kaliningrad, the Russian enclave that lies between Poland and Lithuania on the Baltic coast.

Met by the Base Commander and told to get into something casual, we did a quick change in the mess accommodation, got into a handful of Russian Land Rover equivalents and headed out for the beach and a picnic. When the feast began it was enlivened by a series of toasts, given with due solemnity by some very unsolemn and under-dressed Russian generals. Then it was back to the Mess and time for the 'banya', the Russian sauna. By now the TV team was losing focus and the will to live. Tomorrow couldn't come soon enough for them, as they tried to cope with the steam and the birch twigs, and yet more vodka.

But tomorrow did come, and with it a change of plan — par for the course in Russia. The generals wanted the TV pair to fly in the 'Candid' and film the progress of the flight from its conveniently glazed nose compartment and I would fly in a 'Bear'. Twelve crew members made me welcome and we settled in for some lengthy pre-flights.

I sat in a sonics operator's seat and found the acceleration and take-off surprisingly sprightly. Up we briskly went to 18,000ft and settled into a stable cruise. Noise levels were low, the view out along those enormous wings past contra-rotating props was good, and very soon the opposition appeared — Norwegian and German air defenders came in close, and then Danish. Sadly, the 'Candid' never caught up so all those interceptions went unrecorded. But I had my camera ready as we entered UK airspace, and got some good shots of Tornado F3s slotting in. Down to Fairford we came with typically smooth UK air traffic handling, and a tastefully delicate landing, with parking on the ramp alongside a USAF B-52 and B-1.

Plenty of visitors came and visited the 'Bears'. First and foremost was His Majesty King Hussein of Jordan, himself a pilot. More challenging for the crews was the visit of HRH Prince Michael of Kent, giving a considerable surprise to the navy crew who arrived late and un-briefed to see a dead ringer for Tsar Nicholas II step down from their aircraft and then address them in perfect Russian.

On the second IAT 94 show day only, the air force's Tu-95MS gave a short display routine, and I ran around trying to keep the rest of the delegation from upsetting too many people. For the return trip I was invited up front for the whole performance. Handling the big beast was straightforward, with just the expected lag of response from that big wing in turning manoeuvre. Engine handling was very positive, and despite the slightly ponderous control response at slow speed on the approach to land, it could be put down very precisely on the numbers. It was a surprising and satisfying new experience for me.

We had a final team photograph back on the ground at Tchakalovsky and I went home with a fascinating, unique entry in my flying logbook. Oddly, only the Russian media showed any interest in this genuinely unique event — I don't believe any UK pilot had flown a 'Bear' before. It was a highlight of my time in Russia. I know it was a highlight in the history of the Air Tattoo.

> It was a considerable surprise to the navy crew to see a dead ringer for Tsar Nicholas II step down from their aircraft and then address them in perfect Russian.

Certainly, the Air Tattoo was big, but Paul Bowen, Tim Prince and their colleagues were concerned to ensure that it was the best. With the increasing realisation that airshows were fighting for the public's disposable income with theme parks, sporting events and other outdoor attractions, IAT recognised that it had to take another step forward — that getting larger every year wasn't enough. It was time for the natural showman in Paul to come to the fore. For IAT 95, Fairford was to be turned into the stage for the 'Theatre of the Air'.

Interviewed for *Air Display International* by Mark Ashley, Paul described his thinking. "We're conscious that, for the family, we've got to make the flying display more entertaining. We are in competition with family-orientated theme parks, like Alton Towers and Longleat, and we know we have to come up with the goods. But, just as importantly, we're also acknowledging the needs of the aviation enthusiasts."

Today, Tim Prince puts it thus: "There was great competition out there. There were lots of other airshows in those days, and yes, we were still a celebration

95

RAF FAIRFORD
22 & 23 JULY

It was time for the natural showman in Paul to come to the fore. For IAT 95, Fairford was to be turned into the stage for the 'Theatre of the Air'.

of aviation, but we wanted to do better than the other airshows. And there was the thrill side of things — people could go to Alton Towers, a pleasure beach, football matches or whatever else, and we wanted to get up into that league. Also, we wanted to attract people who wouldn't normally come to an airshow, because one great thing about the Air Tattoo over the years is that youngsters who have come to it have gone away having learned a lot, and if you whack a bit of history in there as well, it's got added value."

Gone was the usual Air Tattoo style of flying display. In its place would come a programme divided into themed segments, some marking significant anniversaries. Within them would, of course, be featured all the traditional solo and team items one would expect at an IAT. But there would also be specially designed set-pieces to reflect the themes, more than the Air Tattoo had ever featured before. When the 'Theatre of the Air' was announced before IAT 95, the official Victory Airshow marking the 50th anniversary of the end of World War Two, some were unconvinced. But even the doubters had to concede that it worked.

IAT 95's historical themes lent themselves to the concept. Hendon Heritage,

recalling the RAF Pageants and Displays in the 75th anniversary year of the inaugural event, brought forth a fort-bombing set-piece in the best tradition. Shuttleworth Collection aeroplanes redolent of the inter-war Hendon heyday — Avro 504K, SE5a, Tutor, Hind and Gladiator — were joined by the late John Fairey's Flycatcher replica, making its final public flying appearance. From there the celebration moved on to a range of warbirds, piston and jet, and modern military items representing the cream of today's flying displays. More of those were to be seen later in a segment dubbed Best of IAT, and an hour-long showcase for sponsor British Aerospace's products.

So fulsome was support for the Victory Airshow that the Saturday and Sunday flying programmes were quite different, just to accommodate everything. Given that, a weekend of glorious weather was all the more welcome, allowing every act that made it — and, with such a big list, a large number of cancellations were inevitable — to fly at some point. However, many items were common to both days, like the two superb Czech Air Force teams. The 'Hinds' were back, but this time a three-ship of Mi-24V variants from the 331. vrlt at Prerov led by Lt Col Jiri Rohacek. Theirs was one of the best rotary-wing displays the Air Tattoo had seen, the prowling low-level

PHOTO: GARRY LAKIN

Top: Kevin Leeson and Amanda Butcher.

Above: RAFCTE director finance, Gordon Harris (right) and commercial manager John Procter chatting with the IAT night duty officers.

Far right: The IAT 95 commentary team.

PHOTO: NIGEL WATSON

PHOTO: MICHAEL EATON

aggression of the Mil battlefield helicopter much in evidence, as well as some very precise flying such as a neatly executed 'carousel'. It was a deserving recipient of the Sir Douglas Bader Trophy. Also new from the Czechs was a team of five Su-22s, mounted by the 321. tl from Náměšť nad Oslavou and dubbed *Duha*, meaning rainbow. Lt Col Jaroslav Kankia and colleagues gave a great account of the 'Fitters', a smooth barrel roll in box four being something not seen in such big strike jets since the days of the Royal Navy's 1960s Buccaneer team, the *Phoenix Five*. To finish, the foursome split asunder before the flare-popping solo Su-22 flew through the middle. Terrific stuff.

The Polish Air Force was attending a British display for the first time, doing so with its *Biało-Czerwone Iskry* team of nine attractive PZL-Mielec TS-11 Iskra jet trainers. The Air Tattoo was also a British bow for the re-equipped *Patrouille Suisse*, now on six F-5Es, though one of the team's former Hunter F58s was flown in for presentation by the Swiss Air Force to the RAF Benevolent Fund. Against those gains, IAT 95 waved farewell to one of the show's, and the British scene's, stalwart acts. The Royal Netherlands Air Force *Grasshoppers*, set to disband at the 1995 season's end, flew their four Alouette IIIs in typically immaculate fashion. Always spectacular, the Italian Air Force RSV's solo G222 was at last able to show its true potential, Maj Luca Rizzi this year being permitted to perform a full aileron roll, while the Italian Army staged a first-time UK demo of an in-service A129 Mangusta attack helicopter. The Swedish Air Force Viggen solo was notable, flown as it was by an SF 37 photo-reconnaissance variant from F 7.

Definitely IAT 95's biggest individual scoop was the debut British public appearance of the Eurofighter 2000, just a month after it had first-footed internationally in Paris. As there, the example involved was BAe Warton's development aircraft DA2, which flew to and from the Lancashire factory airfield for its daily Fairford appearances. But this was no full display, project pilot John Turner not at this stage being allowed to do more than a few gentle passes and turns, under the power of two Rolls-Royce RB199 engines while the type's definitive Eurojet EJ200s were readied for flight.

The show's operational theme for 1995 was SkyTanker, its line-up far wider and more international than had been the case a decade before. The flying element came entirely from the RAF, but very impressive it was, a Tristar C2 — ironically sans refuelling equipment — leading through a VC10 C1K and K3, followed by a VC10 K2 and K4 with pairs of Harrier GR7 'chicks', and lastly a Hercules five-ship including a C1K tanker in the middle. The SkyTanker static featured many 'firsts', its array of Boeing 707/C-135 variants better even than in Fairford's time as a tanker base. Eight of them were USAF Stratotankers, the Ohio ANG's 166th ARS creating a nice piece of historical symmetry by winning the concours d'elegance with its KC-135R, just as the state's 145th ARS had done at IAT 85 with an E-model. But there were also some very rare birds, like a beautiful Canadian

"The defining moment of IAT 95 was the Victory Finale, the showstopper that truly allowed the Air Tattoo team's creative juices to flow."

"On the day, the massed hovering helicopters made so much noise, and were there for so long, that the audience at the front couldn't hear some of what was coming from the loudspeakers. The problem was that we hadn't had a full rehearsal, and nobody had foreseen what a wall of sound so many helos would make."

The finale ending was especially wonderful — the Red Arrows' synchro pair materialised from dead ahead and wrote a huge red victory 'V' in the sky.

Forces CC-137, a French Air Force C-135FR at last debuting on these shores, an Italian Air Force 707T/T (tanker/transport) and a Royal Saudi Air Force KE-3A. Most significant of all, though, was the pristine 707-344 from the South African Air Force's 60 Squadron at AFB Waterkloof, Pretoria. Just as the conclusion of the Cold War permitted Air Tattoo participation by so many east European air arms, so the end of apartheid made possible this first ever visit to a European display by a South African military aircraft.

Another of those former Eastern Bloc countries, Bulgaria, was added to the IAT roster in 1995. Its air force sent a Tu-134A for static display. The Czech Air Force An-30, used as an Open Skies treaty monitoring aircraft, was a UK neophyte; likewise the Finnish Air Force Hawk Mk51A, part of a static line celebrating 21 years of the versatile trainer. A Royal Saudi Air Force Tornado IDS was able to attend after overhaul at Warton. It was a pity the Luftwaffe VFW-Fokker 614 which brought a VIP to Fairford on the Friday couldn't stay for the weekend, as the unsuccessful West German-built twin-jet with its overwing-mounted engines had never been to an Air Tattoo before.

But *the* defining moment of IAT 95 was the Victory Finale, the showstopper that truly allowed the Air Tattoo team's creative juices to flow. Maybe they flowed a little too freely, says Tim: "We'd got the themes as a core, but we saw the ability to turn the airfield into a stage for the VE Day celebrations. The theatrical piece we put on was spectacular, and to have the veterans there with us was tremendous."

They arrived early in the flying display, doing so aboard a fleet of 12 Tiger Moths provided by Charlie Shea-Simonds and his colleagues in the de Havilland Moth Club's *Diamond Nine* team. Among them were veterans of all the wartime RAF commands, together with the Fleet Air Arm, the Air Transport Auxiliary and the Glider Pilot Regiment. Representing Bomber Command was none other than Jack Currie, the Air Tattoo's founding director back in 1971. Inbound from nearby Rendcomb, the Tigers held off while the Czech Su-22s displayed. Says Ken Whitehead, one of the *Diamond Nine* pilots, "The tower advised us that the four-ship was on its final pass and would then be breaking right-hand downwind to land, with us to position left-hand downwind to land after them on the grass. In the event two jets broke right, two jets broke left and 12 Tiger Moths with their veterans broke... well, just about everywhere else!"

As the show drew to a close, there assembled along much of Fairford's runway a line of fast jets from allies old and new, former enemies reunited in reconciliation, with a massed rank of helicopters hovering above. The cacophony all but drowned out a splendid commentary, written by IAT's senior commentator Seán Maffett and his producer Jonathan Ruffle and spoken by BBC Radio 4 announcer Peter Donaldson,

PHOTO: NIGEL WATSON

but everyone got the message. "Not only did the 15-minute duration of the Victory Finale include the orotund tones of the inestimable Peter Donaldson, but we also had live music from the RAF College Band", Seán recalls. "That was, and is, a pretty rare event: it's quite tricky getting a big band to play precisely when you want them to, and to shut up when necessary. That was precisely what we needed them to do to keep the story going in time with the aerial events.

"Of course, on the day, the massed hovering helicopters made so much noise, and were there for so long, that the audience at the front couldn't hear some of what was coming from the loudspeakers. You could only hear it all if you were further back — or if you were listening to what was then called Wings Radio. But the problem was that we hadn't had a full rehearsal, and nobody had foreseen what a wall of sound so many helos would make."

For aviation writer David Halford, what followed displayed "the qualities of good ballet chorography: seamless flow and apparent effortlessness combined with split-second timing". Over the top passed the Tiger Moths, followed by 'missing man' formations of British and American warbirds: the Battle of Britain Memorial Flight Lancaster, Spitfire Vb and Hurricane joined by BAe's Mosquito, B-17G *Sally B* escorted by The Fighter Collection's P-38J, P-47M and P-51D. The 'missing man' tribute was repeated by quartets of RAF Hawks and Luftwaffe Tornados, before a single USAF B-1B thundered through, wings swept back. And then came the pièce de résistance. "For me", says Seán Maffett, "the finale ending was especially wonderful — the *Red Arrows*' synchro pair materialised from dead ahead and wrote a huge red victory 'V' in the sky, and from behind us came a Spitfire, Mustang and Bf 109 to fly through the 'V' and depart rolling. The weather was perfect, the light of the evening sky was just so, and I thought it was a very emotional moment."

That it was. As David Halford wrote, choosing it as his favourite airshow moment of all time, "The British military at its best provides ceremony laced with sentiment, pride and passion. The 1995 finale had this in spades, and the 'Theatre of the Air' never came anywhere near it again". Tim says, "It was probably more than we should have got away with, but we did". Everybody who witnessed the Victory Finalé should still be glad of that.

Air Tattoo Memories: Jeff Bullen

Jeff was pulled from the RAF by Air Marshal Sir Denis Crowley-Milling in 1976 to be his ADC (Additional Duties Commitment). He became IAT's flying display manager in 1991 and later deputy director air operations.

"After 30 years' service there are many, many memories; sadly most would be inappropriate for this book! However, my proudest achievement was my first attempt at organising the flying display programme, which ran to time and was exactly the same as in the pre-printed programme — for the first time ever. A personal highlight was in 1995 when the *Red Arrows* closed the show, with the synchro pair making a victory 'V' in the sky and a Spitfire, P-51 and Bf 109 flying from behind the crowd and through the 'V'. It still brings tears to my eyes — seriously!"

THE ROYAL
INTERNATIONAL
AIR TATTOO

RAF FAIRFORD 20 & 21 July 1996

1971 1996
INTERNATIONAL
25
SILVER·JUBILEE
AIR TATTOO 1996

96

RAF FAIRFORD
20 & 21 JULY

As the Air Tattoo prepared to mark its silver jubilee in 1996, how could it match the previous year? Well, for one thing, it could gain royal assent. Tim Prince recalls, "Air Marshal Sir Denis Crowley-Milling was the man who, as controller of the RAF Benevolent Fund, took us on in 1976. He was such a nice man, and in 1996 he was terminally ill. Paul and I went to see him in hospital in London, and he had a bee in his bonnet. When most people would have been thinking about getting their own affairs in order, he wanted to get the affairs of the Air Tattoo in order, and before he died he wanted to get royal assent for us.

"From his bed, he wrote a letter to HRH Prince Philip — a beautifully hand-written letter, as only an air marshal of that stature would write — and got the ball rolling. He then lobbied anybody and everybody he could who had influence in aviation and government, and as a consequence we were afforded royal status for the Air Tattoo. Very pleasingly, Sir Denis was still alive, and just well enough to come and enjoy that first Royal International Air Tattoo. He was a very special person."

HOME OFFICE
Constitutional and Community
Policy Directorate
Constitutional Unit
Queen Anne's Gate London SW1H 9AT

Sir Roger Palin KCB OBE MA FRAeS FIPD
Air Chief Marshall
The Royal Air Force Benevolent Fund
67 Portland Place
London W1N 4AR

4 July 1996

Dear Sir Roger Palin

INTERNATIONAL AIR TATTOO

Further to Miss Sinclair's letter of 29 May, I write to advise you that Her Majesty has been graciously pleased to grant permission for the Tattoo to be called the Royal International Air Tattoo.

Yours sincerely

S.H. Clarke

Ms S H CLARKE

Paul, Tim and Sir Denis Crowley-Milling celebrating IAT's 25th anniversary.

And there were some very special moments at RIAT 96, even if it didn't hit the previous year's heights. The SeaSearch meet attracted the début at an airshow outside its home nation of an Ilyushin Il-38 'May' maritime patrol aircraft, operated by the Russian Navy's training centre at Ostrov — the same unit as had sent the naval 'Bear' in 1994. With it came the Beriev A-40 'Mermaid' manufacturer's demonstrator, an Air Tattoo debutant, though the four-jet amphibian had displayed at Woodford's 1993 show. In support was an Antonov An-72 'Coaler', Aeroflot-marked but actually on the navy's strength. All were static exhibits, though the 'May' created a bit of unintended action on departure day. When it got airborne, did the crew heed the rule that no flares be let off without permission? No, and few were best pleased at the resulting grass fire.

The Irish Air Corps attended its initial Air Tattoo with a CN235-100MPA Persuader, the Italian Air Force provided the choicest bit of rotary-wing kit in the form of a 15° Stormo AS-61R Pelican, and a Spanish Air Force F27-400MPA attended for the first time since 1981. Victory in the concours d'elegance was taken by 28 Squadron, South African Air Force, whose C-130B Hercules carried colourful markings applied to mark the SAAF's 75th anniversary in 1995. Another rare Hercules never made it into the static park, the Royal Malaysian Air Force C-130H suffering hail damage to its nose while en route to Fairford and departing early for repairs. Pick of a small SeaSearch flying contingent was the Royal Netherlands Navy P-3C-II, rather unexpectedly the first Orion ever to display at the Air Tattoo, which gave a very spirited demo.

Celebrating 30 years since delivery of the first production-representative Harrier, all four RAF squadrons flying the V/STOL aircraft — Nos 1, 3, 4 and 20(R) Squadrons — were represented, and no fewer than 10 of their GR7s and T10s made up the flying display finale. After a mass launch from the runway and northern taxiways, an airfield attack assisted troops deployed from two Hercules C1s in 'securing' the airfield. An 800 NAS Sea Harrier FA2 flew solo prior to the return of the RAF Harriers for box-four flypasts and run-and-breaks to land. To close the show, four of them put on a noisy hovering ballet. Original plans had involved the entire Harrier contingent in a mass hover, but the necessary approval was not gained.

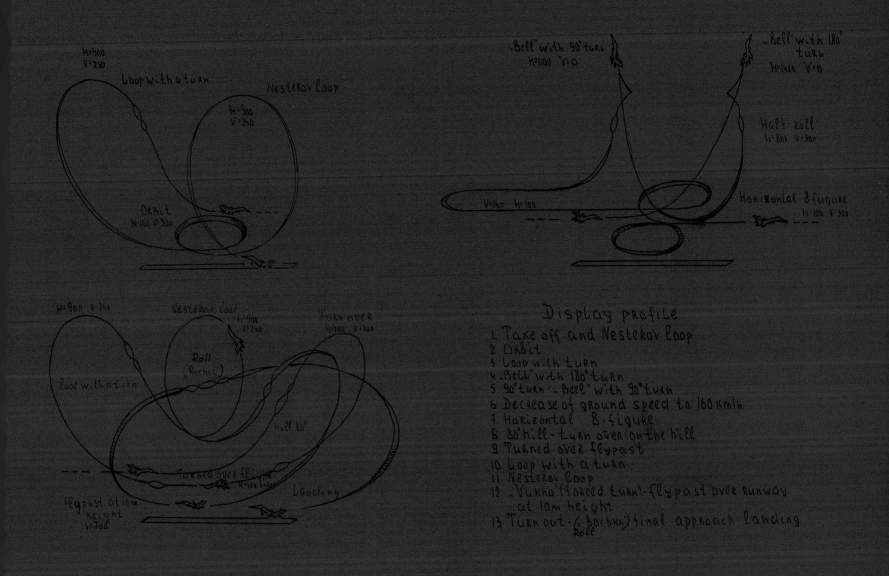

Display flight for aerobatics
by Colonel M. Koval. Su-27 aircraft

H=900 V=250
Loop with a turn
Nesterov Loop
H=900 V=250
Orbit H=100 V=300

"Bell" with 90° turn H=1100 V=0
"Bell" with 180° turn H=1400 V=0
Half-Roll H=800 V=300
V=160 H=100
Horizontal 8 figure H=100 V=300

H=900 V=250
Nesterov Loop H=900 V=250
Turn over H=200 V=300
Roll ("Bochka")
Loop with a turn
Hill 80°
Turned over flypast H=100 V=600
Flypast at low height V=700
Landing

Display profile
1. Take off and Nesterov Loop
2. Orbit
3. Loop with turn
4. "Bell" with 180° turn
5. 90° turn - "Bell" with 90° turn
6. Decrease of ground speed to 160 km/h
7. Horizontal 8-figure
8. 80° hill - turn over on the hill
9. Turned over flypast
10. Loop with a turn
11. Nesterov Loop
12. "Vukho" (forced turn) - flypast over runway at 10m height
13. Turn out - ("Bochka") Roll - final approach landing

Col Nikolai Koval flew his 'Flanker' faultlessly at Fairford en route to winning the Superkings Trophy. "His display was beautiful", Tim enthuses. "It was akin to a ballet performance, and he did it by the book. He really was able to surprise a lot of people with his display flying."

More excitement came from the Ukrainian Air Force's debut. Those, including Tim, who saw its solo Su-27 performing at the Slovak International Air Display in Bratislava in May 1995 might have been forgiven for concern at the prospect of its planned appearance at that July's IAT, what with its manoeuvring towards and over the crowd. In the event, its British premiere was delayed a year, and there were no such worries when Col Nikolai Koval of the 831. IAP flew his 'Flanker' faultlessly at Fairford en route to winning the Superkings Trophy. "His display was beautiful", Tim enthuses. "It was akin to a ballet performance, and he did it by the book. He was a man who, when you saw him, exuded aviation and an understanding of the aeroplane, and he really was able to surprise a lot of people with his display flying."

The Czech Air Force 'Hind' team, which was not to return to RIAT, was backed up by a MiG-21UM 'Mongol' display using an aircraft in the outlandish markings of the so-called 'Stress Team', part of the Letecký zkušební odbor (Flight Test Department). After several years on the circuit, including appearances elsewhere in the UK, the French Air Force's *Raffin Mike* duo of Jaguar Es finally came to Fairford and did well enough to secure the Lockheed Martin Cannestra Trophy. If one national team made an impression it was the Turkish Air Force's *Türk Yıldızları* (Turkish Stars), not so much for the display by their seven NF-5A/Bs but the commentary by Capt Orhan Tamir. His closing gambit was typical: "The supersonic Turkish Stars display was produced by Uniwersal [sic] Studios, Taiwan!"

The 'May' created a bit of unintended action on departure day. When it got airborne, did the crew heed the rule that no flares be let off without permission? No, and few were best pleased at the resulting grass fire.

It really was the final Air Tattoo for Comet 4C *Canopus*, now in the hands of DERA, the Defence Evaluation and Research Agency. Another beautiful routine was this time unencumbered by any need to conserve the venerable transport's fatigue life, so the wingovers looked that bit steeper than they had two years before. The second day saw a unique performance by the Royal Jordanian Air Force Historic Flight, with all four of its aircraft — Vampire FB6 and T55, Hunter T7 and F58. Two more historic aeroplanes in attendance were a pair of retired RAF Chipmunk T10s, which departed during Sunday on the first leg of an abortive round-the-world flight. Also terminated early was the display by Vickers Vimy replica 'G-EAOU'/NX71MY, which suffered a technical problem after take-off on Saturday and made a rapid return.

Two acts featured pilots who had flown in the first ever Air Tattoo. One was 'Bob' Thompson, who in 1971 had been a member of the RAF's *Gemini Pair* team of Jet Provost T5s. For the show's anniversary celebration he was back in the same type, now as wingman to leader Tom Moloney in the civilian *Transair Display Team*. The other was, of course, Ray Hanna. Flying the very same Spitfire LFIX, MH434, now owned by his Duxford-based Old Flying Machine Company, he wowed the audience just as he had at North Weald a quarter of a century earlier. But before a spellbinding solo, he and '434 performed a flypast leading the nine Hawks of the *Red Arrows*, recalling Hanna's time as *Red 1* in the team's Gnat years. Now *that* was aerial theatre.

50 Years of the Air Tattoo: Participating Nations

For half a century, countries from around the world have sent their military aircraft to participate in the Air Tattoo. By way of our appreciation, it is with enormous pride that we display the flags of those participating nations.

ALGERIA

CANADA

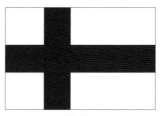

FINLAND

ISRAEL

ARGENTINA

CHILE

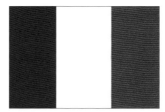

FRANCE

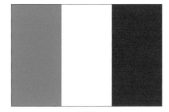

ITALY

AUSTRALIA

COLOMBIA

GERMANY

JAPAN

AUSTRIA

CROATIA

GREECE

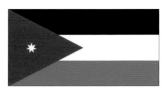

HASHEMITE KINGDOM OF JORDAN

BELGIUM

CZECHOSLOVAKIA/CZECH REPUBLIC

HUNGARY

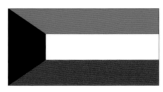

KUWAIT

BRAZIL

DENMARK

INDIA

LATVIA

BULGARIA

ESTONIA

REPUBLIC OF IRELAND

LITHUANIA

LUXEMBOURG (NATO)

SULTANATE OF OMAN

KINGDOM OF SAUDI ARABIA

SWITZERLAND

MALAYSIA

PAKISTAN

SLOVAKIA

TURKEY

MALTA

POLAND

SLOVENIA

UKRAINE

MOROCCO

PORTUGAL

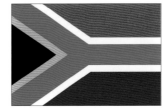

SOUTH AFRICA

UNITED ARAB EMIRATES

THE NETHERLANDS

QATAR

REPUBLIC OF KOREA

UNITED KINGDOM

NEW ZEALAND

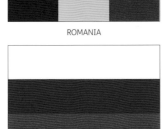

ROMANIA

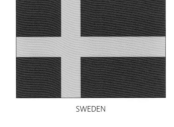

SPAIN

UNITED STATES

NORWAY

RUSSIA

SWEDEN

VENEZUELA

SINGAPORE (2020 VIRTUAL AIR TATTOO)

SRI LANKA (2020 VIRTUAL AIR TATTOO)

119

HRH The Duke of Kent with the crew of B-2A *Spirit of Kansas* at Fairford.

"We'd seen the B-2 over these shores before, of course: first on a single trade day at Farnborough in 1996 and then earlier in 1997 at Mildenhall, its British public début, just for a flyby or two each time. But a landing at Fairford — now that would be something extra-special."

97

RAF FAIRFORD
19 & 20 JULY

Will it land? That was the question on everyone's lips in the run-up to RIAT 97. The subject was the B-2A Spirit, scheduled for a flypast on the Saturday, but rumours abounded that it might touch down for the first time on British soil to help honour the US Air Force's 50th anniversary. We'd seen the B-2 over these shores before, of course: first on a single trade day at Farnborough in 1996 and then earlier in 1997 at Mildenhall, its British public début, for a flyby or two each time. But a landing at Fairford — now that would be something extra-special. "Neither Paul nor I could understand why, when it was coming that far, it couldn't just land on", says Tim Prince.

The then USAF chief of staff, Gen Ronald Fogleman, had become a regular visitor to and a strong supporter of the Air Tattoo, and his assistance proved crucial. Clearly, the opportunity to deploy a B-2 not just on a non-stop 'Global Power' mission, but to have it making a quick crew change at a base that would, in the future, come to host temporary B-2 deployments, was seen as being a potentially valuable one. As Tim describes, "While we were talking to the royal household, it became clear that HRH The Duke of Kent was enthusiastic about seeing the B-2, and when we mentioned this to the USAF they found a way to have it land and stay for about an hour on Saturday. A crew was sent over specially to take it back, and we had it on the ground."

Flown by Capt Roger Forsythe of the 509th Bomb Wing, B-2A 89-0127 *Spirit of Kansas* made a single flypast, escorted by a pair of 48th FW F-15Cs, before it settled onto Fairford's runway that hot Saturday afternoon. It parked on the north side and was inspected at close quarters by the Duke of Kent, from whom the crew received the RAF ensign. They presented him with the stars and stripes, before Capt Steve Basham took the 'stealth bomber' back to its home at Whiteman AFB, Missouri.

RIAT '97 was perhaps the most potent presentation of modern air power the show has ever produced. Witness the presence of no fewer than six other USAF strategic bombers, fully four B-1Bs and two B-52Hs, in an unprecedented show of strength. Unforgettable indeed was the stream launch by three of them, Lancers hailing from Air Combat Command's 37th BS at Dyess AFB, Texas and the Kansas ANG's 127th BS from McConnell AFB, followed by a Stratofortress belonging to Air Force Reserve Command's 93rd BS at Barksdale AFB, Louisiana. This was absolutely a 'Total Force' effort.

In keeping with the 'Theatre of the Air', RIAT opened its two-hour USAF tribute by

Below: The Air Tattoo's unofficial mascot.

RIAT '97 was perhaps the most potent presentation of modern air power the show has ever produced.

reflecting on the service's origins. David Pennell's Spitfire IX, MJ730, flew with Rob Davies's P-51D *Big Beautiful Doll* in recognition of the wartime Anglo-American alliance; moving the scene to the Korean War, the Mustang was set upon by Rolf Meum in the Old Flying Machine Company's Polish-built MiG-15UTI. Later, the 49th FW F-117A Nighthawk brought a different shape to Fairford's skies, the 437th AW C-17A Globemaster III impressed with its agility, and the 48th FW F-15E four-ship 'missing man' formation added emotion. But the greatest rarity was Tracor Flight Systems' F-100F Super Sabre N417FS, bringing back memories of the 'Hun's' long-gone operational heyday as the afterburner on its Pratt & Whitney J57 turbojet engaged with a characteristic bang. Over from its base at Wittmund, where it provided target facilities for the German armed forces, this magnificent jet was piloted by one of the most experienced F-100 jockeys, 'Harv' Damschen, who had flown the 'Hun' in combat over Vietnam.

Another seasoned fighter exponent, Rod Dean, was back in a Hunter. His mount was the Royal Jordanian Air Force Historic Flight's F58, the ex-Swiss example presented to the Benevolent Fund two years before. It and the Golden Apple Trust's F-86A Sabre were part of a show-opening segment saluting 50 years of supersonic flight. "It was very good of RIAT", says Rod. "I said that if I was going to come back in a Hunter, I wasn't going to come back and make a fool of myself by just whistling around. I wanted some practice. So I actually spent the best part of the week prior to the show at Fairford practising, and did a fair number including some in front of the flying control committee to get some proper criticism. That was good, and I felt really back up to speed."

RIAT 97 media launch – with a difference.

With Fighter 97 as the operational theme, there was no shortage of fast jet thunder. The RAF's fighter force showed something of its capabilities in an air defence set-piece, the like of which had not formed part of an Air Tattoo before. No 100 Squadron Hawks played the 'enemy'; No 111 Squadron Tornado F3s, aided by a Sentry AEW1, saw them off. The return of a Starfighter to the Air Tattoo flying after a dozen years' absence was a highly nostalgic moment, the Italian Air Force RSV test unit's F-104S ASA burning up the Fairford skies. But there were also first-rate displays from the Czech Air Force MiG-23ML and Spanish Air Force Mirage F1CE, both new to a British flying programme. The 'Flogger' proved particularly distinctive, trailing after it an afterburner flame that looked practically as long as the aircraft.

Solo routines from a Hungarian Air Force MiG-29UB and Polish Air Force MiG-29A debuted too, but were somewhat overshadowed by the Ukrainian Air Force's new aerobatic team, the *Ukrainian Falcons*, which performed with no fewer than six 'Fulcrums'. On its inaugural western outing, the Kirovs'ke-based outfit looked suitably polished, and the combination of engine smoke trails and wingtip vortices added a certain visual drama. However, the *Falcons* — unlike the Ukrainian Su-27, there for the second show running — were never to return.

In a real coup, RIAT 97 featured another western first: operational fighters from the Russian Air Defence Forces, the IA-PVO. A pair of two-seat Su-30s came from the 148th Combat and Conversion Training Centre, stationed at Savasleyka in the Nizhny Novgorod region. Their arrival was not without incident, as the 'Flankers' and the Il-76 transport leading them were involved in an airprox north of Reading with a British Airways Boeing 737. Then the solo display crew flew their initial rehearsal over the wrong side of the airfield. However, they got it right the second time, and at the weekend Col Evgeny Tikhomirov and Lt Col Mikhail Romanov demonstrated the long-range air superiority jet with professionalism.

In contrast to the heavy metal, the Irish Air Corps contributed one of the true delights of RIAT 97. Its aerobatic team of Fouga Super Magisters, the *Silver Swallows*, almost never ventured to Britain, but here it was for a one-off just before the V-tailed jet's retirement. The four pilots from the corps' Light Strike Squadron at Baldonnel practised only in their spare time, but they flew peerlessly, and were ecstatic winners of the Lockheed Martin Cannestra Trophy for best display by an overseas participant.

RIAT excelled itself in 1997. Clearly the public agreed, and the crowds on Saturday to see the B-2 were quite something. Indeed, they were still leaving well into the night…

From Air Chief Marshal Sir Roger Palin KCB OBE MA FRAeS FIPD

THE ROYAL AIR FORCE BENEVOLENT FUND
REGISTERED UNDER THE CHARITIES ACT 1960

PATRON: HER MAJESTY THE QUEEN   PRESIDENT : HRH THE DUKE OF KENT
Chairman of the Council: Sir Adrian Swire

67 PORTLAND PLACE, LONDON W1N 4AR   TEL 0171-580 8343 (OR VIA GPTN)
FAX 0171-636 7005

Mr P Bowen & Mr T Prince   RP/RIAT
Chief Executive & Director Operations
RAF Benevolent Enterprises
Building 15
RAF Fairford
Gloucestershire GL7 4DL   24 July 1997

Dear Ivns and Tim,

I thought I would write to you in the immediate aftermath of RIAT 97 to congratulate you both on a magnificent event. As I said at the Survivors Dinner, there is only one word that could describe this year's Tattoo - Brilliant. In my mind there is no doubt this was the biggest and the best, and everyone who played any part in its organisation can feel justifiably proud of the final result. Without exception everybody at every level - Royal, CAS, Corporate Sponsor, VIP, aircrew, guest, and spectators expressed their admiration and pleasure at being present, and a wonderfully happy atmosphere pervaded the event. The genesis for this is clearly the "Volunteers" (in which I include the Enterprises permanent cadre, who behave just like volunteers) but it is you and Tim who are the inspiration both behind and at the head of the team. To both of you, my sincere congratulations and my most sincere thanks.

Yours Sincerely

Roger

And so to another RAF anniversary, this time the 80th. Strong themes — Skywatch on the operational side, the Berlin Airlift's 50th as another historical focus — together with a fine line-up of aircraft, new levels of innovation and good weather should have combined to make 1998's a show to remember, and to some extent they did. But this was undeniably an Air Tattoo more beset by difficulty than many, and the RAF celebrations played their part in that.

In devising the year's aerial theatre, RIAT hit upon the idea of presenting RAF aircraft from different eras in the air at the same time, in 'stacks' themed by role. "Again", comments Tim Prince, "we were working hard to put on something unique. We consider it our air force, we're part of the RAF 'family', and we wanted to really do something special for them so we put that package together. Paul, with his air traffic hat on, was really into the idea that you'd have the slowest ones take off first, get them into a racetrack, then keep launching more and more aircraft into the stacks, and if you got the timing right there would be one moment where they would all fly past the datum at the same moment, from the slowest to the fastest. It was a beautiful idea, and lots and lots of planning work went into it. Unfortunately, with a few days to go the RAF decided that it wasn't what it wanted."

The book *Airshow*, by TV director — and former schoolmate of Paul Bowen — Graham Hurley, chronicled the behind-the-scenes machinations in some detail. RIAT had brought in Gp Capt Dave Roome, the man behind many large-scale RAF flypasts including the 168-aircraft

98
RAF FAIRFORD
25 & 26 JULY

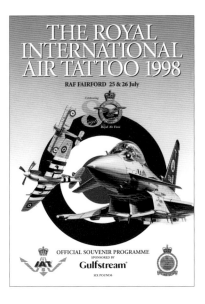

Below: Permanent staff getting to grips with the RIAT 1998 mailout.

For the first time, pre-recorded material on JumboTron big screens was integrated into the flying programme and commentary narrative, a concept intended to come into its own during the Berlin Airlift commemoration.

flyover of Buckingham Palace for the Battle of Britain 50th anniversary in 1990, to co-ordinate it. There were to have been four 'stacks': fighters, ground attack aircraft, bombers and trainers, interspersed with solo displays and 'missing man' formations. But just over a week before the show, RAF Strike Command lobbed a metaphorical laser-guided bomb into those carefully worked plans. "They had some concerns about the management of so many aeroplanes flying at once", says Tim. "We were content with it, but they felt they couldn't sign up to it. Because we were mixing civilian and military aeroplanes, they had the final say on it, so sadly we had to let that go, and we let the RAF put together a less complex package."

That resulted in mixed flypasts of RAF types divided by period — interesting, but not the ground-breaking theatre RIAT had hoped for. Leading them through were SE5a and Sopwith Triplane replicas, followed by the late Ben Cooper in the original Curtiss JN-4D 'Jenny' newly acquired by Vic Norman, with Tutor and Magister in trail. Blenheim, Hind, Gladiator and Harvard depicted the period from the mid-1930s into World War Two; Hurricane and two Spitfires likewise the war years, and Meteor NF11, Vampire, Venom, Hunter and Gnat the early jets. The present-day RAF's offering, meanwhile, combined Canberra PR9, Tornado F3 and GR1, Harrier GR7, Jaguar GR1A and Hawk T1, flying overhead a row of aircraft from overseas air arms lined up along the runway. Each of these formations looked attractive, but having the solos and 'missing man' tributes between them, together with all the related take-offs and landings, created a disjointed feel. The lack of a full Eurofighter 2000 display, BAe only being able to provide a brief appearance by development aircraft DA4 due to the pressures of the flight test schedule, compounded the disappointment. Very much praised, though, was the '80' formation staged using 21 Tucanos from No 1 FTS, perhaps the high point of the RAF finale.

For the first time, pre-recorded material on JumboTron big screens was integrated into the flying programme and commentary narrative, a concept intended to come into its own during the Berlin Airlift

THE ROYAL
INTERNATIONAL
AIR TATTOO 98
RAF FAIRFORD
JULY 25/26

80 YEARS OF THE ROYAL AIR FORCE 1918-1998

No question about it, the Ukrainian Air Force provided the star of the static park in 1998: a Tu-22M3 'Backfire', only the type's second western appearance, and its first in operational service.

commemoration. With seven Douglas DC-3/C-47s — including Aces High's C-47A, returning to airshow flying after a long absence — augmented by the South African Airways Historic Flight's DC-4, Vern Raburn's C-121A, an Air Atlantique DC-6 and, playing the part of a civilian Lancastrian, the BBMF's Lancaster, this was a mighty gathering of propeller-driven heavy metal. The intention was to stage a realistic depiction of the 1948-49 operations, with stream departures and landings, and a re-enactment of unloading operations on the northern taxiway being broadcast live over the JumboTrons. But the general verdict was that the scenario created too little spectacle, with no great airborne 'moment'.

Even so, there were some very fine performances at RIAT 98. Supporters of the Air Tattoo since the early 1970s, the Pennsylvania ANG's 193rd Special Operations Squadron took part in the flying for the first time, offering a flypast from an EC-130E. The latest Hercules, the C-130J, hadn't been seen in this country before, being exhibited by manufacturer Lockheed Martin and demonstrated exuberantly by test pilot Wayne Roberts. A British show debut was made by the Polish Air Force's team of PZL-130TC Turbo Orlik turboprop trainers, the *Zespół Akrobacyjny Orlik*, while the French Air Force *Voltige Victor* duo of Mirage F1s, already well-known around the UK circuit for its brand of extremely close formation work and dramatic opposition passes, came to Fairford for the first time and went back to Reims with the Sir Douglas Bader Trophy. Having been dissuaded from performing full aerobatics with his manoeuvrable mount, Ukrainian Air Force test pilot Lt Col Alexiy Vaneev put on a splendidly graceful performance in the twin-turbofan An-72 transport, winning the Lockheed Martin Cannestra Trophy for his efforts.

No question about it, the Ukrainian Air Force provided the star of the static park in 1998, too: a Tu-22M3 'Backfire', operated by the 185th Guards Heavy Bomber Aviation Regiment at Poltava. It was only the type's second western appearance, and its first in operational service. It also, as Tim puts it, "came with its difficulties. It was flown by the son of a very senior Ukrainian Air Force general, and a lot of very senior Ukrainian VIPs came along in the support aircraft with it, so it was a big logistical exercise. Unfortunately, when it arrived and taxied in there was a bit of a breakdown in communications because they ignored our marshallers and they parked it with the nose right up against the edge of the apron. There was no way to get a tow on it, and it was a real dilemma to get it into the right spot, so we rallied our wonderful Air Training Corps cadets, dozens of them, and got them in a co-ordinated effort to manhandle the thing far enough back to get the towbar and a tug on it! We also had some problems with its departure, because its transponder/IFF [identification friend or foe] system wasn't compatible. We had to do a lot of work to get the UK's ATC system to accept it, but it was then delayed by a day because when we finally got the clearance, they couldn't go because the crew didn't have a night qualification."

Yet, even with the 'Backfire's presence, perhaps the enduring image of RIAT 98 was a German Navy Tornado with one undercarriage leg stuck in a rabbit hole. With just a few hours to go before the gates opened, it caused Tim and many colleagues a long night. "Fairford was built for B-52s, and when they built it allowance had to be made

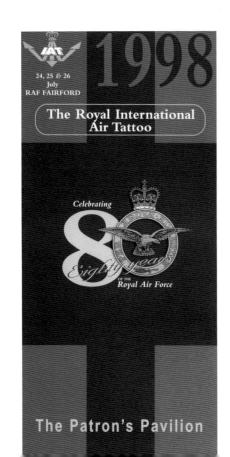

Perhaps the enduring image of RIAT 98 was a German Navy Tornado with one undercarriage leg stuck in a rabbit hole.

for the great span of their wings and the outriggers. I guess money was a concern then, as the taxiways weren't fully hardened edge-to-edge; the outer 20ft or so were just a thin layer of tarmacadam without much support beneath it. Over the years we'd got a bit blasé about this and we'd taxied aeroplanes over it, on the basis that if we kept them rolling they'd be all right. We were towing this Tornado, which unfortunately we'd just refuelled, and one of the mainwheels just sank into the tarmac. It was all the more embarrassing because another German Navy Tornado had arrived on the north side with their admiral in charge of naval aviation, and unfortunately we were rather slow in greeting him. He wasn't best happy, and then when he found out what else had happened... So we went to Swindon and hired a crane, got it out, and parked it exactly where we'd wanted it. Luckily, the tow had been a slow tow, and as soon as the wheel sank in it stopped immediately, so there was no damage to the aeroplane."

Tim doesn't add that, as recounted in Graham Hurley's *Airshow*, the Tornado "was finally put to bed in its allotted parking slot at ten minutes past midnight. All that remained at the site of the incident was a gaping hole in the asphalt and a working party from the Site Team had the ramp operational again by dawn. Tim Prince had stayed with the incident throughout the night..." If you needed an illustration of the Air Tattoo's esprit de corps, there you have it.

LOCKHEED MARTIN

The Chairman of The Royal Air Force Benevolent Fund
and
The President of Lockheed Martin Aeronautics Sector

request the pleasure of the company of

Mr Timothy Prince
at
The Royal International Air Tattoo
to celebrate the
80th Anniversary of the Royal Air Force
in
The Patron's Pavilion
Royal Air Force Fairford
on
Sunday, 26th July 1998

Dress: Lounge Suit (Uniform Optional)
(It is regretted that children cannot be admitted to The Patron's Pavilion)

The Royal International Air Tattoo 1998

GUEST

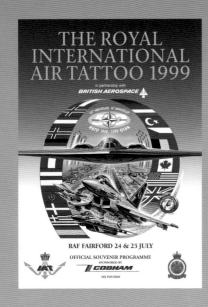

As the North Atlantic Treaty Organization notched up its half-century, on 4 April 1999, it was in the midst of its largest military campaign to date. Operation 'Allied Force', the war against the Yugoslav regime in the wake of its actions in Kosovo, would eventually last for 78 days. By the time it concluded on 10 June, USAF B-1Bs and B-52Hs flying from Fairford as part of the 2nd Air Expeditionary Group had completed somewhere in the region of 230 operational sorties — and there were just six weeks to go before RIAT 99, marking NATO's 50th anniversary.

Several other military airshows in Britain during the 1999 season had to be cancelled due to 'Allied Force'. How did the Air Tattoo avoid going the same way? "We had this gut feeling that there would be a way of going ahead", Tim Prince recalls, "and also we didn't want to let our insurers down. We kept in close touch with the commander of USAFE and went to see him on a number of occasions to make sure he was enthusiastic about the Air Tattoo, and we got on very well with him. As soon as the war came to a close, he could easily have let Fairford not be available by virtue of the relatively slow withdrawal phase, but he saw the benefits and straight away he nominated one of the aircrew there, a full colonel, to stay back to clean the airfield up for us. We were biting our fingernails right up until the time the air war was over, but we knew we had good support there. We had cancellation insurance, but we were determined that if there was a way to do it we'd do it, and the Americans were outstanding in tidying up the airfield so quickly for us."

The last bombers didn't leave Fairford until 23-24 June. Support tanker and transport movements had to follow. At one stage there were rumours within the organisation of RIAT being postponed, maybe until the August Bank Holiday weekend, but Tim scotches those. Postponement, he says, was impossible. "We haven't got that ability because of our total reliance on a volunteer team. Take the air traffic controllers, say. A lot of them came from Manchester Airport and they could only come when they booked leave, which had to be tied in with when everybody else booked their holidays."

That RIAT 99 took place at all was a great achievement. That it proved so outstanding, if a little fraught with incident, was remarkable. B-1s and B-52s were back, of course, but it was the return of a B-2A Spirit that set the show alight. This time the 509th Bomb Wing was able to commit an aircraft, *Spirit of Indiana*, for the entire weekend — and to base it out of Fairford. During 'Allied Force', B-2s had launched from their home base at Whiteman AFB, Missouri, for their 45 wartime sorties. And this was not just a single, high flyby, but a full display, sweeping passes much in evidence, showing the Spirit's unique lines better than ever before.

99

RAF FAIRFORD
24 & 25 JULY

That RIAT 99 took place at all was a great achievement. That it proved so outstanding, if a little fraught with incident, was remarkable. B-1s and B-52s were back, of course, but it was the return of a B-2A Spirit that set the show alight.

NATO 1949-1999
THE ROYAL INTERNATIONAL AIR TATTOO 99
RAF FAIRFORD
JULY 23-25
IN PARTNERSHIP WITH
BRITISH AEROSPACE

CHIEF OF STAFF
UNITED STATES AIR FORCE
WASHINGTON

14 December 1998

Dear Messrs Bowen and Prince

I appreciate your very informative and detailed overview of the Royal International Air Tattoo 1999. As indicated, I will block my calendar for the opening remarks to the symposium in London on 22 July. Unfortunately, the Thunderbirds will be unavailable as their European schedule is set for a May appearance at RAF Mildenhall. I have, however, asked my staff to check into the B-2 availability and possibly, the F-22, for a static display at the Gala Dinner.

I especially thank you both for the wonderful book *"Brace by Wire to Fly-by-Wire"* and the video depicting the 1997 RIAT's dedication to the United States Air Forces' 50th Anniversary. I'm sure they will provide much entertainment. Again, thanks for coming.

MICHAEL E. RYAN
General, USAF
Chief of Staff

Mr. Paul Bowen, Director, RIAT
and Mr. Tim Prince, Executive Director, The RAF
Benevolent Fund
Bader House
Royal Air Force Fairford
Gloucestershire GL7 4 DL, United Kingdom

The most poignant aspect of the weekend was RIAT's tribute to one of the show's staunchest supporters. King Hussein of Jordan had died on 7 February 1999, and a unique flypast tribute took place in his honour.

It was just one act in an extraordinary flying programme, lasting more than nine-and-a-half-hours on the first day, and performed in scorching heat. In honour of another 50th anniversary, No 39 (1 PRU) Squadron contributed a Canberra T4 display by one of two examples it had painted in the colours of English Electric's first prototype. Sqn Ldr Terry Cairns put on a sparkling performance, winning the Steedman Display Sword in the process. A Swiss Air Force F/A-18C Hornet squeezed every drop of vapour from the skies on its British flying display debut, while a C-130H from US Air Force Reserve Command's 731st Airlift Squadron deposited its own moisture by giving the Air Tattoo's first demonstration of the MAFFS (Modular Airborne Fire Fighting System) kit.

It was not an event the G222 crew from the Italian Air Force's Reparto Sperimentale Volo would soon forget. On Sunday, not long after the BBMF's Spitfire IIa had made an emergency landing with a major engine problem, the twin-turboprop airlifter was going through its aerobatic paces when it suffered its own failure. Says Tim, "The de-icing boot on one of the propeller blades broke away and was flung through the fuselage, making a significant hole. Of course, it made the propeller on that side run highly unbalanced, causing horrendous vibration in the cockpit. They didn't actually know what had happened — it was very difficult to see the essential flight instruments — and so did a very rapid descent to land. They got out of the aeroplane very quickly, not knowing whether it was about to explode or what."

The most poignant aspect of the weekend was RIAT's tribute to one of the show's staunchest supporters. His Majesty King Hussein of Jordan had died on 7 February 1999, and a unique flypast tribute took place in his honour. In the lead, fittingly, was the Jordanian Royal Flight's DH104 Dove, JY-RJU. Joining Richard Verrall in the cockpit were two of

NATO took the lion's share of the show, befitting of an event that had always gathered the alliance's aviators, and the static park bristled with rarities from its air arms.

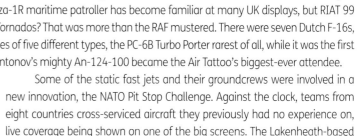

the King's sons — HRH Prince Hamzah on Saturday, HRH Prince Feisal on Sunday — as the de Havilland twin was given close escort by the four Extra EA300s of the *Royal Jordanian Falcons*. Over the top, saluting the 'missing man', came four Jaguars flown by pilots from No 6 Squadron, King Hussein having enjoyed a close relationship with this RAF unit since it was stationed in the Middle East in the 1950s.

But NATO took the lion's share of the show, befitting an event that had always gathered the alliance's aviators, and even more so in this jubilee year. The static park bristled with rarities from its air arms. A platypus-nosed Canadian Forces CT-142 navigation trainer and one of two US Marine Corps AV-8B Harrier II+ variants present caught the eye. So did the 'Speckled Trout', the USAF C-135C used primarily as transport for the service's chief of staff by the 412th Test Wing at Edwards AFB, before it headed home on Saturday afternoon. French Air Force Mirage 2000D and 2000N conventional and nuclear strike jets were Air Tattoo newcomers, the latter a surprise late addition. The sight of a Polish Navy M28 Bryza-1R maritime patroller has become familiar at many UK displays, but RIAT 99 represented a first visit. And, today, some of the multiples almost seem outlandish. Ten Luftwaffe Tornados? That was more than the RAF mustered. There were seven Dutch F-16s, four Italian MB339s, three USAF C-141s. The French Army brought an unprecedented five aeroplanes of five different types, the PC-6B Turbo Porter rarest of all, while it was the first time the Greek and Turkish air arms had attended together. From the civilian world, meanwhile, Antonov's mighty An-124-100 became the Air Tattoo's biggest-ever attendee.

As it landed following Sunday's NATO flypasts, Tim remembers how the Crusader "got into a pilot-induced oscillation. He wrecked the tyre, got it down to the wheel, and caused a lot of damage to the runway."

Some of the static fast jets and their groundcrews were involved in a new innovation, the NATO Pit Stop Challenge. Against the clock, teams from eight countries cross-serviced aircraft they previously had no experience on, live coverage being shown on one of the big screens. The Lakenheath-based 48th Fighter Wing ran out victorious overall, perhaps a reflection of how the USAF had long staged weapons loading competitions of its own.

The theme took over the last few hours of flying, tracing the history of NATO air power. It proved a last hurrah in a British flying display for two charismatic classic jets, the Starfighter and Crusader, which had once been so familiar in the Air Tattoo programme. Even the Italian Air Force F-104S ASA, wearing a very striking black scheme in celebration of the RSV test centre's 50th anniversary, had to give best on this occasion to the French Navy two-ship of upgraded F-8Ps. Their operator, Flottille 12F, had less than six months to run on the Ling-Temco-Vought carrier fighter. Another choice item was a spirited demonstration by a US Navy P-3C-II from VP-30, something not featured in a British show for 18 years.

Gradually each day built to a crescendo, Fairford shimmering in the late-afternoon heat as a phalanx of NATO aircraft took to the runway in a mass line-up, its centrepiece the stunningly painted E-3A from the alliance's own Airborne Early Warning and Control Force. Above them hovered helicopters from 10 countries, their number taking in some of the most unusual participants in an Air Tattoo flying display. Such as a Polish Navy W-3RM Anakonda, a Spanish Army AS532UL Cougar and a US Army UH-1H operated for the HQ US European Command had never flown in the show before, and haven't done so since. Given this, one criticism at the time was the lack of an opportunity to see them closer-up.

There was to have been another element to the helicopter hover. "The plan", says Tim, "was to have all the helicopters with weighted cables beneath them with national flags on. Unfortunately, although a good number of countries had said they would come and do it, when they turned up they found they couldn't for a whole variety of issues, which couldn't be resolved. We had some helicopters that could and some that couldn't, so in the end we had to drop the underslung flags. It was a great shame, as that would have added some extra spectacle."

Overflying all of this, a series of 'East meets West' pairs brought together former Cold War foes. Despite being hit by several cancellations, the flypast proved impressive: Spitfire XVI and Yak C-11, Vampire and Aero L-29 Delfin, Hunter and Soko G-2 Galeb, Slovak Air Force MiG-29 and French Navy F-8P, and RAF Tornado F3 and Ukrainian Air Force Su-27 were the combinations involved. It was, in fact, the last of these big finale showpieces. There was nearly a sting in the tail, as well. As it landed following Sunday's NATO flypasts, Tim remembers how the Crusader "got into a pilot-induced oscillation. He wrecked the tyre, got it down to the wheel, which fell to bits and caused a lot of damage to the runway. We spent a lot of time while the runway was blocked, walking along it to find all the debris so that aeroplanes could get airborne safely after the show."

Make no mistake, RIAT 99 was a superb spectacle. But had it become simply too big? The flying, after

all, overran considerably. "My own view", Tim comments, "was that, without question, we were trying to squeeze too much into the display. We were also cramming more and more aeroplanes into the Air Tattoo overall, each with a crew of varying numbers which our team had to look after. We were starting to push ourselves too far as we endeavoured to ensure that all participants felt welcome and were properly hosted whilst with us in the UK. We should have stood back and said, 'Right, let's do a little bit less, but let's do it better'. We had ended up with crews who felt they hadn't been appreciated, many having travelled such a long way to support us. We were getting the sort of feedback that would clearly do us harm as they submitted their reports internally. We needed their authorities to remain enthusiastic about providing aeroplanes for future shows."

And the next year would be especially interesting. A long-delayed programme of major airfield work was about to close Fairford, leaving the Air Tattoo temporarily without a home. Perhaps a downsizing was inevitable. Whatever the outcome, RIAT would carry on — but where?

Guy Bowen

As the son of one of the Air Tattoo's founder members, Guy Bowen was destined at an early age to have aviation — and more specifically, IAT — flowing through his veins. These images show Guy with his father, Paul; one taken in 1981 and the other in 1999 after he'd flown in to RIAT 1999 at the controls of a Bulldog trainer. Over many years Guy has performed a number of RIAT roles, including hosting guests such as Carol Vorderman, Tim Peake and *Children in Need* winners. His father would have been extremely proud of Guy's achievements to date — which now include his day job of flying long-haul aircraft for British Airways! Guy was also part of the flight crew that displayed the Oasis Hong Kong Airlines Boeing 747-400 at RIAT 2007.

Paul Bowen starts the build of Douglas Bader House, which was designed by volunteer Steve Lacey.

Building for the future...

Since its inception the Air Tattoo had kindly been afforded the use of 'empty' offices on the various airfields on which it had run airshows. Buildings 15/16, which were at the heart of RAF Fairford's site, had the clear advantage of a location which provided easy access to the base commander and his/her staff and the facilities IAT needed to access. They were, however, very old prefabricated pre-war buildings which were in poor order. As such they were scheduled for eventual demolition and, in 1998, it became necessary to move from within Fairford's perimeter to premises elsewhere.

Various options were explored which eventually indicated that a new-build facility at RAF Fairford would be the best solution and would retain an essential and close link with the base. As luck would have it, the USAF had just decided to return its then redundant clinic enclave to the MoD, who in turn offered it for sale. Being alongside the 'fence' it presented a perfect solution. A bid for the land was submitted and thankfully was successful. A year of consultancy reports, due diligence processes, build planning and design then followed. It was no surprise when Steve Lacey and many volunteers stepped up to the plate and helped with the design and build phase.

The issue of funding was another matter! One of IAT's many strengths has been, without doubt, its relationship with its corporate sponsors. This fact was no better demonstrated in 1999 when four of IAT's long-time supporters agreed to provide the money required for the new build through advance sponsorship agreements. This unique and generous funding help by British Aerospace (now BAE Systems), Marshall of Cambridge, Lockheed Martin and Rolls-Royce not only enabled a bespoke HQ for RAFCTE to be built, but was also the precursor to four-year RIAT sponsorship contracts. Once again, RIAT found the way.

Below: An aerial shot of Douglas Bader House following its completion in 2000.

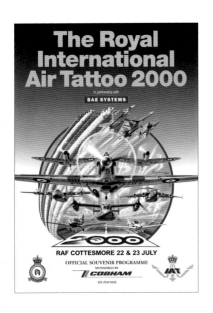

The Royal International Air Tattoo 2000

RAF COTTESMORE
22 & 23 JULY

A new millennium, and a new venue — but where? "The rebuild of Fairford had to happen", says Tim Prince. "We had been given due notice of that — as always, the USAF was very good in that respect. They had made it clear that there was no other USAF airfield that was available". Another seemingly obvious candidate was also ruled out. Since the Air Tattoo team's last show at Boscombe Down, Air Tournament International 92, flight-test activities at the Wiltshire base had been privatised, placed under the auspices of the QinetiQ company While the airfield remained a Ministry of Defence site, using it for an airshow would now be a commercial matter, rather than a case of obtaining agreement from the commandant. Strike one contender.

Very unusually though, a commercial airport operator approached RIAT when it heard of the show's dilemma. As Tim reveals, "We looked at Prestwick, where the airport owners were very keen to see us and offered us a very good deal. There was loads of hardstanding there, and I used to work there — my first operational air traffic job was at Prestwick, and I did my first airshow at Prestwick as an assistant. But then again, 180° of the catchment was basically fish, and the Isle of Arran!

"We went to the RAF and said, 'We need your help. Can you open the door for us with some of your bases?' The truth of the matter was that we'd never been on an operational RAF airfield before, and the RAF didn't have a big stand-by base where there was a catchment area. You might think that St Mawgan was that place, with a nice big runway and lots of hardstanding, but the catchment area is mainly sea. Holidaymakers primarily go down there to spend time on the beach. Yes, there had been shows down at St Mawgan, but the crowd numbers were very small by comparison with ours, and the road infrastructure wasn't up to increasing that. So the RAF said where we could go and where we couldn't go". Another 'no-go' was Brize Norton, ideal in terms of proximity to Fairford, but far too busy even then as a tanker and transport hub.

"There was a spirit at Cottesmore that was reflected by the station commander. He had a great outlook on life — like us, an 'it can be done' approach — and, yes, it worked."

Above: ACM Sir 'Jock' Kennedy with Gp Capt David Walker, station commander at RAF Cottesmore.

Top: Attendees at a RIAT 2000 progress meeting at Cottesmore.

Right: Some of the permanent staff at Douglas Bader House.

Below: Robbie Hancock at the RIAT mail-out.

"To be honest, we were getting quite worried. We were asked to go and look at Yeovilton, but of course they didn't want to disturb their own show. We concluded that the only place that was possible was Cottesmore, the one airfield the RAF had asked us to not go to because they had just done the transition from TTTE [the Tri-national Tornado Training Establishment] to Harriers, there had been a few Harrier incidents and they really wanted the people at Cottesmore to keep their eye on the ball, for all the right reasons. We decided that even though we'd been told we couldn't have it, we'd go and have a look. Paul and I were looking through the fence with our binoculars, trying to recce it, when two Geordie accents piped up from alongside — obviously the lay-by we'd gone to was the one used by enthusiasts — saying 'It's Paul Bowen and Tim Prince! Ah, it's going to be here!' It was two of our FRIAT [Friends of the Royal International Air Tattoo] members, and we'd been caught out. Of course, before we knew it, it was on the web that we were looking at Cottesmore.

"We realised very quickly that we ought to go back to the RAF and try and find a way to open that door, so we went to see the then Chief of the Air Staff, ACM Sir Peter Squire, who used to be station commander at Cottesmore, had run shows there, and was very concerned about not just the Harrier situation but also the road infrastructure. We quickly put together a plan of how we'd do it, went to visit him again, and three hours later, after lunch, he said, 'OK, let's give it a go'. He listened to how we'd go about it, and he said, 'If the station commander's happy, then I'll back it'. As quickly as we could, we met with the station commander, Gp Capt David Walker, and he thought it was a great idea to pull the station together. His words to us were, 'I'll put my trust in you — respect that, and we'll get on well'."

The decision to run with the Leicestershire station was announced in January 2000. Says Tim, "It was a nightmare from the point of view of our permanent staff, an absolute nightmare, because it was a long way to go for meetings. We hired a house there, and so we spent some time in the planning phase sort of living up there, but a lot of the work still had to be done down here, so we were burning the midnight oil with the permanent staff. For the volunteers, they loved the fact that there was a change. There was a spirit at Cottesmore that was reflected by the station commander. He had a great outlook on life — like us, an 'it can be done' approach — and, yes, it worked. It was challenging from the financial point of view to re-establish it, but the industry supported us even though it was a long way from London, and a long way from having the number of nearby hotels they wanted, and the world's air forces supported us. I think the key was the Air Tattoo name. It didn't matter where the airfield was."

THE ROYAL
INTERNATIONAL
AIR TATTOO 2000

RAF COTTESMORE RUTLAND JULY 22-23

IN PARTNERSHIP WITH
BAE SYSTEMS
www.airtattoo.com

Quite apart from the venue, another challenge was posed by the move of the biennial Farnborough show from its traditional September date to a new one in July. In fact, it would run straight on from RIAT, opening for business on the Monday as Cottesmore emptied of aeroplanes. Early press publicity indicated plans for close co-operation between the two — a "two-week long festival of aviation", dubbed 'A Flying Start to the Millennium'. SBAC director of exhibitions Peter Taylor said, "With the two events back-to-back there is much scope for collaboration to provide a seamless event for joint visitors, especially overseas government delegations who will attend both shows". RIAT director Paul Bowen added, "There are many duplicated areas when organising two shows of such a large magnitude, that it makes sense in all respects for us to be collaborating". Major aerospace manufacturers would display some significant wares at Cottesmore as well as Farnborough — US Marine Corps MV-22B Osprey tilt-rotors were set to make a debut deployment to Britain, as would a US Navy F/A-18F Super Hornet, while a full Eurofighter Typhoon display was to be seen at the Air Tattoo for the first time. In the event, it didn't work out like that. The 'festival of aviation' concept seemed to be forgotten, while accidents back home in the US put paid to the Ospreys' attendance, and the Super Hornet and Typhoon appeared at Farnborough only.

And then there was the weather. After three very fine arrival and rehearsal days, Cottesmore remained resolutely clagged-in for the weekend — ironically, while the sun shone at Fairford. Many flying participants were affected, not least the solo jets. One, the USAF F-15C Eagle, never got airborne at all, the cloudbase not high enough for the Air Combat Command demo pilot's minima. All the others were forced into flat routines, but often very impactful flat routines. The year's impressive fast jet newcomer to the flying was the Finnish Air Force F-18C Hornet, in which Capt Kari Korpela from HävLLv 21 at Tampere was able only once to demonstrate his prowess and that of his mount. Somewhat less restricted was the Belgian Air Force CM170 Magister, bringing the butterfly-tailed Fouga trainer back to the Air Tattoo flying after a very long absence. With other items falling by the wayside, Cdt Jean-Charles Kotwicz Herniczek gave two beautiful aerobatic performances on each day, and many considered him unfortunate not to be numbered among the award-winners.

Reflecting Cottesmore's own role as headquarters of the recently established Joint Force Harrier, an RAF Harrier GR7 and Royal Navy Sea Harrier FA2 flew together, accompanying a Nimrod MR2 in a three-ship of assets now under the control of No 3 Group. In a similar vein, a brief role demonstration by an RAF Chinook HC2 and Army Air Corps Gazelle highlighted the formation of Joint Helicopter Command. The University Air Squadrons were entering a new era at the turn of the millennium, as well as their 75th anniversary year. To mark this, outgoing Bulldogs and incoming Grob Tutors were prominent in the static park, and there was RIAT's first look at a Tutor solo display, very well flown by Cranwell-based Flt Lt Mark Williams.

For 2000's 'Theatre of the Air', RIAT looked to the 60th anniversary of the Battle of Britain. Its plans to depict preparation and training for the battle, leading into a large-scale airfield attack and defence set-piece, with archive footage on big screens, were suitably ambitious — and,

Air Tattoo Memories: Es George

Meet & Greet manager Es George recalls a special moment at Cottesmore in 2000:

"We parked the Greek and Turkish F-4s next to each other. I did the meet and greet on both, the Greeks arrived first and I gave them the traditional welcome. Their ground crew had arrived by road so, once they'd done the formalities, the aircrew were straight into airshow party mode. It was a different matter for the Turkish pair and it was clear that one had a problem. It took a while to shut down, clearly the two crews were chatting on the radio to each other and after a while and a resigned headshake, they gave up and switched off. I don't know what the problem was but it seemed to be the sort of thing that could have been prevented (the RAF crews would call it a 'switch pigs'). Anyway, I gave them the traditional welcome and before I was able to finish, one of the Greek pilots had wandered over and asked if there was a problem. The response was a bit reserved, but the Greek guy says, "My engineers, they will take look?" At this point, there were smiles all round. I put my arms around one of the Greeks and one of the Turks and said, "This is what we love about RIAT, we forget what's outside and come together.""

Praise went to the Canadian Forces for its salute by a quartet of CF-188s. They performed a 'missing man' formation tribute to the overseas pilots who flew in the Battle of Britain.

alas, destined to fall somewhat flat. The fundamental problem was the withdrawal of almost all the representative German aircraft. Only the Deutsche Lufthansa Berlin-Stiftung's Messerschmitt Bf 108 and Arado Ar 79, the latter making its only British flying display appearance, depicted the 'other side'. All the Bf 108s, and the Belgian-owned Buchón, that were to have played the Luftwaffe attackers, fell by the wayside as the show date loomed. Using the South African DC-4 to portray a German bomber kept the scenario on track, but did not look historically credible, while the routines by two Hurricanes and five Spitfires were, this author wrote in *Aircraft Illustrated*, "simply too sedate to create much impact."

More praise went to the Canadian Forces for its salute by a quartet of CF-188s, among eight examples from 4 Wing that stopped off at Cottesmore en route back to Canada from a detachment to Aviano, Italy. They performed a thunderous scramble and 'missing man' formation tribute to the overseas pilots who flew in the Battle of Britain. With slightly more favourable conditions on Sunday, four RAF Tornado F3s repeated the 'missing man' gesture, while BBMF Hurricane LF363 flew through with the *Red Arrows*.

The biggest achievement of RIAT 2000, however, was squeezing the Air Tattoo's quart into Cottesmore's pint pot. Using computer-aided design to lay out the static park, making maximum use of the more limited space available, was one means of achieving this. Stressing to aircrews the importance of arriving on

time, thus not disrupting the intricate parking plan, was another. It worked, and the Rutland base proved more than capable of hosting all the 'heavies' involved in the year's operational meet, Airlift. Twenty Hercules, eight KC-135s — the numbers stayed up to Fairford standards. Remarkable was the line of Antonov transports, six in all, among them Open Skies An-30s from Bulgaria, Russia and Ukraine. There was more in the air, too, an early chunk of the programme being given over to the Airlift theme and bringing about some excellent displays. Perhaps most notable was the Polish Navy M28 Bryza, a perennial static exhibit but not seen in the air at a UK display before or since. A spirited showing included a short landing, 360° turn on the runway and short take-off. Beat that, Harriers!

At one stage the Ukrainian Air Force committed 17 aircraft to the show, but operational and financial constraints cut this to four. Star among them was inevitably the Tu-22M3, the first occasion on which a 'Backfire' had visited an operational RAF station — and, as it turned out, surely the last. It was parked next to a French Air Force Mirage IVP, a remarkable meeting of Cold War nuclear bombers. RIAT 2000 may not have shone as planned in the air, but the event's strength in depth was still there. But the crowds weren't. "The real problem at Cottesmore were the attendance figures — the numbers were dramatically down on previous Tattoos at Fairford", said Paul Bowen afterwards. Even so, with many lessons learned, it would be Cottesmore again for 2001, and this time the sun would shine on RIAT's endeavours.

In reflecting on Air Tattoo history, some years inevitably stand out, and there have been few more enjoyable than its 30th anniversary. Somehow the show being on an active RAF base had a particularly good feel to it. Even after just two years, it felt settled at Cottesmore. It almost seemed a shame to go home...

There was no great 'Theatre of the Air' this time, and, by comparison with some seasons, relatively little that hadn't been seen before, though the Training theme was new. Instead, RIAT 2001 was simply a superb modern military airshow, and all the better for it. Take the RAF contribution. An entire apron was filled with present-day aircraft from the service, 48 of them in all, the second C-17A delivered to No 99 Squadron acting as a centrepiece. As a showcase of modern UK air power in the early 21st century, it could scarcely have been bettered.

Yet there was still room for historical reflection. For the Hunter's 50th anniversary, Rod Dean led a six-ship formation in Kennet Aviation's F6A, accompanied by the rare ex-Fleet Air Arm PR11 operated by the Classic Jet Aircraft Company, and a mixed quartet of Swiss-owned F58s and T68s. "The nice thing

about that", Rod recalls, "was that they gave us something like about a 25-minute slot, so we could do some close formation, then split into sections and do different parts". After initial passes by the sextet, the Swiss were given their chance to shine, especially Ueli Leutert in 'Papyrus', the Fliegermuseum Altenrhein's F58 painted to represent the specially liveried example from the disbandment of Swiss Air Force unit Flieger Staffel 15. The two British-based machines having flown together, how better to finish than with another of Rod's exemplary solos, as good in 2001 as in 1972 when he became the Air Tattoo's inaugural trophy-winner. Now he was victorious again, the Hunter team collectively being awarded the King Hussein Memorial Sword for best overall flying demonstration.

This was one of two historic aircraft displays to leave with silverware. The other was Rolls-Royce's Spitfire PRXIX PS853, in the hands of Andy Sephton, who claimed the Sir Douglas Bader Trophy for the top individual display. He also led a trio of Cottesmore-based Harrier GR7s in a 'missing man' tribute to wartime fighter ace and wing leader AVM J. E. 'Johnnie' Johnson, who had died in January. Johnson had been station commander at Cottesmore, then a Victor bomber base,

144

01

RAF COTTESMORE
28 & 29 JULY

The Royal International
Air Tattoo
2001

RAF COTTESMORE 28 & 29 JULY

OFFICIAL SOUVENIR PROGRAMME
SPONSORED BY
COBHAM

SIX POUNDS

Paul, Tim and Peter March cutting the IAT 30th anniversary cake at RAF Cottesmore.

An entire apron was filled with present-day aircraft from the RAF, 48 of them in all, the second C-17A delivered to No 99 Squadron acting as a centrepiece. As a showcase of modern UK air power in the early 21st century, it could scarcely have been bettered.

PHOTO: FERGAL GOODMAN

In a static park with many rarities, the Armed Forces of Malta's BN-2B Islander and Bulldog T1 were among the best, Malta being a nation new to the event.

Air Tattoo Memories: Gordon Harris

Gordon joined as company secretary in 1996, retiring as director finance in 2007.

"My abiding memory of the Air Tattoo is the quality of the people we had — both volunteers and permanent staff. Each year, as the show grew nearer, the pressure on everyone tangibly increased. Those who handled the pressure best were capable of retaining their sense of humour even when faced with the most difficult situations. And they gave their all! I remember at RAF Cottesmore asking John Procter, our commercial co-ordinator, if he wanted a beer to mark the end of a successful show. He smiled, said he'd love to but added that he simply had 'nothing left in the tank'. Like so many on the team, he had given everything! It struck me just how exhausting — and rewarding — staging each airshow could be."

from 1957-60. The flypast by a No 10 Squadron VC10 C1K, meanwhile, saluted the passing in March of the great Brian Trubshaw, who flight-tested so many of these majestic Vickers transports and was long a member of the Air Tattoo's flying control committee.

Almost uniformly, the RIAT 2001 flying was at an especially high level. This time the Finnish Air Force F-18C could be shown to the full, earning Capt Jyri Selvenius of HävLLv 11 the Solo Jet Aerobatic Trophy. But there was tough opposition, the Canadian Forces CF-188, over from 441 Squadron at Cold Lake, Alberta, and Royal Netherlands Air Force F-16AM both running it close — and sporting extremely attractive special markings to boot. But the Hungarian Air Force MiG-29, back in the hands of Maj Gyula Vári, eclipsed them all. Since his appearances at Fairford in 1997-99, Vári had revamped his routine to feature expansive, flare-firing tailslides, and here they took full advantage of the blue skies. Both the Lockheed Martin Cannestra Trophy for best display by an overseas participant, and the As the Crow Flies Trophy judged by the FRIAT membership, were deservedly his. They added to the trophies won on his previous RIAT outings, making Vári one of the show's true 'Top Guns'.

With such a full flying programme, the two MiG-29 displays were originally scheduled to 'toggle' between the two days: the Hungarian on Saturday, the German example on Sunday. However, so good was the Hungarian's performance that it was inserted into the Sunday schedule too. The Luftwaffe pilot from Jagdgeschwader 73 then blotted his copybook with an extremely low pass, leading to an immediate 'red card' from the flying control committee.

The Romanian Air Force made a UK display debut, the well-flown routine from a two-seat MiG-21UM LanceR B, operated by Grupul 86 at Borcea-Fetesti, also representing a welcome return for this classic Warsaw Pact-era fighter. Accompanying it, on show in the static park, were a single-seat MiG-21 LanceR C fighter and a C-130B Hercules. But there should have been still more from the Romanians: a true show-stopper indeed in the form of a Harbin H-5, the Chinese-built variant of the Ilyushin Il-28 twin-jet bomber.

PHOTO: ANDREW SHAW

Above: Long-serving staff member Claire Lock accepting her retirement gift from Paul Bowen.

Sadly, it was not to be. Just a week before the show, having conducted a training sortie at Borcea-Fetesti, the H-5R earmarked for the trip to Cottesmore suffered a crosswind landing accident. The crew was unharmed, but the freshly overhauled reconnaissance aircraft's starboard wing was torn off. This example had been specially outfitted for the journey with western-compatible navigation aids and radios, meaning none of the three other H-5s still operational in Romania could substitute.

Most recent USAF B-1B flying appearances had been fairly limited affairs, but not so the efforts of the crew from the 34th Bomb Squadron at Mountain Home AFB, Idaho. This was the Air Tattoo's most striking Lancer display to date, concluding on Sunday with a climbing double roll. Some onlookers outside the airfield boundary felt the full force of the 'Bone' during Friday's rehearsals, a number of minor injuries being sustained as it powered up for take-off. Choosing to stand directly behind a B-1's jet blast was not, shall we say, the most sensible choice they'd ever made.

The single-flypast appearance by a 509th BW B-2A might not have seemed especially notable, but it was. The same aircraft, *Spirit of Kansas*, was involved on both days, flying to and from its base at Whiteman with just a three-and-a-quarter-hour turn-around between sorties. A 49th FW F-117A operated out of Lakenheath, though there was another example in the static park, its rear aspect the subject of especially tight security. Bowing out was the 62nd Airlift Squadron C-141B, which gave the last ever Starlifter display at a UK show.

Every Air Tattoo has its surprises, and for Tim Prince, this one was no exception. In a static park with many rarities, the Armed Forces of Malta's BN-2B Islander and ex-RAF Bulldog T1 were among the best, Malta being a nation new to the event. Come the Friday night though, RIAT airfield manager John Thorpe needed the locked Islander moving and the crew was nowhere to be found. What to do? Well, Tim is an AA member, and one 'phone call later Peterborough patrolman Terry Kirton found himself at the airfield, using his master keys to gain access to the Maltese machine. It was in its designated position come Saturday morning. Unfortunately, Malta has never sent aircraft to the Air Tattoo since.

They had been two entertaining years at Cottesmore, 2001 especially so, but there was no doubting the commitment required on the part of a front-line RAF base to host an event on RIAT's scale. Despite the immense support given from the station commander down, the degree of disruption meant this could only ever be a temporary move. The airfield work at Fairford was still far from finished though — and, in the meantime, the terrorist attacks of 11 September 2001 made returning to a USAF installation all the tougher. What would RIAT 2002 bring?

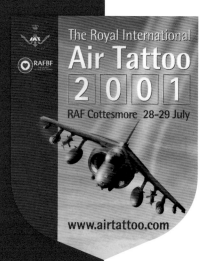

The Royal International
Air Tattoo
2 0 0 1
RAF Cottesmore 28–29 July

www.airtattoo.com

01

PHOTO: NIGEL BLAKE

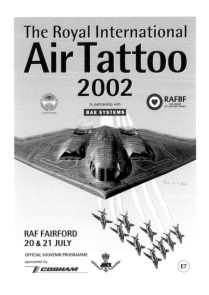

The Royal International
Air Tattoo
2002

In partnership with
BAE SYSTEMS

RAFBF
THE HEART OF THE RAF FAMILY

RAF FAIRFORD
20 & 21 JULY

OFFICIAL SOUVENIR PROGRAMME

sponsored by
COBHAM

£7

02

RAF FAIRFORD
20 & 21 JULY

This was a USAF-dominated year, marking the 60th anniversary of the United States Army Air Forces' arrival in Britain during World War Two.

The challenges of RIAT 2002, at a new-look RAF Fairford, were enormous. "Firstly, we'd been away for two years", Tim Prince recalls. "The airfield had been rebuilt, but it wasn't quite finished and there was still work going on. They were still taking bits of the airfield back from the contractor. All of our local agencies and organisations had had two years off, and some of the people had retired, some had moved away, so it was almost like coming to a new airfield again. Secondly, '9/11' had happened, and we came back to effectively a new regime from a security point of view. It wasn't a matter of 'Oh, it's the Air Tattoo, we can trust them' — it was very high-level stuff — but thankfully, both the USAF and the RAF were very much on-side."

"We realised quite quickly that we couldn't argue against parking off-base, having just done it at Cottesmore where there was nowhere on-base there to park. We literally had to reassess and renegotiate everything we wanted to do on the airfield where enhanced security was the overriding priority. Straight away, costs

were soaring. We now needed armed policemen to be on the airfield to protect certain assets, and armed police don't do long shifts because their protective gear is so heavy, so we had to fund many more to cover more shifts. We also had to rent more fields, and although it was a blessing that the farmers had the fields available, it was money that we were losing very quickly.

"We had to keep a very close eye on whether it would even be viable to run the show or not. It was a near thing. We did it, we ran it, and financially it worked, but because we were out of kilter with how to run a show at Fairford anyway, and with the new regime of security, there were some rough edges. From the public's point of view, 2002 wasn't an enjoyable experience getting in or getting out, and the same applied for our sponsors and our invited guests. We took a huge reputational hit that year, and it took a long time to recover from it."

Traffic had always been a problem in the narrow Cotswolds lanes, but the combination of so many attending with the new security arrangements led to RIAT's worst ever queues. There were reports of visitors on one route facing delays of up to four hours — and that was before they got to the airfield. What, eventually, they found when inside the showground were vast new areas of concrete, with huge aprons and taxiways expanded significantly in width. The new space in the showground enabled

As a nod to the Queen's golden jubilee, a big contingent of classic 1950s-era aircraft was brought in for static display, perhaps the most distinctive feature of this particular RIAT.

the national aerobatic teams, the volunteer-crewed British Airways Boeing 777-236s that brought in passengers in aid of RIAT's Flying Scholarships for the Disabled, and visiting and charter aircraft, to be parked around the south-eastern stretch of the taxiway loop, which in turn freed up slots on the north-side aprons.

The sight of the Italian Air Force G222 crew from the RSV exiting their stricken aircraft on the runway was an unfortunate reminder of a similar incident at the 1999 show. This time a heavy landing after the traditional Khe Sanh approach was to blame, the twin-turboprop airlifter bouncing onto its nose undercarriage leg, which duly collapsed. The G222 slid to a stop, a small fire breaking out and entering the cockpit via the nosewheel bay. There were no injuries, but much consternation. With the runway blocked, there was no option but to rejig the flying schedule before heavy lifting gear arrived to move the obstruction. The *Utterly Butterly Barnstormers* Stearman wingwalking formation and the RAF Gliding and Soaring Association's *Team Condor* duo of ASK-21s flew in earlier than planned from their operating bases, the two sailplanes able to land comfortably in the remaining distance; an RAF Hercules C3 and Army Air Corps Islander that happened to be active in the local area kindly gave impromptu flybys; and, gradually, other acts untroubled by the need to use 6,000 rather than 10,000ft of runway came forward to plug the gap.

Most importantly, the show's USAF hosts were very forgiving. Tim recalls with a smile, "They had just spent £100 million on the base, and Gen John Jumper [the then USAF Chief of Staff] was up on the balcony of the control tower talking to our flying display director Geoff Brindle when the G222 scraped the brand-new runway. That's testament to the relationship, in that Gen Jumper was able

The return after nine years of the Chilean Air Force Halcones in their Extra EA300s drew admiring glances, especially the drawing in smoke of a five-point Chilean star.

to say, 'Not a problem'. Later, he became a volunteer, as a RIAT vice-patron."

This was a USAF-dominated year, marking the 60th anniversary of the United States Army Air Forces' arrival in Britain during World War Two, and as part of a Salute to Bomber Crews. There were impressive B-1B, B-2A and B-52H flypasts, as well as an F-117A display, a 'missing man' salute from four Aviano-based 31st FW F-16Cs, and a F-15D from Lakenheath in the hands of Air Combat Command's West Coast Demo Team pilot, plus 'safety pilot' in the back. On Sunday, the Eagle was joined by The Fighter Collection's P-47M Thunderbolt and Robs Lamplough's P-51D Mustang for RIAT's first look at a USAF Heritage Flight, the two piston fighters being piloted by visiting American warbird maestros Steve Hinton and Ed Shipley. They also flew with B-17G Flying Fortress *Sally B*, while the BBMF Lancaster and the Aircraft Restoration Company's Blenheim made a very rare duo in closing the bomber tribute, wartime American and British veterans taking the salute.

In the run-up to RIAT 2002, the flying programme was looking decidedly overloaded — one draft in the author's possession has a running time of close on 10 hours. Late withdrawals cut it to a more manageable length, but reduced the rarity quotient. For many, 899 Naval Air Squadron's Sea Harrier FA2 duet, performed by Lt Cdr Rob Schwab and Lt Will Hynett, was the pick for spectacle — the Steedman Display Sword and As the Crow Flies Trophy were theirs. The return after nine years of the Chilean Air Force *Halcones* in their Extra EA300s drew admiring glances too, especially the drawing in smoke of a five-point Chilean star. Pleasingly, the two Chilean support aircraft, a Boeing 707-351C that flew the dismantled Extras to Brize Norton and a Gulfstream IV VIP transport, stayed to join the static line.

As a nod to the Queen's golden jubilee, a big contingent of classic 1950s-era aircraft was brought in for static display, perhaps the most distinctive feature of this particular RIAT. Some were notable in their own right: de Havilland Aviation's Sea Vixen, still then in its RAE Llanbedr drone scheme, Martin-Baker's recently reflown Meteor T7 WA638 and Golden Apple's F-86A Sabre, back in the air after a lengthy overhaul, were bona fide stars of any show. With hindsight, this was the shape of things to come: fewer military assets for the static park, more civilian ones. In the post-'9/11' world, in-service aircraft would be in short supply. RIAT would see more manufacturers' aeroplanes, too, especially in Farnborough years. The world debut of the Pilatus PC-21 was an unexpected feature in 2002, again pointing the way ahead.

Paul Bowen said afterwards, "I think actually we did well to come out with an event". Its effects, though, were far-reaching. As RIAT 2002 ended, much had already been revealed about plans for 2003: it would celebrate 100 years of powered flight, and incorporate Defence 2003, the latest in a series of official events conceived to replace the Royal Tournament. The ambition was boundless. Would it succeed?

Air Tattoo Memories:

Max R. Rothman
Lieutenant Colonel USAF (Ret'd)

02

Lt Col Rothman was base commander at RAF Fairford/RAF Welford from May 2002 to May 2004.

"I will never forget Saturday 20 July 2002. I was the new US Air Force base commander of RAF Fairford. I had a newly resurfaced runway on base and was anxious as I was thrust into the midst of final planning phases for the 2002 Royal International Air Tattoo.

"I was conscious that the US Air Force had spent millions of hard-gotten US taxpayer dollars resurfacing the Fairford runway and the fact that it would be needed for many decades to come. I felt every ounce of that weight on my shoulders as I turned over its use for the Tattoo into the capable hands of two extraordinary gentlemen, Paul Bowen and Tim Prince. The RIAT team was run by amazing professionals who worked hard to include me and gain my trust. As with all aviation professionals, they had a mission, and I was in a position to help them execute it. I knew my main job would be providing a US connection point and guaranteeing preservation of the new runway. What could possibly happen to a runway anyhow?

"I gained nothing but respect for the RIAT team as I watched every aspect of their thorough preparation unfold before me. Then, just at mid-day on Saturday, at the height of the main show, an Italian G222 made an extremely hard landing and bounced onto its nose gear, collapsing it. It skidded with flames under the fuselage to a stop, leaving all those watching quite concerned. Responses were perfectly co-ordinated, and the crew were safe. The incident was so well handled by the resident Fairford and RIAT trained rescue crews, I was quickly allowed to go out onto the runway to inspect it. On so doing, I couldn't believe my eyes. That darned G222 had left a long, deep gash down the centerline of my brand new runway. As a pilot I understood... but as the new base commander I took it almost personally! I almost missed the fact that the crew were safe. I missed the fact entirely that the RIAT crews handled the incident with poise, grace and supreme professionalism, keeping the huge crowd assembled both safe and entertained as all of this unfolded!

"In the end, I took a wonderful life lesson from this incident. Long a professional at what I do, others too are extraordinary professionals at what they do. Surround yourself when you can with people like Paul, Tim and the RIAT team, and then stand back and let them do what they do best, even if at times it may mean one's pride may have to be put aside (or an eventual gash in one's proverbial runway may need mending!) This lesson has stuck with me ever since and not only has my professional aviation outlook changed, but my personal and business outlooks have

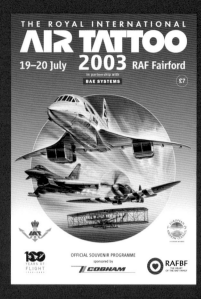

Perhaps it requires the passage of time to fully appreciate it, but the 100 Years of Flight exhibition at RIAT 2003 must go down as one of the most outstanding depictions of aviation history ever staged in Britain. It ranks alongside the *Daily Express* 50 Years of Flying event at Hendon in 1951, or 1968's RAF 50th anniversary at Abingdon. In fact, given its size and scope, it should perhaps be rated ahead of them. This is no idle boast; rather, an accurate reflection on the array of aeroplanes — static museum-pieces, airworthy historic machines and current service types — brought in from home and abroad.

Of all 2003's celebrations of the Wright brothers' epoch-making feat, the Air Tattoo's was the broadest and most imaginative. Around the western end of the base was arrayed a chronological series of vignettes from the pioneers to the present day, each with suitable 'set dressing' — as far as was possible on a modern airfield, of course. Several aircraft had been specially refurbished beforehand, among them the Wright Model B 'Flyer' replica belonging the Yorkshire Air Museum, without which the occasion would hardly have been complete. It and the other airframes from Elvington — among them the Blackburn Mercury replica that sat alongside the 'Flyer' in the opening pavilion — were flown in specially aboard an RAF C-17. Re-enactors and artefacts enhanced the World War One and Two displays; commentator Seán Maffett had recorded period airshow narrations for broadcast over loudspeakers in the areas covering barnstorming and the Hendon pageants.

Of course, there were many aircraft highlights. Perhaps the most striking element was the almost unbelievable array of post-war jets. At the start, the RAF Museum's Gloster F9/40 prototype DG202 sat alongside two later Meteors, the Jet Age Museum's F8 WH364 and the Craig-Wood brothers' airworthy NF11 WM167. Walk a little further on and you found another RAF Museum exhibit, Saunders-Roe SR53 XD145, taking its place in a line-up also containing Javelin FAW9 XH903 from the Jet Age Museum, Murray Flint's Lightning T5 XS420 and Brooklands' P1127 XP984. Supermarine's early jets were represented by the part-restored fuselage and wings of Swift F7 G-SWIF and the then Southampton Hall of Aviation's Scimitar F1 XD332, neither having been seen in public for some years. To have John Bradshaw's immaculate Fury, G-CBEL, in the line of Fleet Air Arm carrier fighters and fighter-bombers

The 100 Years of Flight exhibition must go down as one of the most outstanding depictions of aviation history ever staged in Britain.

was a delight, given how seldom it ventured out. Nearby there was a gap, two wreaths filling the space the Royal Navy Historic Flight's Firefly should have occupied, had it not been for the fatal accident at Duxford the weekend prior.

On the display went, the chance to see so many museum exhibits out in the open especially appreciated. There were historic British rotorcraft galore, light transports and plenty of other front-line types. Then came the present-day equipment, RAF Tristar, Sentry and C-17 looming largest. It was very much a journey through aviation history through British eyes, but not exclusively so. Most types on hand had been used at some point by the UK's or the Commonwealth's flying services, but not all. By any standards, what RIAT dubbed the 'Flightpath to Fame' was unrivalled.

But it was not without its problems, as Tim Prince remembers. "It was costly in emotions, it was costly in money. We set that world record for having 535 aeroplanes here — again, we probably overstepped the mark a bit, because we were borrowing beautiful assets from museums, and we were relying on all sorts of ways to get them here. Just occasionally, people weren't as caring in returning them as they might have been. That was unforgivable. But overall, we made it happen, and it was a high spot."

What RIAT 2003 actually looked like was quite different to the initial plan. Much of that involved the tri-service Defence 2003, for which the permanent Air Tattoo team was bolstered by a specific organising cell headed by an RAF group captain with more than a dozen air force, army and navy staff. "Again", says Tim, "it gave Paul a chance to really go for it". Pre-show interviews with Bowen bear this out. Fairford's eastern end was to become a fictional state called 'Riattica', which, he said in *Aircraft Illustrated*, was to have "an internal political destabilising problem. Once inside Fairford the public will find big screens set up depicting the growing situation in this mythical country... in that third of the airfield the public will see an FMB, a forward mounting base, taking place showing a UK force deployment in action". Aircraft would be "coming and going throughout the deployment, exactly as it would happen for real... The whole story will evolve throughout

03

RAF FAIRFORD
19 & 20 JULY

THE ROYAL INTERNATIONAL
AIR TATTOO
2003
19–20 July   RAF Fairford
in partnership with
BAE SYSTEMS

www.airtattoo.com

Presentation of an original painting as a retirement gift to the then Chief of the Air Staff Sir Peter Squire (fifth from left), from the RAFBFE directors and staff.

Max Rothman, US Air Force station commander at RAF Fairford, is presented to HRH The Duke of Edinburgh.

the day, culminating in victory in Riattica following a battle."

None of this was to happen. In March 2003, with British forces freshly engaged in coalition operations in Iraq, it was announced that Defence 2003 had been postponed for a year. However, RIAT remained on, despite Fairford's use as an operating base for USAF B-52s. The focus now was on the powered flight centenary, as well as the year's operational theme, Ocean Watch. And there was an opportunity to focus on the aircraft and crews involved in the Iraq war, though this ended up being quite a low-key feature. Given the controversy that surrounded the conflict, not to mention the death the Thursday before the show of government weapons expert Dr David Kelly, this was understandable.

Even leaving the 100 Years of Flight display aside, the static park was among the finest RIAT had mustered in recent times. With so many operational commitments, USAF participation was well down, but did take in an inaugural Air Tattoo appearance by an E-8C JSTARS from the 116th Air Control Wing. France's Aéronautique Navale offered the British show premiere of a Flottille 4F E-2C Hawkeye, and in-service Rafale Ms from 12F. By contrast, the specially marked duo of Swiss Air Force Mirage IIIRS recce jets was doing the rounds of a select few European airshows before the type's retirement by Flieger Staffel 10. The single Italian Air Force TF-104G from the 20° Stormo was, as events turned out, giving the Air Tattoo its final sight of an in-service Starfighter. The Latvian Air Force debuted in Britain, with a Mi-8MTV-1 rescue helicopter and L-410T, the 'Hip' going home with the rotary-wing Ocean Watch concours d'elegance trophy. The fixed-wing equivalent deservedly went to the Polish Navy M28 Bryza-1R, painted as an RAF Wellington operated by No 304 (Polish) Squadron in tribute to the 60th anniversary of the Battle of the Atlantic.

There was proof of the Eurofighter Typhoon's progress into RAF service, with the arrival for static display on Saturday morning of a two-seat T1 in the markings of No 17 (Reserve) Squadron, the operational evaluation unit for the type. This particular jet, ZJ802, was yet to be handed over, though at least one RAF crew member was on board. At the helm of instrumented production aircraft IPA1 from the BAE Warton fleet was Alenia test pilot Maurizio Cheli, at last bringing a full Typhoon display to the Air Tattoo, and doing so with panache.

The King Hussein Memorial Sword for best overall flying demonstration went, rather unusually, to an item that performed just one pass. It was a memorable one, though: the combination of *Red Arrows* and USAF F-117A, the latter flown by Sqn Ldr Richie Matthews, then the RAF exchange officer with the 49th

Even with the 100 Years of Flight display, the crowd was substantially down. "That", Tim Prince says, "was because of 2002. It takes about three years to regain visitor confidence after lots of people had the unfortunate experience of being stuck in their cars for hours."

Other British shows would put on the aerial pageants. RIAT's strength in 2003 was on the ground.

Fighter Wing. This time the 509th BW deployed a B-2A to Mildenhall for the RIAT weekend rather than flying it to and from Missouri, original plans to land it at Fairford falling through. After a dozen years, a full A-10A display was back, flown by East Coast Demo Team pilot Capt Matt Kouchokos in a Spangdahlem-based 52nd FW machine.

The first Boeing 757-2K2 delivered to the Royal New Zealand Air Force gave a very dashing demonstration in the hands of No 40 Squadron 'boss' Wg Cdr Tony Davies. Following it on the programme, and highlighting RIAT's growing industry support, a primer-painted Airbus A330-203 flew past with two German Marineflieger Tornados in close attendance. The logo of the AirTanker consortium on the tail of the A330 — which was actually destined for EVA Air in Taiwan — illustrated how the type was being offered for the MoD's Future Strategic Tanker Aircraft contract.

The flying part of the centenary celebration was left wholly to industry. EADS supported appearances by two aircraft, the Albatros B.II replica from Historischer Flugzeugbau at Fürstenwalde, east of Berlin, and the Amicale Jean-Baptiste Salis' CASA 352L (Spanish-built Junkers Ju 52/3m). Then there was the regular attendance of Rolls-Royce's Spitfire PRXIX, somewhat oddly the sole British historic aeroplane on the programme. It did seem strange to have an Air Tattoo without even the BBMF in the air, but its charges were all part of the static display. Other British shows would put on the aerial pageants. RIAT's strength in 2003 was on the ground.

But even with the 100 Years of Flight display, and security arrangements significantly improved, the crowd was substantially down. "That", Tim says, "was because of 2002. It takes about three years to regain visitor confidence after lots of people had the unfortunate experience of being stuck in their cars for hours." In turn, there were wider consequences. "There was a concern on the part of our parent charity over the volatility associated with what we were doing in all respects, whether it was '9/11', the financial outlay or whatever else. It was beginning to unsettle the Benevolent Fund and we had to be very, very tight in managing everything we did". And, as if that wasn't enough, RIAT 2003 turned out to mark the end of an Air Tattoo era.

More Air Tattoo People

Over 50 years, the Air Tattoo's army of volunteers and supporters may have changed, but their significant support and enthusiasm has never wavered. A further snapshot of some of these incredible people — to whom a huge debt of gratitude and thanks is owed — appears here.

BRITISH AIRWA

THE ROYAL INTERNATIONAL
AIR TATTOO

D Day
Entente Cordiale
Information
First Aid
Toilets
Shopping Mall
Green Car Park
Red Car Park
Blue Car Park

WW2 veteran Geoffrey Wellum
with Wg Cdr Jon Hitchcock.

Regular RIAT visitor David Jason
seen here with Carolyn Grace and
her two-seater Spitfire.

04

RAF FAIRFORD
17 & 18 JULY

Paul Bowen died in hospital on 19 May 2004. The Air Tattoo had lost its guiding light, and Tim paid heartfelt tribute. "He was quite simply the heart of the Tattoo", he said. "RIAT is very much a family affair and now that family has lost its father."

Even with the need to rein things in somewhat after 2003's poor financial out-turn, there seemed little reason to assume RIAT 2004 wouldn't be like any other. In Tim Prince's words, "We were getting on all right with plans, industry was still behind us, and the 100 Years event had actually put us in fairly good stead even though the numbers weren't what we'd wanted on the public days. Then, over Christmas, Paul was taken ill. That was the start of his lung cancer. In fact the team didn't see Paul again from when we closed the office for Christmas.

"Douglas Bader House was already running 'light' following some restructuring, so then there was more to be done. We divided up Paul's work between us while at the same time endeavouring to support him, Janet and his son Guy during this awful time for them. Leading into the show, it was challenging, and of course Paul was wanting to know that we were getting it right."

Paul Bowen died in hospital on 19 May 2004. The Air Tattoo had lost its guiding light, and Tim paid heartfelt tribute. "Paul was quite simply the heart of the Tattoo", he said. "RIAT is very much a family affair, a 2,000-strong family of volunteers, supporters and staff who are committed to staging a world-class event each year. Now that family has lost its father."

But there was still a show to run. Paul wouldn't have wanted it any other way. Tim looks back on this time with, he says, "Very mixed emotions. I didn't have much time to think — I was scrabbling around trying to ensure that all stakeholders still had

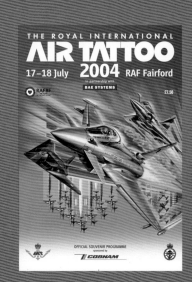

As one of the Extras pulled up and away, Maffett's words harked back to Paul Bowen's roots in air traffic control: "Cleared for unrestricted climb..."

confidence in us, along with the team here at Douglas Bader House. The volunteers were outstanding in their support. In effect, we just got on with it. We were a very tight-knit team, because we wanted to do it for Paul, and I have to take my hat off to everyone for rallying behind me and supporting me. What we achieved was actually a highly successful, highly profitable event."

An emotional one, too. Its memorial to Paul juxtaposed a perfectly judged tribute by commentator Seán Maffett with a 'missing man' formation comprising a PA-28-140 Cherokee used by RIAT's Flying Scholarships for the Disabled, which Paul was instrumental in establishing, and the Extra EA300s of the *Royal Jordanian Falcons*. As one of the Extras pulled up and away, Maffett's words harked back to Bowen's roots in air traffic control: "Cleared for unrestricted climb..."

The MoD having called off Defence 2004, citing "the continued high level of operational commitments", official tributes to the 60th anniversary of D-Day and the centenary of the Anglo-French Entente Cordiale took its place. Neither represented, many felt, the apogee of aerial theatre. In trying to tell the story of the 1944 Allied invasion, the finale scenario forsook excitement for realism. Quartets of Spitfires and Mustangs flew fairly sedately and seemed under-used, while elements such as Jim Buckingham's Miles Messenger — the veteran Bristol-based pilot making the last of many Air Tattoo appearances — and a Piper L-4 artillery spotting sortie were simply lost along the vast crowdline. Not seen in the UK for six years, Didier Chable's TBM-3E Avenger was nice to have in the show, even if its undercarriage kept extending itself. The centrepiece of the Entente Cordiale celebration, a Jaguar

PHOTO: GERHARD SCHMID

Boeing test pilot Ricardo Traven was presented with three awards for his F/A-18F Super Hornet display.

Air Tattoo Memories: Hugh Lohan

Hugh's and IAT's paths first crossed when, as a lieutenant colonel and CO of the Army's Queen's Division depot, he 'joined forces' in helping IAT put on the Bassingbourn Anglo-American Air Festival in Cambridgeshire in May 1978. He soon became involved with IAT as a volunteer where, over the years, his roles included: emergency services manager, marketing co-ordinator, MRC commander and show operations – flying complaints! A man with vast Air Tattoo experience, this is how Hugh Lohan sums up what being part of the show's family meant to him....

"What's so special about volunteering at RIAT? The friends I've made and the staff and volunteers I've met over the years. Being part of a team dealing with challenges, some critical — met and dealt with. Being allowed to set up a system that informed and pacified local animal farmers, stable owners and families with pets. Calming extremely unhappy visitors who had a problem. I remember when the B-1B Lancer was cancelled at the last moment. A whole family upset and demanding money back and wanting to confront Paul Bowen. So, I said 'Let's have tea all round and discuss the problem'. My explanation was accepted by the visitors. Out of interest, I asked "Why is it so important to see the B-1B?" Their reply... "Oh, we don't come to see it, we come to hear it!"

Hugh Lohan is a man of many talents. He is also a very capable visual artist who specializes in drawing cartoons. Below are a few of the many Air Tattoo related cartoon drawings which Hugh has produced over the years.

PHOTO: GERHARD SCHMID

PHOTO: GERHARD SCHMID

PHOTO: GERHARD SCHMID

DEPARTMENT OF THE AIR FORCE
WASHINGTON DC

OFFICE OF THE UNDER SECRETARY

Air Force Pentagon
Washington, DC

Mr. Tim Prince
Director of The Royal International Air Tattoo
PO Box 1940
Fairford, Gloucestershire
GL7 4NA
United Kingdom

AUG 1 1 2004

Dear Mr. Prince,

Greetings to the exceptional staff of the Royal International Air Tattoo. I am writing to express my sincere appreciation for your wonderful hospitality during my trip to Fairford three weeks ago. This was my first opportunity to attend an airshow in the UK and your organization certainly has demonstrated how to do things with professionalism and style.

The gala dinner Friday night was a tremendous way to begin the events and I especially enjoyed the flying demonstrations over the weekend. The corporate sponsors were a large part of the airshow, but your organization brought it all together—it was a class act all the way.

Please accept my warmest regards and highest professional esteem.

Sincerely,

BRUCE S. LEMKIN
Deputy Under Secretary of the Air Force
International Affairs

31 AUG 2004	
DATE RECEIVED	
FILE NO.	
PAB	
TP	
GH	
ACTION	TP
INFO CC:	LJ CL

Tim Prince
Director of Operations
The Royal International Tattoo
Dougla Bader House
Horcott Hill
Fairford
Gloucestershire GL7 4RB

20 July 2004

Dear Tim Prince,

I would like to thank you most sincerely for a wonderful day on Sunday, and I congratulate you on a superb feat of organisation. My wife Judy and I could not have had a more enjoyable time, meeting friends old and new and of course having a grandstand view of a sensational air display.

Paul Bowen's death was a great tragedy, but his spirit and his lifelong work lives on in all that you have done. I am sure he was there, nodding in approval!

With kindest regards,

George Martin

Sir George Martin, CBE

The Royal International Air Tattoo 2004
in partnership with **BAE SYSTEMS**

A   **A**

GALA DINNER

Name: _____   Contact Number: _____   09719

Vehicle Registration: _____   Organisation: _____

GR3/Mirage 2000C paired run over a pyrotechnic French flag, proclaimed as the "largest single ignition of fireworks ever detonated in the UK", was possibly more impressive in the idea than the execution.

Leaving no-one disappointed was the thunderous display by Boeing test pilot Ricardo Traven in the F/A-18F Super Hornet. Such a combination of brutishness and agility had seldom been seen in a fast jet until the big US Navy strike fighter came along, and Traven was its leading exponent. He was awarded the King Hussein Memorial Sword for the top overall demonstration and the Friends of RIAT's As The Crow Flies Trophy, while the colourful VFA-2 'CAG-bird' also scooped the FRIAT award for best livery. Other newcomers this year were a limited demo by an in-service RAF Typhoon T1 and the Finnish Air Force *Midnight Hawks* team, while the Swiss Air Force formation flypast of the *Patrouille Suisse* F-5Es and the solo F/A-18C added a touch of imagination.

Never again would the Air Tattoo, nor any other British event, be graced by an Armée de l'Air Mirage IVP, so the static appearance by one of Escadron de Reconnaissance Stratégique 1/91's remaining examples was one to log in the memory bank. The type was retired early the following year. USAF participation was up, bolstering considerably the Hercules 50th anniversary meet — operational commitments meant RAF and Italian examples were the only European-based C-130s present. With fast jet rarities increasingly hard to come by, the unusual training, transport and support types were assuming greater importance, and the Estonian Border Guard Air Wing debuted, bringing an L-410UVP-T. None could match the panache of the Italian Air Force Piaggio P166DL-3 on arrival, though. On its first flyby prior to

Air Tattoo Memories: Air Marshal David Walker

David Walker was Station Commander at RAF Cottesmore when the Air Tattoo was staged there in 2000 and 2001, and was instrumental in helping to secure the show's future in 2004.

"You must be mad!" — a comment I remember receiving more than once as station commander at RAF Cottesmore in 2000 and 2001. We had volunteered to HQ Strike Command to host RIAT after it faced having no venue while RAF Fairford was being refurbished. Mad we may have been, but the sense of achievement and success we all felt after the last aircraft left and quiet returned to rural Rutland was enormous and more than made up for any accusations of insanity that may have been offered.

Looking back, it is so clear that it was the right thing to do. For the members of the station it provided a great and novel challenge that brought all sections of the station together. Working with the fantastic RIAT team of volunteers, who transformed our operational airfield into an international event venue in the space of just over a week and then returned it to us as if nothing had happened a week or so later, was inspirational. It demonstrated just how much could be done if people worked together and shared a common sense of delivery, hospitality, and operational excellence. It was so good to watch the station staff after the show where these values inspired them in what they could achieve and do together.

It was also right to offer an airfield so that RIAT continued uninterrupted. RIAT in 2000 was, as now, the foremost airshow in the world. And as someone whose love of aviation and the RAF was kindled at airshows on US bases in East Anglia in the 1960s, RIAT had a special place in the hearts of the aviation community and it simply needed to go ahead. Anyone who has been involved with the RIAT team would be enormously impressed by the good the airshow does on so many levels. Whether it was keeping aviation in the public eye, enthralling young people to a future career, raising funds for RAF charitable work, or just simply providing a fantastic day out for families and friends, RIAT needed to be able to operate and it was a privilege to be part of the Cottesmore team that was able to help out.

In 2004 it was my turn to offer an exasperated exclamation when, as the Assistant Chief of the Air Staff, I was passed a letter written to the Chief of the Air Staff from the RAF Benevolent Fund informing him that they were no longer able to parent RIAT. It was August in MoD, and I had a very short time to try and find a solution that preserved RIAT but didn't expose the RAF to unlimited liability. By comparison, providing an airfield and its facilities for RIAT in 2000 was child's play. Luckily, the RIAT team of ACM Sir Mike Knight, Alan Smith, Fred Crawley, David Bywater, Oli Delany, Tim Prince, David Higham, Caroline Rogers and Gordon Harris were as determined as me that RIAT would survive, change, and prosper.

Since leaving the RAF I have been privileged to be the president of the Royal British Legion and a commissioner with the Commonwealth War Graves Commission, and have learnt a great deal about the charity and not-for-profit sector. In August 2004, I knew nothing. But it was clear that RIAT needed an overarching structure under which it could operate and flourish. A charitable trust linked by name to the RAF seemed to offer a way ahead, and after a considerable amount of discussion and cross-checking the Royal Air Force Charitable Trust (RAFCT) was formed. The RAFCT Enterprises was set up alongside to raise funds and act as the trading arm of the trust. Since 2004, the RAFCTE has run RIAT brilliantly and raised significant funds for the trust whose subsequent grants have had such an impact on air cadets and on front-line stations where the investments have been so gratefully received.

Although making Cottesmore available in 2000 may have been important, I suspect being part of the team that established the trust in 2004 was even more significant. RIAT is a fantastic organisation, founded on people who share a love of aviation. Happy 50th anniversary and every success for the next 50 years.

---

landing, the pilot rolled it. On its second, he did the lowest beat-up seen during Air Tattoo arrivals for many, many years. It would have earned him a straight red card had he been taking part in the display.

A different RIAT, then: smaller, more conventional, but also more profitable. The run-up was dominated by talk of whether the show could survive another difficult year. As it was, 168,000 people attended, a five per cent increase on the previous show. Having budgeted for a repetition of 2003's crowd figure, this was a good result. With renewed sponsorship from some of the aerospace industry's biggest players and some judicious pruning of organisational costs, the ship was on a steadier course. But a new obstacle was just around the corner.

PHOTO: PAUL EMERY

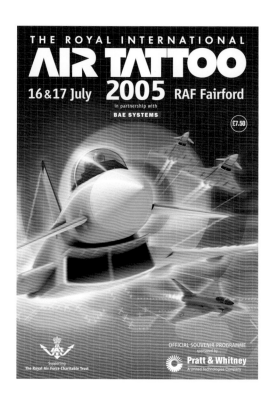

RAF FAIRFORD
16 & 17 JULY

RIAT 2004 had seen to it that Paul Bowen's legacy would live on. This, however, wasn't enough to change the RAF Benevolent Fund's mind about no longer wanting to be in the airshow business. It had developed a concern, according to Tim Prince, "that there was a volatility associated with what we were doing in all respects, whether it was '9/11', the financial outlay or whatever else". But the RAF, which relied upon RIAT in furtherance of international defence diplomacy and recruiting, lent its support to make sure this wouldn't spell the end. Along with a number of very loyal volunteer supporters and with the assistance of the RAF, a new charity, the RAF Charitable Trust, was established in early 2005 specifically to ensure that RIAT would continue.

This change cemented the show's relationship with the service. It seemed fitting, therefore, that RAF items should take the aerial limelight. Surveillance was the operational theme, so a unique three-ship of photo-reconnaissance Spitfires — Peter Teichman's PRXIX, Rolls-Royce and BBMF PRXIXs — flew together, and in formation with the *Red Arrows*. Hitting the headlines for other reasons was the No 29(R) Squadron Typhoon T1, in its debut season of full solo aerobatic displays. It was heart-in-mouth time for all who were watching Sqn Ldr Matt Elliott's Friday rehearsal, when a small positioning error led to an extremely low recovery over the grass between crowdline and runway. Allowed to fly again later in the day following discussions with the flying control committee, this slightly modified sequence was duly approved for the weekend public show.

The RAF's airlift fleet had a special part to play. A No 99 Squadron C-17A featured in the flying programme for the first time, opening the show with a brief flypast and landing — on Saturday, it deposited an air force pipe band on the runway. Adding the most poignant note to proceedings, the component squadrons of the Lyneham-based Hercules wing flew a 'missing man' formation to honour the nine crew members and Royal Signals passenger who lost their lives in January 2005 when XV179 was shot down over Iraq.

The only real overseas newcomer in the air was a flare-popping Royal Netherlands Air Force AH-64D, 301 Squadron's Maj Wandert Brandsen and Capt Raymond Laporte winning the Sir Douglas Bader Trophy for the best individual display and FRIAT's As The Crow Flies Trophy. But there was entertainment from other quarters, such as the biggest Royal Navy contribution for many seasons, four-ships of Sea Harrier FA2s and Jetstream T2s among it. Honda-sponsored aerobatic pilot Will Curtis was part of a Guinness world record-breaking effort, seeking in his

Oli Delany, Sir Mike Knight, RAFCTE commercial director Caroline Rogers and Tim Prince.

PAUL ANTHONY BOWEN

18 February 1947 – 18 May 2004

was instrumental in the founding of the Air Tattoo in 1971
and bringing the now Royal International Air Tattoo
to RAF Fairford in 1985.

Hangar 1200 – the venue for the internationally famous
RIAT Gala Dinner – received his name in 2005
in recognition of his achievements.

THE ROYAL INTERNATIONAL
AIR TATTOO
16 – 17 July 2005 RAF Fairford
BAE SYSTEMS
eyes in the sky
TIGERS
ROAR·05
surveillance
www.airtattoo.com

Honda-sponsored aerobatic pilot Will Curtis
was part of a Guinness world record-breaking
effort, seeking in his Sukhoi Su-26 to set new
benchmarks for limbo flying and inverted
ribbon cuts.

Sukhoi Su-26 to set new benchmarks for limbo flying and inverted ribbon cuts. In the former he was successful, in the latter he just missed out, but no-one who saw it will quite put out of their mind the pronounced sink towards the runway...

Another item was like no other seen in the UK. The Boeing ScanEagle gave the country's inaugural demonstration of an unmanned aerial vehicle, but it had to fly so far from the crowd that it literally went out of sight. It was certainly impossible to see its British military roundels with the naked eye, these illustrating how the ScanEagle had been undergoing trials with the Joint UAV Experimentation Programme, including operations from a Royal Navy warship. Real-time downlinked imagery from its camera was broadcast on two big screens, but didn't seem to draw the crowds.

If the unmanned future didn't inspire, a quite superb static park did. The comeback of some meaty East European hardware saw the Polish Air Force's tiger-striped Su-22UM3K sharing ramp space with four Romanian AF MiG-21 LanceR Cs that were concluding a deployment to the UK. For the Surveillance meet the French military provided two aircraft rarely seen at airshows in their own country, let alone abroad — the Armée de l'Air Transall C-160G Gabriel electronic intelligence platform and an ALAT AS532 Cougar HORIZON battlefield surveillance helicopter received much attention on their debuts. Outstanding support too came from the Italian services, the Guardia di Finanza taking its British bow with an ATR-42-400MP patrol aircraft and two AB412s, and the Marina Militare sending examples of the AV-8B and TAV-8B Harrier II. And, at long last, the RAF deigned to bring a No 51 Squadron Nimrod R1, for so long the most secretive asset in its inventory.

RIAT 2005 took place just over a week after the al-Qaeda terrorist bombings in London, difficult circumstances for any public event, but especially one so large and high-profile. Security was tight, for public and volunteers alike, yet efficient and far from overbearing. The 160,000 crowd, an increase of about seven per cent, enjoyed a fine airshow in glorious weather — and there was better to come.

Air Tattoo Memories: Air Chief Marshal Sir Michael Knight

Sir Michael Knight, RIAT honorary vice patron and former chairman of the Royal Air Force Charitable Trust, reflects on the formation of the charity in 2004.

Imagine the scene... recently retired elderly gent (REG), ensconced in an unobtrusive coffee-house in the centre of Taunton, awaiting the arrival of three good friends from his Royal International Air Tattoo days, who'd suggested a meet-up as they made their weary way back to Fairford from 'somewhere or other'.

He had just heard the almost unbelievable news that the skids appeared to be well and truly under the Air Tattoo, following the unexpected decision of its Ben Fund parent charity to wind down the show just one month after yet another triumphant annual extravaganza. While that event had, as ever, enthused and delighted the Great British Public, it had failed to realise the sort of profit which the fund considered appropriate — and which, as a service charity, it required. A further problem had arisen from a formal governance review, which had concluded that the continued management of what had become a major public (and now thoroughly commercial) event was no longer compatible with the strictly charitable objectives of the fund.

Not only was this decision a veritable 'bolt from the blue', but its obvious consequence would see the disbandment and redundancy of the team which had grown the Tattoo over the 34 years since its first staging as a rather informal fly-in to the former Battle of Britain airfield at North Weald in Essex.

Thus the background to the Taunton gathering. It was not in the nature of the RIAT team to admit defeat — whatever the odds, and the Taunton-bound trio was determined to fight on. It consisted of the chief executive Tim Prince (a founder member of the Tattoo), his right-hand colleague Caroline Rogers and a wise and determined supporter in retired Air Cdre Oliver Delany. The 'REG' realised not only the true purpose of this 'informal' meeting, but that it would be useless to deny it. Indeed, he was fully prepared to add to the 14 or so commitments he'd taken on since leaving the service; and, even had he not been invited, RIAT would have been very high on his personal list.

The result was, therefore, never in doubt. RIAT would be re-born under new management, and would continue as the show-piece and primary fund-raising element of a brand-new operation — the Royal Air Force Charitable Trust. All that remained was the agreement of the Air Force Board — and, that, with the impressive support of the then Assistant Chief of Air Staff, AVM David Walker, was duly achieved.

If all this appears to be a simple and undemanding exercise in administrative accounting — pray think again. It called for a protracted period of dedicated and intensive effort by a small nucleus of folk, determined to prove that RIAT and the new charity would maintain and extend the remarkable growth of what many had long designated 'the world's greatest military air show'.

Despite the enforced cancellation (in 2008) of one Tattoo by reason of incessant bad weather and the flooding of its car parks, the show continued to offer an annual fiesta of aviation-related activity until COVID-19 forced it — and almost every other major national event — into postponement or cancellation. This has served merely to inspire the ever-aspirational Air Tattoo management as they look to the future of the airshow.

THE ROYAL INTERNATIONAL
AIR TATTOO
15 – 17 July 2005 RAF Fairford
in partnership with

EYES IN THE SKY

06

RAF FAIRFORD
15 & 16 JULY

In many ways, RIAT 2006 was the very model of a modern military airshow. It painted a potent picture of where military aviation found itself — much downsized, older types gradually disappearing, a new generation of multi-role combat jets, trainers, helicopters, tankers and transports in or nearing service, civilian contractors in the ascendancy, and global operational commitments and financial pressures leaving air arms at full stretch. Yet this was surely the best Air Tattoo for some years.

Never had the event seen such high-profile aerospace industry involvement, and not just in the form of sponsorship. Many of these companies — including AleniaAermacchi, BAE Systems, Bell, Boeing, EADS CASA, Omega Air, Pilatus and the Russian Aircraft Corporation (RAC) MiG — brought their latest hardware, in several cases providing UK flying display debuts. As a 'shop window', allowing manufacturers' representatives to mingle in relative informality with military pilots and top brass, RIAT was proving ever more effective. And, against azure skies, the public weekend flying displays provided great entertainment. The programme was notably slick, and mixed the familiar with the new — in some cases, the downright stunning — in utterly professional style.

To have the inaugural UK showings of the tilt-rotor Bell Boeing MV-22B Osprey and the three-dimensional thrust-vectoring MiG-29M OVT in the same flying programme was truly exceptional, and neither disappointed. The Osprey, from US Marine Corps test and evaluation unit VMX-22 but flown by company test pilots Steve Grohsmeyer and Marty Shubert, was presented with great confidence in almost the full variety of its flight modes — at speed, transitioning and in the hover — and impressed and intrigued in equal measure.

But it was swivelling nozzles, and not tilting rotors, which set the pulses racing. Sharing their mount over the two days, RAC MiG test pilots Pavel Vlasov and Mikhail Beliaev gave the most masterly demonstrations

To have the inaugural UK showings of the tilt-rotor Bell Boeing MV-22B Osprey and the three-dimensional thrust-vectoring MiG-29M OVT in the same flying programme was truly exceptional.

of 'supermanoeuvrability' in the MiG-29M OVT, setting a new standard for Air Tattoo fast jet displays. The aircraft had only appeared once before in the west, earlier that year at the ILA Berlin Air Show, but since then Vlasov — a hero of the Russian Federation and chief test pilot of RAC MiG's A. V. Fedotov Flight Test Centre — and Beliaev had expanded its airshow envelope, showing even more of their ability to deflect the thrust-vectoring nozzles by up to +/-15° in all directions. "We are including a new manoeuvre – a flat rotation, which we do nearly at the end of the programme," said Vlasov. "At the time of Berlin, we were still finding out how to show this at a safe altitude, but now that's completed."

Much of this incredible performance — multiple somersaults, flat spins and all — was conducted with the Klimov RD-33 OVT engines in full reheat. Vlasov explained, "The aircraft can do all these manoeuvres without using the afterburner, but this is a display, so during the short time of the display we must show as much as possible. That's why we use the afterburner for nearly the whole flight without turning it off". It all added to the spectacle of what was a genuinely dramatic but beautifully controlled piece of flying. The Russian pair left as recipients of the King Hussein Memorial Sword and the As The Crow Flies Trophy.

It says a lot for the conventional combat jets that many were far from outclassed. Flying a very plain-looking F/A-18F, Boeing's Ricardo Traven followed the MiG and did his very best to look impressive in comparison; he succeeded, but the older Swiss Air Force F/A-18C in the hands of Capt Michael 'Elvis' Reiner was generally regarded as superior. It won the Paul Bowen Solo Jet Trophy ahead of such enduring staples as the French Air Force Mirage 2000B, Royal Netherlands Air Force F-16AM and the snappiest USAF F-15C sequence seen for some time, flown by West Coast Demo Team pilot Capt Tony Bierenkoven.

The Spanish Air Force Typhoon took part in one of the weekend's three unique formations involving the national jet aerobatic teams present. It undertook a flypast on Sunday led by the *Patrulla Aguila*, this following an earlier combination in which the *Red Arrows* had accompanied No 101 Squadron's red-tailed VC10 C1K as a salute to the big jet tanker/transport's 40 years of RAF service. A swathe of Swiss red and white was the order of the day for the third combine, as the Pilatus PC-21 kept up comfortably with the F-5Es of the *Patrouille Suisse*.

Pavel Vlasov receiving the As The Crow Flies Trophy from Fred Crawley and FRIAT members.

Kevin Leeson with HRH Prince Feisal.

PHOTO: ANTHONY NOBLE

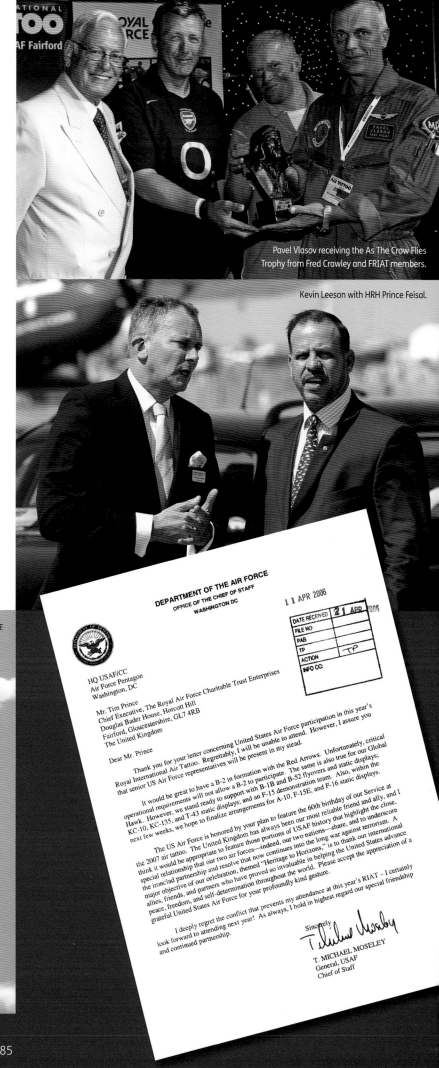

DEPARTMENT OF THE AIR FORCE
OFFICE OF THE CHIEF OF STAFF
WASHINGTON DC

11 APR 2006

DATE RECEIVED	21 APR 2006
FILE NO	
PAB	
TP	TP
ACTION	
INFO CC:	

HQ USAF/CC
Air Force Pentagon
Washington, DC

Mr. Tim Prince
Chief Executive, The Royal Air Force Charitable Trust Enterprises
Douglas Bader House, Horcott Hill
Fairford, Gloucestershire, GL7 4RB
The United Kingdom

Dear Mr. Prince

Thank you for your letter concerning United States Air Force participation in this year's Royal International Air Tattoo. Regrettably, I will be unable to attend. However, I assure you that senior US Air Force representatives will be present in my stead.

It would be great to have a B-2 in formation with the Red Arrows. Unfortunately, critical operational requirements will not allow a B-2 to participate. The same is also true for our Global Hawk. However, we stand ready to support with B-1B and B-52 flyovers and static displays; KC-10, KC-135, and T-43 static displays; and an F-15 demonstration team. Also, within the next few weeks, we hope to finalize arrangements for A-10, F-15E, and F-16 static displays.

The US Air Force is honored by your plan to feature the 60th birthday of our Service at the 2007 air tattoo. The United Kingdom has always been our most reliable friend and ally, and I think it would be appropriate to feature those portions of USAF history that highlight the close, special relationship that our two air forces—indeed, our two nations—share, and to underscore the ironclad partnership and resolve that now continues into the long war against terrorism. A major objective of our celebration, themed "Heritage to Horizons," is to thank our international allies, friends, and partners who have proved so invaluable in helping the United States advance peace, freedom, and self-determination throughout the world. Please accept the appreciation of a grateful United States Air Force for your profoundly kind gesture.

I deeply regret the conflict that prevents my attendance at this year's RIAT – I certainly look forward to attending next year! As always, I hold in highest regard our special friendship and continued partnership.

Sincerely,

T. MICHAEL MOSELEY
General, USAF
Chief of Staff

PHOTO: PETER STEEHOUWER   PHOTO: RAMON VAN OPDORP

THE ROYAL INTERNATIONAL
AIR TATTOO
15–16 July 2006 RAF Fairford
airtattoo.com

" This is THE best airshow! "

Buzz Aldrin Apollo 11 Astronaut

THE ROYAL INTERNATIONAL
AIR TATTOO
sponsored by BAE SYSTEMS
2006
B 14
Name:
Vehicle Reg:

THE ROYAL INTERNATIONAL
AIR TATTOO
sponsored by BAE SYSTEMS
2006
PUBLIC HOURS
SHOWGROUND
NON - PUBLIC HOURS
Name:
Vehicle Reg:
Contact Number:
Organisation:

RIAT
Staff
Reception

So, RIAT 2006 contained the new, the futuristic, the imaginative — and there was still room for the nostalgic. Sqn Ldr Terry Cairns, the RAF's oldest serving pilot, gave an utterly magnificent farewell display in a soon-to-be-retired No 39 (1 PRU) Squadron Canberra PR9. His zoom climb into the blue towards the end of Sunday's show, ending inverted and rolling off the top, was a moment for the ages.

This was the high point of RAF involvement, which included the lowest number of static aircraft from the service for many years. Operational commitments took their toll, right up until the start of the show weekend. Yet there were other rarities and 'firsts', none more significant than the debut western airshow appearance by the Pakistan Air Force. It provided an L-382B Hercules from No 6 Squadron, the sole example of this former civilian C-130 variant in Pakistani service, for the Rapid Global Effect operational theme as a way of thanking the international community for its support in earthquake relief efforts during 2005. The crew's work in creating the transport's special scheme, including illustrations of humanitarian flights on the tail fin, was rightly rewarded with victory in the concours d'elegance and the competition for the best livery.

The times had changed for military airshows, and none more so than RIAT. "We had to drop the Theatre of the Air", says Tim Prince — "we couldn't do it any more, we hadn't got the finances for it and costs were roaring up for a whole variety of reasons. We decided to go a bit smaller, because the world couldn't afford to provide that many aeroplanes with the way the economy was even then, but also to go for 'specials'." There were many of those in 2006, a year for the Air Tattoo annals.

Air Tattoo Memories: Brian Hughes

Brian was one of IAT's long-standing volunteers — contributing in a number of different ways over many years. Senior roles included security command, followed by show operations control co-ordinator and finally chief of staff.

"Memories? Hot Gossip at the hangar party at Greenham Common in '77 or '79 – or was it in the Big Top at South Cerney? Very nice. I was a lot younger then! The navigator ejecting from the Phantom on take-off at Bournemouth and the long lines of C-130s at the meet at IAT 1979.

"Another abiding memory was the two MiG-29s colliding in 1993 and one of the Russian pilots reaching for his cigarettes after he landed, just like the Marlboro man — this coupled with the eerie silence that followed it. Then there was the G222 landing and the crew leaving the aircraft at speed! The first flypasts by the B-2 will also stay long in my mind.

"The rain and its aftermath in 2008 was also unforgettable, with the rain cascading off peaked caps and bouncing up to waist height as the parade marched off after the presentation of the colours by Her Majesty The Queen, who stayed dry throughout."

There was to be only one major European celebration of the US Air Force's 60th anniversary, and RIAT was its host. After all, no other event on this side of the Atlantic — nor, indeed, many in the States — can boast the same level of USAF involvement as can the Air Tattoo. With the air force's chief of staff, Gen T. Michael 'Buzz' Moseley, in attendance to watch the show's first appearance by the _Thunderbirds_ and displays by other front-line USAF types, it was truly a high-powered gathering.

No other display team in the world presents such an exacting list of requirements as does the USAF Air Demonstration Squadron, something to which European organisers are largely unaccustomed. Fitting the _Thunderbirds_ into a UK flying programme, on the rare occasions it happens, can prove challenging. But RIAT proved it is worthwhile. Having deployed specially across 'the Pond', the six F-16C/Ds put on a genuinely slick, dynamic routine, one very different from the European teams, but refreshing for it.

Concluding a short British tour for the F-15E Strike Eagle Demo Team, Capt Al 'Jewel' Kennedy and Capt Jack 'Woody' Stallworth from the 4th Fighter Wing at Seymour Johnson AFB notched up a second appearance on these shores in a week aboard a borrowed 48th FW jet. The Heritage Flight display that followed was a two-ship affair, Ed Shipley taking the controls of The Fighter Collection's 'new' TF-51D Mustang _Miss Velma_ to join the F-15E. This, plus

07

RAF FAIRFORD
14 & 15 JULY

There was to be only one major European celebration of the US Air Force's 60th anniversary, and RIAT was its host. With the show's first appearance by the Thunderbirds and displays by other front-line USAF types, it was truly a high-powered gathering.

Plane Sailing's Catalina and Golden Apple's F-86A Sabre, made up the historic USAF flying content. A pleasing static park of American warbirds was assembled, but they seemed lacking in the air.

However, the most spirited B-1B displays for some time helped make up for this. The 7th Bomb Wing crew grabbed the attention with topside passes, a roll to the inverted at the top of a zoom climb on Saturday and then, on Sunday, a condensation-wreathed entry from behind the crowd. Many will also have been pleased by the banked run and low overshoots by the 49th FW F-117A, as it made the type's final European showing before (official) retirement. Handling the Nighthawk was Lt Col Peter York, one of the last group of F-117 pilots — or 'Bandits' — to graduate from the aircraft's formal training unit in November 2006.

Given reports of how the Sukhoi fighter performed against USAF F-15s in Exercise 'Cope India', it was ironic that the brief flying appearance by an Indian Air Force Su-30MKI ended up following the Strike Eagle on Saturday's schedule. There was no comparison between the two, as the Indians didn't bring a display pilot over and chose to make a couple of short passes, turns and climbs, but its

Air Tattoo Memories: Colonel Joe Dill

Col Joe Dill was USAF base commander at RAF Fairford from July 2007 to October 2009.

In July 2007, Joe Dill (pictured right with artist David Bent) — or 'camel' as he was introduced and better-known to all RIAT staff and volunteers — was immediately taken into the hearts of all those who had the privilege of meeting him. When asked what RIAT had meant to him, Joe said he had many memories juggling around in his head — some heartfelt, others funny, but he thought this photograph "tied up everything nicely in a small bundle". Joe wanted this particular photo included in the book as it shows, in his words, "what RIAT means to many — dreams and aircraft zealots enjoying life... and well-known *Red Arrows'* artist David Bent to boot! RIAT is the airframe that makes Airpowah dreams come true!"

THE ROYAL INTERNATIONAL
AIR TATTOO
14 – 15 July **2007** RAF Fairford

BAE SYSTEMS

airtattoo.com

IL-78MKI

PHOTO: PETER RUSSELL

RIAT 2007 progress meeting at Douglas Bader House.

HRH The Duke of Kent, KG

ST. JAMES'S PALACE
LONDON SW1A 1BQ

4th September 2007

Dear Michael,

Thank you very much for your letter of 23rd July, which I found on my return from holiday.

It was most kind of you to write and report on what must clearly have been an extremely successful International Air Tattoo. It certainly seems that the organisers were remarkabley lucky with the weather and it says a great deal, I believe, for the Tattoo's standing and reputation that the attendance was so good in spite of forbidding weather forecasts.

I need hardly say that I am sorry not to have been able to be there, particularly when you tell me that the Red Arrows put on the best show anyone had seen for many years. I hope, however, I shall have opportunities in the future of seeing those splendid red aircraft performing.

The Gala Dinner on the Friday evening was indeed most enjoyable and I am sure most of your guests will have found the unplanned fire practice added, if anything, to the entertainment, rather than otherwise.

As to RIAT 2008, I obviously cannot commit myself at this moment, but certainly hope I shall be able to be there.

Yours ever,

Air Chief Marshal Sir Michael Knight, KCB, AFC, FRAeS, FRGS

07

> "It certainly seems that the organisers were remarkably lucky with the weather and it says a great deal for the Tattoo's standing and reputation that the attendance was so good in spite of forbidding weather forecasts."

attendance — along with that in the static display of two more Su-30MKIs from 30 Squadron, together with their support Il-78MKI and a pre-delivery Hawk Mk132 — was welcome. India had never before provided aircraft to the Air Tattoo.

It was much to the RAF's credit that, in spite of reduced flying participation, it provided two star items. One was the formation flypast by the *Red Arrows* and the Battle of Britain Memorial Flight's four original fighters, Hurricane LF363 and the trio of Spitfire PRXIXs, celebrating the 50th anniversary of the BBMF's establishment as the Historic Aircraft Flight. Their extremely lively tailchase was one of the more effective multi-warbird sequences RIAT had seen for some while. The other was the new RAF role demo. The fact that it was again possible to spare the Tornado F3s and GR4s, Hercules, Sentry and Chinook that formed the 'friendly' forces was even more laudable when one considers how only 16 RAF aircraft (including five gliders) were to be found in the static park — the smallest showing by the 'home team' in the Air Tattoo's history.

At least there was a Jaguar on hand, thanks to QinetiQ's Fast Jet Test Squadron which sent T2A XX833 for a final British airshow outing. The list of other static highlights was long and varied. Leaving aside the Indians, many gave top honours to the Turkish Air Force's pair of immaculate NF-5Bs, making the inaugural appearance in the UK by standard squadron Freedom Fighters from this air arm. The debut of a Brazilian Air Force R-99A ran them close, this extraordinary-looking airborne early warning and control platform having made the trip from Anápolis via Lisbon just to attend the Air Tattoo.

Yes, the show remained a major draw for the world's air arms, even if they had fewer and fewer assets to commit to displays. The battle with defence bean-counters was just one of many RIAT had to fight, but thanks to its continued prestige and increasing importance as a 'meeting point' for industry and air force chiefs, it managed to do so most effectively. The onset of another big RAF anniversary would surely build on that — wouldn't it?

When Paul met Del and Tel...

Paul Lindsay – RIAT airfield group manager

Well, who would have thought that, having seen a note in RAF Brize Norton's Engineering Wing orders seeking volunteers to help out at an airshow, I would still be a volunteer at that same show 35 years later?

At the time I was serving in the RAF and a large number of RAF volunteers, coupled with a few civilians, pitched up at Fairford under the guise of the Engineering Team headed by Wg Cdr Peter Liddell, affectionately known as the 'ginger tornado'. That was July 1985.

Now, 35 years later, I head up that team of volunteers which is comprised of very few RAF personnel and many civilians. How times have changed. However, the job remains essentially the same — prepare the airfield for aircraft of various shapes and sizes, park the aircraft on arrival, welcome the crews, refuel, make everything safe, barrier/rope and cone and then wait for the crowds. All very easy really...

In addition, we often welcome VIP visitors and two in particular are fondly remembered. In 1996, actor David Jason, then best known as 'Del Boy', visited the show for the first time. He flew in, in the front seat of a Harrier T10 from No 20 Squadron at RAF Wittering, with a media throng among those eagerly awaiting his arrival. Unbeknown to him, the Air Tattoo had arranged to borrow the Trotters Independent Traders' Reliant Robin from a museum in the Lake District and we attached a follow-me sign to its roof (the follow-me sign appears on specially liveried vehicles that escort an aircraft to and from its parking bay). However, as the Harrier landed, the Reliant stalled. Had it not been for Andy Budge, a stalwart volunteer of many years and several other guys, we would have missed this great PR opportunity. The boys pushed, I dropped the clutch and the 'beast' burst into life just in time for me to perform the follow-me role. When the canopy opened, David Jason assumed the part of 'Del Boy', providing great entertainment for press and visitors alike.

On another occasion we helped host a visit by the legendary broadcaster Sir Terry Wogan, who joined us as part of a BBC *Children In Need* auction prize. He was accompanied by Pudsey Bear, whose attendance was largely due to Mike Pomeroy from RIAT's site team, who had said he could arrange Pudsey's visit as he 'had contacts'.

The following day I took Sir Terry, his friend and BBC travel reporter Lynn Bowles and Dr Wally (aka Pauly Walters, Terry's much-loved producer on *Wake Up To Wogan*) on a tour of the airfield so they could see the static and flying display aircraft. Needless to say, the laughter and banter in the car was wonderful.

For over half of my life spent as a volunteer, the Air Tattoo has provided many unforgettable memories — all of which I will treasure for the rest of my days.

PHOTO: MICHAEL BRAZIER

08

RAF FAIRFORD
12 & 13 JULY

The Air Tattoo had coped with all sorts of difficult circumstances, yet nothing — not even wars, peace demonstrations and short-notice searches for new venues — had stopped it in its tracks. Then came the worst the English summer weather could throw at Fairford, and the unprecedented cancellation of both public show days of RIAT 2008. It was a decision, it goes without saying, that was not taken lightly.

The event had enjoyed a lucky escape 12 months earlier. Just a couple of days after the 2007 airshow, the Cotswolds were awash with the worst flooding seen for many years. Come 2008, again it hadn't been a summer to remember, and when the first RIAT arrivals day on Wednesday 9 July dawned grey and wet, with forecasts offering little hope for the day ahead, events began to unfold. True to form, it didn't ease off until well into the night. Several participants made it through, but others were delayed, awaiting a better outlook.

They arrived on Thursday, when the morning's blue skies held out more promise. In the late afternoon, though, the rain came again — and with a vengeance. The runway, aprons and taxiways were soon awash, and the large grass areas due to fill up with trade stands and spectators started to look saturated. Sunshine and showers were again on Friday's agenda, with the potential to disrupt the RAF 90th anniversary ceremonies

The Royal Air Force celebrates its 90th anniversary

The RAF 90th anniversary ceremonies constituted the closest the Air Tattoo got to staging a flying display in 2008. The prelude to the flypast, staged on the Friday before the weekend show, was the presentation of new Queen's Colours to the RAF in the United Kingdom and the RAF Regiment, for which was staged the service's largest parade since the Silver Jubilee Review at Finningley in 1977. The Queen herself came in aboard Sikorsky S-76B G-VONB from PremiAir, entirely appropriate in times of ever-growing private sector involvement in defence.

For a while, it was touch-and-go as to whether the flypast would take place. After one of the week's many heavy showers had passed through towards the end of the parade, would the cloudbase be high enough? Thankfully, it was. The skies cleared just a few minutes before the 90 aircraft came into sight, navigation lights twinkling against the dark sky to the north

as they headed for the datum point, Fairford's control tower. The series of formations was, by today's standards, impressive, imaginative and comprehensive. Such heavily committed fleets as the support helicopters, Hercules, Nimrod, VC10, Tristar and Harrier were all represented, and the nine-ships of Typhoons, Tornado F3s and GR4s looked immaculate.

A short historical pageant following the flypast brought forth the excellent *Great War Display Team* and the Battle of Britain Memorial Flight, before a four-ship of Typhoons provided the closing act, powering into a head-on break that would have done a display team proud. Almost immediately, Her Majesty was back in the S-76 and away — whereupon the heavens opened again. That the 90th was able to be commemorated as planned proved to be one of the few pieces of good fortune RIAT 2008 enjoyed.

In concert with The Queen's Colour for the Royal Air Force in the United
The Royal Air Force Regiment Colour was then slow marched onto parade.
both Colours were received with a Royal Salute.

The Escort Squadrons then marched past in slow and quick time.

Colour Bearer: Flying Officer J D Hall RAF
Colour Warrant Officer: Warrant Officer R Hargreaves MBE RAF
Colour Escorts: Sergeant Morris
Sergeant Giddings
Colour Orderly: Corporal M Nuttall

The parade then advanced in Review Order and gave a Royal Salute.
Her Majesty was then given three cheers by the parade. Her Majesty then left the
parade ground and went on to a day at the Royal International Air Tattoo,
in celebration of the 90th Anniversary of the Royal Air Force.
The Parade was then marched off.

Elizabeth R

Air Comm
Com

14th July, 2008.

Dear Tim,

The Queen and The Duke of Edinburgh have asked me to write to you to convey their thanks for the contribution RAFCTE made to the events to mark the presentation of Colours to the RAF and RAF Regiment on Friday. The support that you provided was greatly appreciated both on the day and during the preparations beforehand. It was most unfortunate that the torrential rain of last week meant that the ground became water-logged to the extent that the Air Tattoo had to be cancelled on Saturday 12th and Sunday 13th July. Her Majesty and His Royal Highness were very sorry to hear this and have asked me to send their sincere commiserations to you and everyone at RAFCTE.

Please pass on my thanks to Caroline Rogers for all her excellent work in the lead up to the RAF Colours presentation.

Yours sincerely,

Doug King
Assistant Private Secretary to The Queen

Tim Prince, Esq.

involving HM The Queen. She and the celebratory flypast may — just — have missed the downpours, but hardly anyone else did. When they came, they were positively monsoonal.

Flying display rehearsals, aircraft arrivals and other preparations for the weekend went on, even though, by this stage, serious questions were being asked about the condition of the off-airfield car parks and areas inside the showground. Already, the organisers had decided not to sell any admission tickets on the gate in an effort to keep visitor numbers manageable. Efforts were made to render the car parks usable, but the show was fighting a losing battle. Even before the final aircraft movements took place on Friday evening, the decision was made to call off Saturday's show. Having looked at the state of the site, the organisers then had no option but to cancel Sunday as well.

Anyone who saw the effects of the rain will have realised this was inevitable. Any grass on which vehicles had parked or been driven was totally churned up, and the unused car parks and much of the crowdline had turned into a swampy morass. It was simply impossible to imagine these areas coping with tens of thousands of spectators come the weekend. Even by a dry and sunny Sunday afternoon, many places were simply impassable on foot.

Most of the participating aircraft had turned up and a good proportion of the flying items had rehearsed in the preceding days, so there is no doubt the first European public appearance by the USAF's F-22A Raptor would have stolen the show. Maj Paul 'Max' Moga's practice display was the most outstanding to be seen during the week, the gloomy skies making the condensation generated by the Raptor's vectored-thrust manoeuvring and the shockwaves in its afterburner flames all the more dramatic. We'd seen thrust-vectoring being shown to great effect before, of course, but what made the Raptor exceptional was the fact that this was an in-service, production aircraft being flown by an operational pilot.

Moga was disappointed at not being able to fly the F-22 in front of the public, and all his display pilot counterparts shared that frustration. Several others would also have been performing in the UK for the first time, such as 1st Lt Tomas Merta in the Czech Air Force JAS 39C Gripen, Canadian Forces CF-188 demo pilot Capt 'Billy' Mitchell with his specially marked jet from Bagotville, and the Portuguese Air Force's Asas de Portugal pair of Alpha Jets. You had to feel most sorry for the Brazilian Air Force *Esquadrilha da Fumaça*,

PHOTO: MARK FAIRHURST

08

Flying display rehearsals, aircraft arrivals and other preparations for the weekend went on, even though, by this stage, serious questions were being asked about the condition of the off-airfield car parks and areas inside the showground.

PHOTO: TIM FELCE

Turkish Stars

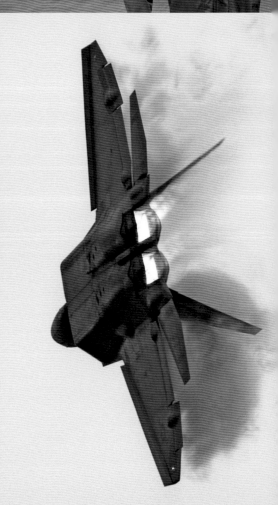

The Fumaça's rehearsal showed them to be a classy outfit, and it was a great shame so few were able to watch their imaginative display.

The insurers paid out, and the will to continue remained undiminished. That there would be a RIAT in 2009 was never in question.

which brought eight T-27 Tucanos all the way from their home base at Pirassununga for this one show, including an over-water stretch lasting some eight hours, and involving a big logistical effort — and never got to fly in public. The *Fumaça's* rehearsal showed them to be a classy outfit, and it was a great shame so few were able to watch their imaginative display. Tim Prince recalls how, "when they were here and saw the problems we had, they were rolling their sleeves up and said, 'What can we do to help?'"

The crew of the star static item, the Pakistan Navy P-3C Orion from 28 Squadron at PNS Mehran, made the best of it by manning their souvenir stall virtually all weekend despite the lack of people. As so often with air arms visiting RIAT for the first time, a lot of effort had been made to present the aircraft, which bore tail artwork proclaiming, 'A Civilisation 5,000 Years Old'. A specially produced leaflet was even being given out to help explain the painting.

And, despite the show's cancellation, there was still something significant to salvage from the weekend. "Industry still derived benefits from it, as did the chiefs", says Tim Prince. "Their programme kept going, to the extent that they wanted to come back". Caroline Rogers adds, "We had all these guests there, and we had no option but to continue. It wasn't as if the public was kept out and the champagne-drinkers carried on — we had to continue a programme, because we had a hotel full of air chiefs, we had chief execs here, there and everywhere, and they still needed to do their thing."

Above all, though, cancelling RIAT 2008 was the hardest decision Tim and the rest of the Air Tattoo team had needed to take. "It was horrible", he says, "horrible because of feeling we'd let so many people down". But there was no question of stopping. The insurers paid out, and the will to continue remained undiminished. That there would be a RIAT in 2009 was never in question.

09

RAF FAIRFORD
18 & 19 JULY

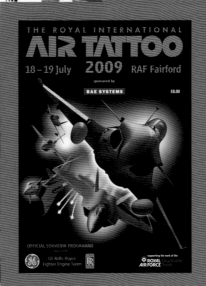

THE ROYAL INTERNATIONAL
AIR TATTOO
18 – 19 July **2009** RAF Fairford
sponsored by
BAE SYSTEMS
£8.00

OFFICIAL SOUVENIR PROGRAMME

GE Rolls-Royce
Fighter Engine Team

● ROYAL
AIR FORCE Charitable Trust

Gala Dinner hangar setting.

One could have been forgiven for feeling a sense of déjà vu, as the elements left RIAT 2009 decidedly bedraggled. But measures — expensive but crucial measures — had been taken to try and avoid a repetition of 2008.

"The discussions with our insurers", Tim Prince remembers, "really had highlighted the fact that if we were going to protect the show in the future with insurance cover, we had to put a lot of things in place to make sure we were robust". Thanks to the USAF, on-base car parking was allowed once again in the south-eastern and south-western areas of the airfield, in an effort to avoid problems in case of inclement conditions, while all the external car parks and many grass areas on the airfield had large quantities of 'trackway' matting put down. Perhaps the biggest change was to make RIAT advance ticket-only, putting the show, as Tim phrased it, "in control of its own destiny". And in reference to 2008, he said in the run-up to 2009, "the overseas air forces haven't held it against us that they came all that way for nothing."

They included the Algerian Air Force, a UK first-timer with a

In recalling the Cold War days of the NATO alliance, there was no better aircraft to have back at the Air Tattoo than Vulcan B2 XH558. On both days the imminent appearance of the majestic delta brought the crowd literally to its feet.

THE ROYAL INTERNATIONAL
AIR TATTOO
sponsored by
BAE SYSTEMS

RIAT 2009
RESIDENT

supporting the work of the

ROYAL
AIR FORCE
Charitable
Trust

C-130H in the static park. The Brazilian Air Force was back, a gaudily painted C-105A Amazonas — the local designation for the C-295 — being the most notable attendee in the year's SeaSearch meet. It highlighted how the type had operated far into the Atlantic the previous month while searching for remains of the crashed Air France A330. Two of the world's main maritime aircraft, the Atlantic and P-3 Orion, were completely absent, but there were compensations. One was a specially marked French Navy Lynx HAS4, its colours marking the successful completion of NATO's Operation 'Impartial Behaviour', a naval task force enforcing an international ban on arms-smuggling off the Lebanese coast. It tied together both the SeaSearch and NATO 60th anniversary themes of the show.

In recalling the Cold War days of the NATO alliance, there was no better aircraft to have back at the Air Tattoo than Vulcan B2 XH558. The great delta-winged 'V-bomber' would have starred the previous year, had the show gone ahead, having just returned to the display circuit in civilian hands. Now it was well-established on the scene once more, but, with funds still short, there were few more important showcases for the Vulcan to the Sky Trust. On both days the imminent appearance of the majestic delta brought the crowd literally to its feet, and they were not to

Left: USAF General John P Jumper is greeted by Tim Prince on arrival at Fairford.

CHIEF OF STAFF
UNITED STATES AIR FORCE
WASHINGTON

4 AUG 2009

Dear Mr. Prince Tim

Thank you for hosting Suzie and me during our recent visit to the Royal International Air Tattoo. We truly enjoyed the warm hospitality and your generosity. All the events were top-notch! It's clear that you and your staff worked extremely hard to ensure that every detail was covered. It was an honor and a privilege to attend such an outstanding occasion. Thanks again!

Sincerely

NORTON A. SCHWARTZ
General, USAF
Chief of Staff

Mr. Timothy Prince
Chief Executive, RAF Charitable Trust
Douglas Bader House
Horcott Hill
Fairford
Gloucestershire, GL7 4RB
UK

be disappointed. This went especially for Sunday as Kev Rumens, taking over the captain's seat from Martin Withers, pushed the port wing well beyond 90° at the peak of a vertiginous take-off climb.

Spirits had lifted further between the downpours as Maj Joseph Babone and his 20th Bomb Squadron crew in B-52H *War Hog* thundered back and forth upon returning from the Vigo Air Show in Spain, eventually positioning above the Vulcan just as XH558 readied for its take-off roll. Their joint taxi down the runway once the Stratofortress had recovered was unfortunately in the middle of a very heavy shower, but still provided the spectacle that lingered once others from RIAT 2009 had faded.

Often wreathed in condensation, the solo jets gave of their best. For years French Air Force Mirage 2000s had swept most before them in the fast jet display stakes, but now the Rafale assumed the honours. The initial RIAT outing by Cne Cédric Ruet, in a two-seat Rafale B belonging to Escadron de Chasse 1/7 'Provence', proved it to be a more than worthy successor. From the outset the multi-role machine's outstanding qualities were shown to the utmost, seamlessly changing pace between full-on 'turning and burning' and slow-speed manoeuvring in a

way no other type could quite demonstrate. Ruet returned to Saint-Dizier with the Sir Douglas Bader Trophy and FRIAT's As The Crow Flies award, and that after stiff opposition from a record three Hornets — Finnish, Spanish and Swiss — and two Gripens, a Hungarian Defence Forces example lining up for the first time alongside its Swedish counterpart.

With no role demo and a reduced number of solo items, the RAF's participation was low-key, its static presence amounting to barely 20 aircraft and just four full display items backing up the *Red Arrows* and BBMF, though a full air force crew was aboard the Nimrod MRA4 that BAE Systems contributed. Nonetheless, the Typhoon FGR4, Chinook and King Air put on especially fine displays, the King Air creating a great moment on Sunday when Flt Lt Leon Creese's accompanying music, ELO's 'Mr Blue Sky', produced just that — a sudden, welcome respite from the rain.

There was a need in 2009 for the Air Tattoo to regroup after the cancelled year. Despite the weather's best efforts, this it managed to do, aided significantly by the participants' professionalism. The display aircraft rose magnificently to the weekend's meteorological challenges, and produced some first-rate performances against constantly changing skyscapes.

Very unusually, it was the Royal Navy that dominated the 2009 Air Tattoo.

Its Fly Navy 100 celebration, marking the centenary of the Admiralty's first order for an airship — the ill-fated His Majesty's Airship No 1, dubbed 'Mayfly' — was staged at several venues that summer, and Fairford was one of them. The number of aircraft fielded by the Fleet Air Arm, Cobham, FRADU and others varied daily, but by Sunday there were 20 helicopters and 21 fixed-wing aircraft in the 'Balbo'. Led by Lt Cdr Mike Pamphilon in one of four Merlin HM1s, it included seven Sea Kings of different marks, with HU5SARs, ASaC7s and three HC4 'Junglies', plus a lone Lynx AH7 behind.

A quartet of Lynx HAS3s and HMA8s was inserted between the two groups of Sea Kings, with four Squirrel HT1s at the rear. Passing above the rotorcraft were four Jetstream T2s, while up at 1,500ft and overtaking the lot as the 'Balbo' reached display centre were the larger fixed-wing aircraft, with two Falcon 20s and four Hawks in tight formation, then de Havilland Aviation's Sea Vixen FAW2 and two Naval Strike Wing Harrier GR9As. Three Grob Tutors, the RN Historic Flight's sole flying aircraft at the time, the Chipmunk T10, and a Slingsby Firefly box-four completed the stream.

The main naval helicopters re-formed before sweeping back in a low hover in front of the crowd as the two Harriers powered over the top. The collective victory of all the Royal Navy items in the contest for the King Hussein Memorial Sword, for the best overall flying demonstration, was richly deserved. Only a reappearance by the Sea Vixen would have set the seal on this salute, but alas the RIAT budget did not stretch to a full demo by this most dramatic of classic jets.

FLY NAVY 100

PHOTO: DAVE KEY

PHOTO: TIM FELCE

PHOTO: ALDO BIDINI

PHOTO: DAVE KEY

PHOTO: DAVE KEY

Below right: Luftwaffe Bf 109 pilot Hans-Ekkehard Bob (right) meets RAF Battle of Britain veterans Tony Pickering, Ken Wilkinson and Bob Foster.

To mark 70 years since the exploits of 'the Few', the accent was on a more ceremonial style with an international military element alongside the warbirds. The consensus was that it worked extremely well.

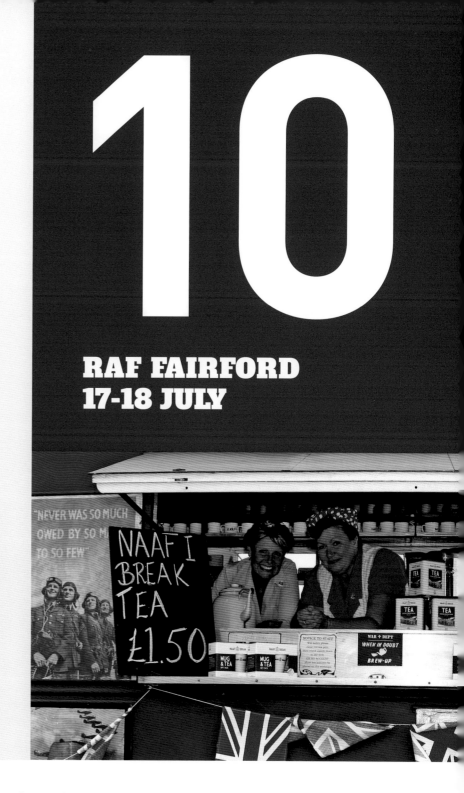

10

RAF FAIRFORD
17-18 JULY

The Air Tattoo's past treatment of major anniversaries relating to the Battle of Britain had involved not just commemoration, but also re-enactment. For 2010, to mark 70 years since the exploits of 'the Few', it took a different tack, playing to RIAT's strengths. So, while the Biggin Hill and Shoreham shows staged pyrotechnic-laden set-pieces, and September's Duxford display offered the most invigorating Spitfire and Hurricane formations and tailchases, at Fairford the accent was on a more ceremonial style with an international military element alongside the warbirds. The consensus was that it worked extremely well.

Playing a major role was No 19(R) Squadron, which brought a number of Hawk T1s and new T2s from Valley. Some of the T1s bore special markings, not only celebrating 19's own 95th anniversary but also its role as a Duxford-based Spitfire unit in 1940. The names of Spitfire pilots from 19 who took part in the Battle of Britain, such as Sgt George Unwin and Flt Lt Brian Lane, were painted below their canopy rails. A Hawk quartet performed a 'missing man' formation as the 14 warbirds lined up on Fairford's runway 27, before making a stream take-off and forming up to the east.

The original intention had been for the warbirds to make just one flypast before a run-and-break, but what transpired was rather more. Led overall by Battle of Britain Memorial Flight commanding officer Sqn Ldr Ian Smith, two each of finger-fours and vic-threes flew a series of formation passes, the elements quite widely spaced but the formations tight — not least given the lack of a full

215

Triple award-winning USAF F-22A Raptor pilot Major Dave Skalicky receiving the As the Crow Flies Trophy from RAFCTE chairman Fred Crawley.

THE ROYAL INTERNATIONAL
AIR TATTOO
17 – 18 July   RAF Fairford
2010   airtattoo.com

Bringing together the fighters of yesteryear and today, the show was closed each day by the RAF's brilliant 'synchro pair' of the BBMF Spitfire LFIXc and a No 29(R) Squadron Typhoon.

rehearsal. The lead combination was especially noteworthy, bringing together the BBMF's Spitfire IIa and Peter Vacher's Hurricane I, both veterans of the 1940 air war, Spitfire Ltd's Spitfire LFIXe and the EADS Heritage Flight's Messerschmitt Bf 109G-4 'Red 7', enjoying a long-awaited debut on these shores. It was a shame there was no opportunity for Klaus Plasa to display the Bf 109, given its long trip over from Manching in Bavaria, but there would be future opportunities. Behind came the Historic Aircraft Collection's Spitfire LFVb and Hurricane with the Aircraft Restoration Company's Spitfire IXT and Buchón; then a trio comprising Spitfire Ltd's Spitfire LFXVIe, the Hangar 11 Collection's Hurricane and Peter Monk's Spitfire HFIXe; and finally the 108 Flying Group's Nord 1002 (Bf 108) leading the BBMF's Hurricane LF363 and Spitfire LFIXe. As the last element turned away from each pass, so the first ran back in, the sound of those Merlins and the Bf 109's Daimler-Benz DB605 an evocative one.

With the warbirds back on the ground, No 19(R) Squadron's Hawks led the multi-national flypast, callsign 'Dowding Formation', with tucked in right behind a Tornado F3 from No 111 Squadron making the type's last in-service RIAT appearance, though sadly it was unable to land due to operational requirements. A Royal New Zealand Air Force Boeing 757-200 was escorted by two US Air Force F-15Cs from the 493rd Fighter Squadron, one of which, in a fuel-critical state, had taken the arrestor cable at Lyneham after Friday's rehearsal owing to a hydraulic failure. Bringing up the rear was a tight trio of a French Air Force Mirage 2000B and two Belgian Air Component F-16A MLUs. The efforts of those overseas pilots who flew in the battle were not to be forgotten.

The disruption caused by Sunday's weather conditions was unfortunate, the crosswind being outside the Spitfire IIa's limits. 'Smithy' took over the BBMF's MkIX to lead, and the 108 was rather oddly singled out for a solo while the rest joined up, meaning the flypasts consisted of three four-ships. A weather-related decision was also taken to scrub all but the Hawks from the multi-national flypast, but at least there had been a chance to watch the whole salute the day before.

The greatest contrast of all to the Hurricanes, Spitfires and Messerschmitts was the stunning USAF F-22A Raptor demo performed by Maj 'Zeke' Skalicky from the 1st Fighter Wing in a 3rd Wing aircraft. After the cancelled RIAT of two years earlier, this marked the type's UK public flying display debut, and it did not disappoint. Bringing together the fighters of yesteryear and today, the show was closed each day by the RAF's brilliant 'synchro pair' of the BBMF Spitfire LFIXc and a No 29(R) Squadron Typhoon, with Sqn Ldr Dunc Mason and Flt Lt Rich Walton at their respective controls. Both these items were deserving recipients of awards at the Sunday night prizegiving, the Raptor taking a record three.

On the ground, a Polish Air Force Su-22M4 remembered the largest overseas contingent to join the RAF in 1940, and the sight of historic unit codes on the 800 Naval Air Squadron Harrier GR9, and No 41 Squadron's Tornado GR4 and Harrier GR9, showed great

recognition of history. The codes 'SH-M' on the 800 NAS Harrier were those worn during the battle on a No 64 Squadron Spitfire Ia flown by Sub-Lt Francis Dawson-Paul, the Fleet Air Arm's first ace of the war. He scored seven confirmed kills — Bf 109s, Bf 110s and a Dornier Do 17 — before being shot down over the Channel on 25 July and dying of his injuries six days later.

The other major theme, that of training, was to have been ably reflected by a number of very unusual USAF flying items. Variable weather, unserviceability and other circumstances somewhat blunted the plans, which had included an Altus AFB-based 97th Air Mobility Wing KC-135R demonstrating the refuelling of a C-17A from the same unit. They never got to perform that sequence, but in low cloud on the Sunday both aircraft were shown off separately and punchily, the tanker flying the full length of the runway 'dirty' at barely 50ft. The C-17A, named *Spirit of Denali*, was also able to drop the USAF Academy *Wings of Blue* parachute display team on Saturday. In its hold was brought to Fairford a Let TG-10C Kestrel glider operated by the academy's 94th Flying Training Squadron in Colorado Springs, which was to have shown the aerobatic prowess of this military derivative of the Blaník. But it was not to be. Saturday's conditions would have been ideal, but the tug aircraft's pilot arrived at his airfield ready to deploy to Fairford, only to discover he had left his hangar keys at home, and so would miss his slot. In Sunday's clag, the chance to put on anything like a full show was gone.

Perhaps the most memorable individual display, F-22 aside, was the first British outing by Airbus Military's new A400M transport. To see the second prototype put through its paces so vigorously by chief test pilot Ed Strongman, only seven months

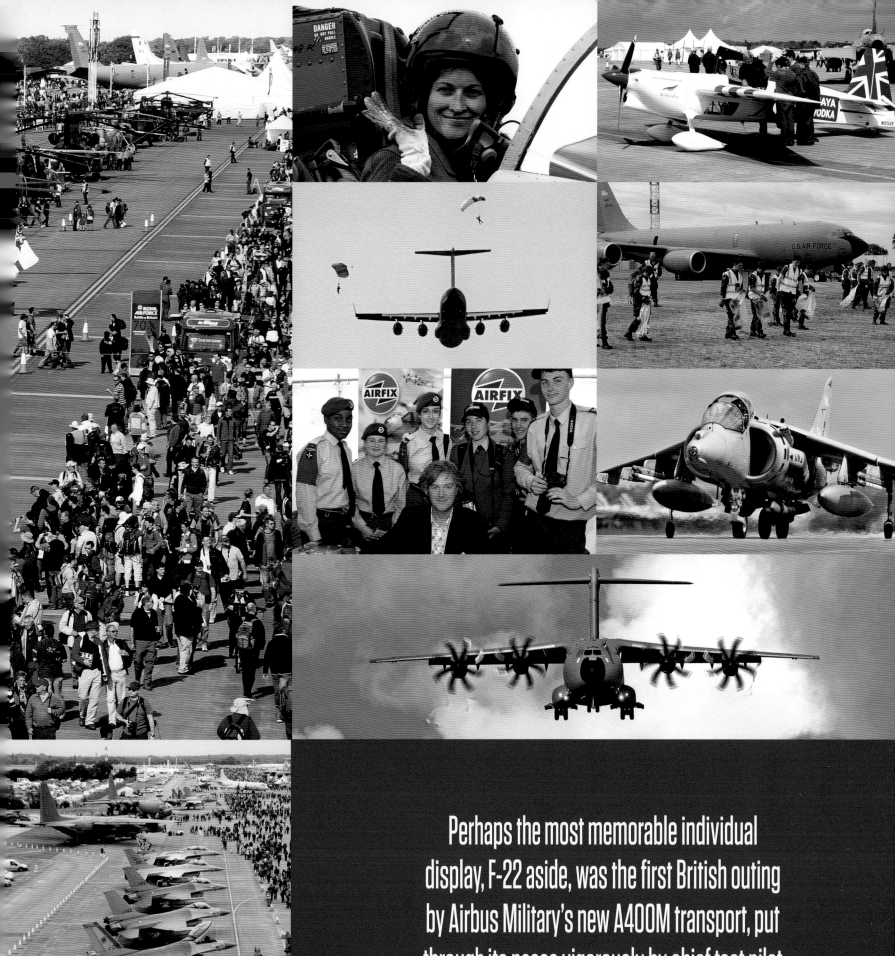

Perhaps the most memorable individual display, F-22 aside, was the first British outing by Airbus Military's new A400M transport, put through its paces vigorously by chief test pilot Ed Strongman.

The Italy-based WeFly! team provided one of the show's finest moments. Two of the three pilots are paraplegic, and it was humbling to see them slowly easing themselves into their cockpits before producing a very polished three-ship display.

on from the type's maiden flight, was truly impressive, 120° wingover and all. Another piece of manufacturer support came in the form of the new Sukhoi Superjet 100 regional airliner, sent over from Farnborough for a single pass.

Though the national display teams — *Red Arrows, Patrouille de France, Royal Jordanian Falcons* and *Patrouille Suisse* — performed immaculately as always, three diminutive Fly Synthesis Texan 550 light sport aircraft of the Italy-based *WeFly!* team provided one of the show's finest moments. Two of the three pilots are paraplegic, and it was humbling to see them slowly easing themselves into their cockpits before producing a very polished three-ship display. RIAT flying display director Geoff Brindle had seen *WeFly!* performing at the Al Ain Aerobatic Show earlier in 2010, and invited them to Fairford with the link to the Flying Scholarships for the Disabled charity very much in mind. It proved an inspired decision, very much in keeping with the spirit of the Air Tattoo.

Alexandra Burke. Ask some for their main recollection of the 40th anniversary Air Tattoo, and the appearance of the 2008 X-Factor winner, rather than any aircraft or display team, sticks most in the memory. RIAT had identified the need to appeal to a wider audience, and the introduction of more non-aviation content on the ground was the result. Though it was through no fault of the excellent performer, staging a concert of any type was something that the organisers decided not to repeat.

That it came in a year when the world's air forces were harder-pressed than ever, in the aftermath of NATO-led military action over Libya, was unfortunate. For the Burke concert to coincide in part with the Merlin music of the Old Flying Machine Company's Spitfire IX and P-51D Mustang duo, present in honour of MH434's appearance at the very first Air Tattoo in 1971, was hard for aficionados to swallow. RIAT 2011 lacked its expected celebratory sparkle, a situation exacerbated yet again by the weather. On both days, low cloud and rain delayed the start time, and with the programme not being rejigged — primarily for safety reasons and concern about being seen to prioritise certain acts over others, in the eyes of visiting pilots and their chiefs — unfortunately the *Patrulla Aguila* never got to perform at all.

But when conditions permitted, the show actually saw some very fine flying. In the absence of a solo RAF Typhoon, withdrawn from the season because of the Libya operations, BAE Systems stepped in with Typhoon FGR4 test aircraft ZJ700, in the hands of test pilot Mark Bowman. This posed an interesting regulatory challenge for the show: a military-registered, civilian-owned aircraft flown by a civilian test pilot. It also involved a significant cost for BAE in taking the aircraft out of its test programme. But, says Tim Prince, the military regulatory authorities — since early 2010, the Military Aviation Authority — were "satisfied that the work-up could be done in a simulator at Warton". The resulting demonstration, with 12 of ZJ700's 14

11

RAF FAIRFORD
16 & 17 JULY

THE ROYAL INTERNATIONAL
AIR TATTOO
16-17 July 2011
sponsored by
BAE SYSTEMS
RAF Fairford
airtattoo.com

THE ROYAL INTERNATIONAL
AIR TATTOO
16 – 17 July **2011** RAF Fairford

sponsored by
BAE SYSTEMS

FORTY YEARS
IAT

OFFICIAL SOUVENIR PROGRAMME
sponsored by

ROYAL Charitable
AIR FORCE Trust
promote support encourage

£10.00

hardpoints loaded with four Paveway IIs, four AMRAAMs and two ASRAAMs, and a couple of tanks, proved very impressive. Bowman was duly awarded the Steedman Display Sword for best display by a UK participant.

Other solo highlights included the debut of *Solotürk*, the Turkish Air Force's flamboyant F-16C display — one of four Fighting Falcons to perform — and the return of a solo US Air Force 'Warthog', now in upgraded A-10C form, a 52nd Fighter Wing jet from Spangdahlem being displayed by West Coast Demo Team pilot Capt Joe 'Rifle' Shetterly. The Italian Air Force C-27J was now permitted to present its full repertoire of rolls and a loop, and to great effect. Majs Severino de Luca and Francesco Ferreri won both the Sir Douglas Bader Trophy for best overall flying demonstration, and the FRIAT members' As The Crow Flies equivalent. The Royal Saudi Air Force made its first ever appearance in the Air Tattoo flying programme with its *Saudi Hawks* team, much assisted by past members of the *Red Arrows*, and mounted on six attractively painted Hawk Mk65/65As. A Hunter 60th anniversary tribute saw four examples from *Team Viper* joined initially by Jonathon Whaley's unmistakeable F58A *Miss Demeanour* and the Swiss Hunter Team's tiger-striped T68, but the weather scrubbed any appearance on Saturday. Closing the display, an attractive combine of *Breitling Wingwalkers* and *Breitling Jet Team* filled the sky with Stearmans, L-39Cs — and a lot of smoke.

One of the less showy, but nevertheless more striking, moments was the stately progress across the airfield of the Air Cadets' 70th anniversary flypast. The on-tow glider cavalcade of vintage Sedbergh, Cadet and Swallow joined by

The Italian Air Force C-27J was now permitted to present its full repertoire of rolls and a loop, and won both the Sir Douglas Bader Trophy for best overall flying demonstration and the FRIAT members' As The Crow Flies equivalent.

THE ROYAL INTERNATIONAL
AIR TATTOO

FREE
Car parking

sponsored by
BAE SYSTEMS

Under-16s
go FREE

16-17 July
RAF Fairford Nr Swindon

supporting the work of the
ROYAL
AIR FORCE

airtattoo.com

МІНІСТЕРСТВО ОБОРОНИ УКРАЇНИ

КОМАНДУВАЧ ПОВІТРЯНИХ СИЛ
ЗБРОЙНИХ СИЛ УКРАЇНИ

-21- 07 2011 р.
№ 350/_1_/ _1416_ /пс

21007, м. Вінниця-7, Військова частина А0215

Royal Air Force Charitable
Trust Enterprise Chairman
Air Chief Marshal
Sir John CHESHIRE

Dear Marshal!

Let me express my sincere gratitude for your efforts in organization and leading of the Royal International Air Tattoo 2011. For me personally and for the Air Forces of the Armed Forces of Ukraine this event was very fruitful and the United Kingdom of Great Britain and Northern Ireland has left amazing impressions.

On my personal persuasion the experience got during this event will be very useful for the Ukrainian side. I hope, that the meetings we have had, will promote a new impulse in development of military cooperation between air forces of our countries.

Take this opportunity to extend the gratitude for your hospitality, I ask you to retell gratitude to all who worked with application on organization of the visit. The changeable English weather could not prevent the irreproachable success of the airshow and special warm atmosphere of the visit.

I deeply value our good relations that we have established and I look forward to our future meeting.

Take this opportunity to extend the highest respect for you, your country and Royal Air Force.

Sincerely,

Lieutenant-General

S.I.ONYSCHENKO

A much-needed boost to this anniversary RIAT was provided by the Ukrainian Air Force's comeback after more than a decade.

modern Viking, following on from motorised elements comprising first Tiger Moth, Chipmunk, Bulldog and Tutor elementary trainers, and then Venture and Vigilant motorgliders, battled hard against very difficult wind conditions to recall how the seed of enthusiasm was first sown in so many future aviators.

The year's operational theme, STAR (Strike, Attack and Reconnaissance), rather blended into the background, not aided by the commitment of so many relevant types to actual combat operations. Airbus Military's new C295 AEW platform, only flown the previous month, was thus doubly welcome in the static park; likewise the return of a USAF RC-135V. Elsewhere there was evidence of the RAF's tanker/transport future, the service's second A330 MRTT flying in from Boscombe Down to be officially named Voyager in a ceremony on the eve of the show.

A much-needed boost to this anniversary RIAT was provided by the Ukrainian Air Force's comeback after more than a decade. "We needed to get our post-Soviet friends back", says Tim, "but it was a challenging thing to get them back because there was still an element of funding being needed. However, their chief of the air staff was brilliantly supportive. They weren't offering a flying display, only a static". To this end, a two-seat Su-27UB was accompanied to Fairford by an Il-76. After a weekend sitting on the ground, their pilots were obviously keen to put on a departure show come Monday. The result Tim describes, cautiously, as "quite interesting". That it was, the Il-76 retracting its undercarriage too quickly, resulting in at least two blown tyres, while the Su-27 performed a low-level roll. Spectacle, for sure, but not quite as the show would have wanted...

HRH Prince Michael of Kent with Ukrainian crew in front of their Il-76 transport aircraft.

Naming ceremony for the RAF's new A330 Voyager tanker/transport.

Richard Noble, Bloodhound land speed record project director, in the Techno Zone.

AIR TATTOO event services

Gradually, RIAT had left the business of helping run other people's airshows. In the 2000s it had dipped its toe in the seafront show water, organising the flying displays for Airbourne, the Eastbourne International Airshow, and for the Sunderland International Airshow. However, this didn't last. Says Tim Prince, "The challenges after Paul [Bowen] died [in 2004] were extreme, and we had to shrink the organisation". There was also the end of the tie-up with the RAF Benevolent Fund, and the change-over to the RAF Charitable Trust. All of this took time and effort. "We had to just focus on the core activities, and we identified those core activities as the Air Tattoo and the concerts... We let go of a few things that were quite enjoyable, but didn't produce the bottom line we needed". So, the work on those seafront shows ended, long-time RIAT team members Ian Sheeley and Dave Walton tying up with ex-*Red Arrows* manager Ray Thilthorpe to form TSA Consulting, and taking on those contracts.

By 2010, however, things were more stable within the RIAT and RAF Charitable Trust Enterprises organisation. That September saw Airbus staging the last ever Families' Day at Bristol's historic Filton airfield, and an Air Tattoo team headed by display director Geoff Brindle

put on the flying programme. An impressive affair, it took in such heavyweight items as an A380, Vulcan XH558 and an RAF VC10.

The decision was then taken to establish Air Tattoo Event Services (ATES) as an arm of RAF Charitable Trust Enterprises, providing consultancy services to outside event organisers. The most visible manifestation came in July 2011, when ATES took on organisation and management of the flying display at the East Fortune Airshow, staged annually by Scotland's National Museum of Flight. It has remained in the role ever since, with Norm Webster as flying display director. Despite a lack of RAF items, caused by a late change of date, that 2011 East Fortune event proved a great success. Subsequent years have seen some very choice international participation in the skies over East Lothian, at what has become known as Scotland's National Airshow: the *Royal Jordanian Falcons* and a full display by a Royal Norwegian Air Force P-3C Orion in 2015, the Swiss Air Force *PC-7 Team* the following year. Sometimes inclement weather has done its worst — indeed, virtually the entire flying programme in 2017 was wiped out. But East Fortune has become a true favourite for those of us involved, and long may it remain so.

It all seemed horribly familiar. A rain-soaked Friday at Fairford, the Cotswolds wreathed in low cloud, and a feeling that an outstanding Air Tattoo could go for a burton. But, in lots of ways, this wasn't 2008. The 'weather-proofing' measures taken since that year's cancellation in order to satisfy the show's insurers were "hugely expensive", says Tim Prince, but they were "essential". Moving to an advance ticket-only model, providing acres of trackway for areas of soft ground, ensuring there was redundant capacity within the car parks — all of this, and more, made a difference.

But RIAT 2012 was still a close-run thing. Tim remembers it all too well. "I was in our Friday gala dinner and came out halfway through to talk to [operations director] Chris Murray, who was running Show Operations Control (SOC), at about 10 o'clock at night. It was still raining, but the view was that we actually could still continue. It was one of those discussions when I had to be satisfied that we were on top of things, and that the rain was starting to ease. It was very much knife-edge stuff."

This was, of course, the London 2012 Olympics year, hence an earlier-than-usual Air Tattoo date. It also saw HM The Queen's Diamond Jubilee, and the world's air arms turned out in particular strength to help celebrate. Three were new to the show, two to a UK public event. "The really good thing", Tim reflected later, "is that the world's air chiefs believe in what we do. When Paul and I, with the team, were working our way forward, we realised the future was in knowing them and them seeing the value of what we did. We continued to develop that side of it, with lead-in global air chiefs' conferences — and, while those are going on, ensuring that the spouses of the air chiefs have a good social programme when they come to the show. For all of them to get on makes a difference. When the chiefs go home, they've achieved a huge amount of value from rubbing shoulders with their counterparts, because each of them is only in post for two to three years and one visit to the Air Tattoo saves them the time and expense of travelling to each other's countries to meet up... There's an operational reason for coming."

Attracting the Republic of Korea Air Force and its aerobatic team, the *Black Eagles*, was testament to the show's long-term view. "We went to the South Korean embassy many times", says Tim, "and their story was, 'If you had North Korea just north of you, would you send your aircraft half-way around the world to attend an airshow?' But their *Black Eagles* team members

This was a modern-day Air Tattoo at its best.

The *Black Eagles* team and supporting personnel of the Republic of Korea Air Force.

12

RAF FAIRFORD
7 & 8 JULY

PHOTO: REPUBLIC OF KOREA AIR FORCE

Flying very tight formations, the Black Eagles demonstrated an appreciation of what other world-class display teams had achieved, but combined it with their own distinctive inventiveness.

Royal Air Force A400M Atlas naming ceremony.

came without their aircraft for two or three years running, and in 2004 the team leader had come up to me at the Sunday night party. They were somewhat at their wits' end, because they couldn't find our transport boss. I looked around at the sea of thousands of volunteers and participants, and couldn't see how to delegate this problem. So, I told them to hop into my courtesy Range Rover. They all squeezed in, and I drove them to the other side of the airfield, getting myself totally lost looking for their car. Eventually we found it, and I led them out to the gates so they could return to their hotel. About a month later I received a lovely letter from the major, saying how much he'd enjoyed coming, but how he was bowled over with the fact that I took time out to help, and that if he got into a position of power he'd make sure the Korean team would come. Whether he did help oil the wheels or not, I don't know, but it was all part of it."

Scarcely less notable was the first ever appearance at a British show by an in-service aircraft from the Japan Air Self-Defense Force, a Boeing KC-767J tanker/transport from 404 Hikotai at Komaki.

THE ROYAL INTERNATIONAL
AIR TATTOO
The
Patron's Pavilion
Sunday 8 July
2012

At that time, back in 2004, the *Black Eagles* were still equipped with the veteran Cessna A-37B Dragonfly, but when this author interviewed the team at Fairford, they told him of plans afoot. Team commander Lt Col Jong Chan Lee confirmed the hope to re-equip with the Korea Aerospace Industries (KAI) T-50 Golden Eagle advanced jet trainer, being developed in conjunction with Lockheed Martin, in the relatively near future. Speaking for Lee, left wingman Capt Dong Soo Son said, "If we change our aircraft to the T-50, we think we will be able to come here in the near future and show our display". That transition took place in 2009. Given Korea's — and Lockheed Martin's — desire to demonstrate this very potent machine, the prospect of a RIAT visit gained momentum and became a reality.

It was confirmed publicly at the beginning of May 2012, along with details of how the T-50Bs

THE GLOBAL AIR CHIEFS CONFERENCE
5 July 2012

ROMANIA Major General Fanica Carnu, SOUTH AFRICA Major General Johan Pelser, SINGAPORE Major General Chee Meng Ng, SWEDEN Major General Micael Byden, THAILAND Air Chief Marshal Itthaporn Subhawong,
UAE Major General Mohamed Sowadian Al Qamzi, URUGUAY General Del Aire Washington R Martinez, USA Lieutenant General Herbert Carlisle
MALAYSIA General Tan Sri Dato' Sri Rodzali bin Daud, USMC Lieutenant General Robert Schmidle Jr, NATO General Mark Welsh III, NETHERLANDS Lieutenant General Alexander Schnitger,
NEW ZEALAND Air Vice-Marshal Peter Stockwell, OMAN Air Vice-Marshal Mattar bin Ali Al-Obaidani, POLAND Lieutenant General Lech Majewski
ESTONIA Brigadier General Valeri Saar, FRANCE Lieutenant General Guillaume Gelee, GERMANY Lieutenant General Peter Schelzig, HUNGARY Brigadier General Albert Safar, IRELAND Brigadier General Paul Fry,
ITALY Lieutenant General Giuseppe Bernardis JAPAN Lieutenant General Yoshiyuki Sugiyama, JORDAN Major General Malek Habashneh
AUSTRALIA Air Vice-Marshal Gavin Davies, AUSTRIA Brigadier General Wolfgang Katter, BELGIUM Major General C Van de Voorde, BRUNEI Brigadier General Jofri bin Haji Abdullah, CAS Air Chief Marshal Sir Stephen Dalton,
CANADA Lieutenant General Andre Deschamps, KENYA Major General Jeff Ottend, CZECH REPUBLIC Brigadier General Jiri Verner, DENMARK Major General Henrik Roeboe Dam

— 10 in all, eight for the display plus two spares — would come to Britain. They needed to be dismantled and flown across in freighter aircraft, specifically Boeing 747-400Fs of Korean Air Cargo, which arrived at Manchester Airport in the second half of May onwards. This display team appearance required a logistical effort like no other. From Manchester, each T-50B airframe was taken by road to RAF Leeming and reassembled there, the North Yorkshire base offering suitable undercover accommodation (in its hardened aircraft shelters) to reassemble the Golden Eagles. Having all been air-tested, it was time for display work-ups to begin.

On the back of their visit for RIAT, the *Black Eagles* had also agreed to participate at the RAF Waddington International Air Show the week prior, and there the team's prowess was apparent for all to see. RIAT brought more of the same, the performance by the T-50Bs demonstrating what an outstanding display team mount the Korean trainer is — more powerful, and with greater presence, than most jet trainers. Flying very tight formations, they demonstrated an appreciation of what other world-class display teams had achieved, but combined it with their own distinctive, dynamic imagination and outstanding, fluid inventiveness, adding numerous flourishes not employed by others. At one point in their high display, two aircraft drew the Taegeuk, the 7th century symbol that appears in the centre of the South Korean flag. Under the team leader, Maj Wook Cheon Jeon, the team proved outstanding ambassadors for their country, and worthy winners of the King Hussein Memorial Sword for the best overall flying demonstration as well as FRIAT's As The Crow Flies Trophy.

Scarcely less notable was the first ever appearance at a British show by an in-service aircraft from the Japan Air Self-Defense Force (JASDF), a Boeing KC-767J tanker/transport from 404 Hikotai at Komaki. For years, the thought that any of the Japanese air arms might attend may have seemed highly unlikely, given the country's entirely defensive military posture. However, RIAT kept working on it. "We were always made very welcome", says Tim. "It was normally a naval captain running the military side of the embassy, and I thought the first aeroplane we would likely see from them would be a helicopter from the back of a frigate."

However, this reckoned without the help of the RAF's Chief of the Air Staff from 2009-13, ACM Sir Stephen Dalton. "He had always enjoyed the event and clearly understood the value of it, so whenever he was meeting his counterparts he would be an ambassador for the Air Tattoo. He and Lady Anne, when they went to Japan, clinched the deal and persuaded the authorities to send the 767 — and, wonderfully, the Taiko drummers as well. That added the extra dimension. The enthusiasts got the aeroplane; the public got the aeroplane, the people and the drums, and the vibrancy they brought. Going to the Japanese embassy and other embassy receptions since, it's been remarked on just what a big step that was for Japan. It helped industry, and the RAF started up an exchange scheme with the Japanese."

For the first time in, it must be said, some while, the static park felt like an Air Tattoo of old. The Skylift 2012 theme filled the line with more transport and tanker aircraft than had assembled at Fairford for a long time, the 10-strong Hercules contingent — but sadly not one from the RAF — recalling the heady 1980s, when the minimum expectation would be at least 15 lined up wingtip-to-wingtip.

PHOTO: MICHAEL HALL

B-2A Spirit of New York emerged from the rain shortly before 19.15hrs on the Friday, its arrival betokening the favoured treatment RIAT can command from across the Atlantic.

BUCKINGHAM PALACE

Tim Prince, Esq., OBE
Chief Executive
Royal International Air Tattoo
RAF Fairford
Douglas Bader House
Fairford
Glos
GL7 4DL

26 July 2012

Dear Tim,

A very belated but nonetheless sincere note to congratulate you and your marvellous team at Bader House on a wonderfully successful Diamond Jubilee Royal International Air Tattoo. I can only imagine what stresses and strains you all were under as once again we fought the rigours of the British climate. I certainly admired the cheerfulness of you all in the face of adversity. From my perspective, everything went very well indeed and, in particular, the arrangements in the Patrons Pavilion this year really embedded themselves down. I would be grateful if you could pass my thanks on to Caroline and all your other colleagues.

Yours ever
David

Air Marshal Sir David Walker
Master of the Household

They came from as far afield as the UAE, Brazil and Colombia, the latter adding another country to the RIAT participation roster. Indeed, the Colombian Air Force's specially marked C-130H from Escuadrón de Transporte 811 brought a surprise bonus in its hold: a T-90 Calima trainer, also brightly painted, which went on to be exhibited at Farnborough as a means of publicising this Colombian licence-built development of the Lancair Legacy.

Having a B-2A on the ground also recalled Air Tattoos of the past. *Spirit of New York* emerged from the rain shortly before 19.15hrs on the Friday, its arrival — with an RAF exchange pilot on board — betokening the favoured treatment RIAT can command from across the Atlantic, rather like the US Marine Corps MV-22B Ospreys that seemed to be constantly coming or going. In the past, security around the 'stealth bomber' had always been ultra-tight, but this time it was much more relaxed, the 509th Bomb Wing crew milling around, happy to answer the crowd's questions.

The B-2's attendance had been confirmed for a while, but initially the USAF would not allow it to be revealed. This posed Tim a problem. "We'd had a friendship for many years with a lady called Betty Isaacs in the USAF chief's outer office, who always would come to the show with the chief. I rang her up one day and said, 'Help'. I asked her what she could do, because we had this aeroplane coming but we weren't selling enough tickets and I needed to announce it. She got on the 'phone, oiled the wheels with the public affairs departments at Whiteman and other places, and magically got approval for us to announce it." Still the authorities wouldn't allow the Spirit's arrival time to be publicised, but all the enthusiasts knew...

The 'special relationship' was symbolised on Sunday morning when the Battle of Britain Memorial Flight Lancaster took Sir Stephen Dalton on an early sortie alongside Gen Norton A. 'Norty' Schwartz, the USAF chief of staff. Schwartz had presented the US Legion of Merit the previous evening to Air Cdre Colin Basnett, RAF — now a volunteer non-executive director of RAF Charitable Trust Enterprises — for his 'meritorious service' when running the Combined Air and Space Operations Center in Al Udeid during 2010. Once back from the Lancaster trip he swept off in

RAFCTE non-executive director Air Cdre Colin Basnett with the US Legion of Merit award presented by US Air Force Gen Norton A. Schwartz (right).

From: Air Chief Marshal Sir Stephen Dalton GCB ADC LLD BSc FRAeS CCMI RAF

Chief of the Air Staff

Zone I
5th Floor
Ministry of Defence
Main Building
Whitehall
London
SW1A 2HB

Mr T Prince OBE FRAeS
Chief Executive
Royal Air Force Charitable Trust Enterprises
Douglas Bader House
Horcott Hill
FAIRFORD
Gloucestershire
GL7 4RB   17 July 2012

Dear Tim,

Thank you for another superb Royal International Air Tattoo (RIAT) and for your assistance with facilitating the Global Air Chiefs' Conference. Both events were huge successes and the International Engagement opportunities, quality of the arrangements and impression left on our guests is undoubtedly one of excellence in organisation, professionalism and utter quiet proficiency; in short, it was fantastic!

This event would not have been possible without the help and assistance of your staff. Their outstanding commitment efficiency and courtesy was greatly appreciated and the events were both significantly enhanced as a direct consequence. Whilst all of your staff, without exception, deserve to be congratulated on their hard work and dedication there are just a few who deserve particular mention. Caroline Rogers, Sophie Bennett and David Czepeck were involved from the start and their cheerfulness, knowledge, assistance and above all patience were exceptional throughout. Through their excellent leadership and determination the complex organisational and protocol challenges were handled impeccably and they are superb examples of the highly capable RAFCTE/RIAT team that you have. One particular volunteer also deserves mention, Sarah Palmer-Pearce was the VIP Host at the Marriott Hotel and her cheerfulness, willingness to help and complete mastery of all she surveyed was exemplary; her assistance and sheer good nature, at all stages and for all events, ensured success and contented visitors.

Thank you again for all your assistance and that of your staff; I hope that they know that their excellent help was absolutely at the heart of the success of both the attendance of so many international air force chiefs and, equally importantly, the good feeling that they helped create amongst the visiting air and ground crews. I look forward to RIAT next year and our continued cooperation with what remains the world's most outstanding and well managed airshows: A brilliant job for a fantastic course run and enabled by the most well-motivated and effective airshow team!

Yours sincerely

Stephen

his C-37A back to the US, leaving behind a wide selection of USAF assets.

The RAF's static presence was 17 aircraft, more than half of them trainers, and the only large machine a VC10 C1K. In the air, though, the Skylift combine contained one each of the major Brize Norton-based transport and tanker types, starting with another VC10 and ending with an A400M demonstrator. The outstanding RAF flypast — with a Royal Navy element, too — was the immaculate Jubilee 'E II R' formation of 27 Hawks, though it could only be mounted on Sunday for weather reasons. Adding a deeply poignant touch, the two-ship Tornado GR4 role demo team from No XV(R) Squadron gave a scintillating performance only a few days after the tragic loss of three of their colleagues in a mid-air collision. Their Sunday performance concluded with a 'missing man' pass, dedicated to Flt Lt Hywel Poole, Flt Lt Adam Sanders and Sqn Ldr Sam Bailey, as well as to former Tornado GR1 pilot Trevor Roche, killed the previous weekend when the Shuttleworth Collection's DH53 Humming Bird crashed at Old Warden.

The return of a 'Fulcrum's' smoke trails to the Fairford skies was long-overdue, and the Polish Air Force MiG-29 from 1.elt flew immaculately in the hands of different pilots on each day, Lt Col Artur Kałko and Capt Adrian Rojek. The Poles brought an arguably even better machine for the static park, a first-time UK show visit by an ageing Polish Navy Mil Mi-14PL anti-submarine helicopter that needed an eight-hour flight to reach Fairford. This and the eight days spent on the 'Orca' scheme were well worth it, as the 'Haze' crew from 29 Eskadra took home to Darłowo the prize for the best livery.

In a show heavily loaded with rarities, RIAT was host to the debut outside the Middle East of the UAE Air Force's *Al Fursan* team. Flying seven Aermacchi MB339NATs, seven being the number of Emirates in the UAE, the team was clearly influenced by the assistance of the *Frecce Tricolori*. Other flying 'firsts' included the Irkut Corporation's stylishly presented Yak-130 jet trainer with dummy stores, and the DHL Boeing 767-3JHF freighter which repeated the display profile flown by the same crew on Saturday in a 757, albeit rendered all the more imposing by the 767's extra bulk. The seal was set perfectly on a first-rate weekend by the JASDF Taiko drummers' performance at the Sunday-night hangar party, leaving crews and volunteers spellbound with their energy. Could this quality be carried forward to future seasons? The team would try, it went without saying. But new obstacles were on the horizon.

U-2 can make your RIAT dreams come true...

When nine-year-old Ellie Carter from Devon wrote to the Air Tattoo in late 2011 asking if her favourite aircraft could be invited to the following year's event, little did she know what lay in store. Ellie's letter asked if the airshow would invite a US Air Force U-2 spyplane because she loved the fact it flew on the edge of space and that teamwork was required to operate and land the aircraft safely. However, in her enthusiasm Ellie only gave her name, age and the fact she lived in Devon, leading to an international 'hunt' for the youngster. This captured the attention of the US unit at Beale Air Force Base in California.

Inspired by Ellie's letter, the U-2 crew arranged for her to come to RAF Fairford in 2012 and be shown around the aircraft. She was also given the rare opportunity to sit in the chase car, travelling at approximately 120mph, as it attempted to keep up with the landing U-2, which had just completed a 12-hour flight from Sacramento at altitudes on the edge of space.

The Air Tattoo's Richard Arquati said: "Even then, it was clear that Ellie's passion for aviation and her determination would help drive her to achieve great things." And achieve she did, becoming, at the age of 16, Britain's youngest solo pilot of a powered aircraft. Richard added: "We're hugely proud of Ellie and the small part we played in helping her reach for the stars and fulfil her dream."

Adding a deeply poignant touch, the two-ship Tornado GR4 role demo team from No XV(R) Squadron gave a scintillating performance only a few days after the tragic loss of three of their colleagues in a mid-air collision.

'Sequestration' was a word few on this side of the Atlantic had heard of. Suddenly, in the military aviation world, it was on everyone's lips. The US Congress was unable to agree on spending cuts and fiscal prudence measures by its deadline that year, which brought the consequences of disarray on Washington's Capitol Hill into sharp and painful focus well beyond America's borders.

Half of the US$85.4-billion cuts, or sequestrations, in fiscal year 2013 were defence-related. They forced the US Air Force and other parts of the American military to rein in spending sharply, all USAF activities except essential military training exercises and war-fighting being immediately affected. Numerous airshows at US military bases were cancelled, while the prospect of any USAF heavy metal filling the static display at RIAT rapidly looked unlikely. But Tim Prince's concern went beyond that. "It was, 'Will Fairford still be a US Air Force base?' The base had already undergone change to cut costs into a facility run solely by a civilian team. Could sequestration, potentially, be its death-knell?

"What would we do, as we had understood that the RAF probably didn't need the airfield? Fortunately, though, the incumbents in the command chain in the UK and Europe still saw Fairford as a very flexible and important facility. On the aeroplane front, it would be our first time without American assets which was daunting. But everyone rallied round, and we hired in some more privately operated aircraft". Several of those were

13

RAF FAIRFORD
20 & 21 JULY

PHOTO: MATT HANCOCK

A4000

ROYAL AIR FORCE

ROYAL AIR FORCE

ROYAL AIR FORCE

ROYAL AIR FORCE

THE ROYAL INTERNATIONAL
AIR TATTOO
sponsored by **BAE SYSTEMS**

2013

A

ROYAL Charitable
AIR FORCE Trust
promote support encourage

Name: _____ Organisati
Vehicle Reg: _____

THE ROYAL INTERNATIONAL
AIR TATTOO
sponsored by **BAE SYSTEMS**

2013

B **14** **G**

ROYAL Charitable
AIR FORCE Trust
promote support encourage

Name: _____
Vehicle Reg: _____ Mobile No: _____
_____ Organisation: _____

V22903

Warbird and modern military were paired in a 70th anniversary commemoration of the Ruhr dams raid, an appropriately marked No 617 Squadron Tornado GR4 accompanying the BBMF Lancaster.

American warbirds. "We wanted to show the Americans that we supported them in their time of need, spending some money to show what they had been, as we couldn't demonstrate what they are and what they're going to be."

Uniquely in the Air Tattoo's history, not one USAF aircraft appeared in the static park, let alone displayed in the air, while virtually all US base personnel disappeared from public view. Just one USAF machine, a C-21A making a very quick stop-off with a VIP visitor on Sunday morning, was seen all weekend. Many who had been present on the arrivals days, however, knew a U-2S was also on the airfield. It happened to be present as part of the 9th Reconnaissance Wing's regular rotation of airframes through Fairford. Could it be put on display? "They worked very hard to try and get approval, and we were willing supporters", Tim remembers. "But in the end the position was put politely, but quite clearly, to me: 'Tim, how can we do this without shooting ourselves in the foot given the embargo on any US military participation in all airshows within the USA itself?' This was a more than fair point so, with about two days to go, I realised it was the time to back off". The U-2 stayed hangared.

The American warbirds were a nod to 'absent friends', but little more. Over from Salzburg, the Flying Bulls' immaculate B-25J Mitchell — debuting at a British show — and F4U-4 Corsair flew very nicely, Raimund Riedmann and Eric Goujon doing the honours, and on Sunday providing 'top cover' for Plane Sailing's Catalina. The first day had seen B-17G *Sally B* back over Fairford after more than a decade. But, without being woven into a particular theme of the show, these fine machines somehow seemed a little lost.

One thing RIAT 2013 definitely got right was Saturday's formation of a British Airways Airbus A380, the flag-carrier's first, and the Red Arrows.

It was, indeed, a different RIAT. "It stemmed from the reality that our attendance was going down, rather than up", Tim explains. "We had realised that it was going down and done a lot of survey work to find out why. We found that the enthusiasts were still fairly pleased with what we were doing, but needed to see more exotic aeroplanes — and more aeroplanes, ideally. But, as importantly, our public weren't enjoying the experience as much. The weather had been very, very bad, and big airfields when it's really wet aren't the nicest places to be. We hadn't got many 'creature comforts' for them when the weather was inclement. So, we brought on board Nigel Samuels, a gentleman who'd had more consumer market experience. Our chairman, Alan Smith, and his colleague Dr Jim Glover — both non-executive directors and volunteers — also had good experience in the consumer world.

"When we closely analysed what we were doing, we knew we were getting it right for the participants now, having slightly fewer aeroplanes but looking after them better. Industry was really valuing it, finding that the informal 'Pimm's in the Cotswolds' with the visiting air force chiefs, and with each other, was working for them. The chiefs were getting huge value out of it. But from the public's point of view, we needed to do more. We needed to provide more wi-fi, have better toilets, service stations, baby-changing facilities. It had to be more comfortable for our audience. We spent a huge amount of money to establish all these facilities in a way where the public could easily find them and use them, and enjoy using them. The reality was, it was worth the spend. We didn't need to go back to having pop stars, but what we did need were these fundamental elements. We had some really good feedback that year albeit we didn't get the toilets quite right, but in other areas we came on streets ahead of the past."

One thing RIAT 2013 definitely got right was Saturday's formation of a British Airways Airbus A380-841, the flag-carrier's first, and the *Red Arrows*. How it happened is a story in itself. According to Tim, "The approach started off with the chairman of our parent charity, Air Marshal Sir Kevin Leeson, talking to the chairman of British Airways about the fact that the '380 was about to be delivered to the airline, and whether it could fly through. Quite quickly, that turned into, 'If we're going to do it, let's do it in style'. Before we got into the loop properly, British Airways were talking to the *Red Arrows* about the work-up.

"It was a wonderful thing to work on, but fraught with challenges. Following a few incidents, the *Red Arrows* were cutting back on what they were allowed to do and the amount of time they could devote to extraordinary activities. There was the Military Aviation Authority's interest in it, the Civil Aviation Authority's interest in it. But many people saw huge value in this opportunity. Work-ups were done in simulators, and — after a lot of debate — flights were done with a *Red Arrows* Hawk behind the A380 to determine where there was acceptable turbulence and where there wasn't. Although it was a little bit eleventh-hour, it did happen, and it was a fantastic display and an exceptionally good thing to have done."

The chairman of British Airways, Martin Broughton, and his wife were there to watch as the A380 made two passes accompanied by the *Reds*. Even better, pilot-in-command Capt Charles Everett — an ex-RAF Jaguar flier — then came in alone for a low go-around, the Airbus behemoth's starboard wingtip

looking barely out of reach. The *Reds'* formation act was repeated on the Sunday with the A400M, in the hands of an Anglo-German flight crew comprising Tony Flynn and Karl-Heinz Mai, taking the place of the A380.

Several other unusual combinations leavened the parade of fast jet solos and team routines. Behind the trailing refuelling hoses of an Italian Air Force KC-767A from the 14° Stormo were tucked an Italian EF2000 and RAF Typhoon FGR4. Warbird and modern military were paired later in a 70th anniversary commemoration of the Ruhr dams raid, an appropriately marked No 617 Squadron Tornado GR4 accompanying the BBMF Lancaster. On the ground, they were parked alongside Vulcan XH558, completing a unique threesome of former 617 equipment.

Not all the flying passed off without incident. The Armée de l'Air didn't have the best day on Sunday: the solo Rafale blocked the runway for about 15 minutes after landing, an attempt to 'bow' to the crowd having apparently jammed the nosewheel steering, while the sole weekend display by the *Patrouille de France* was aborted when one Alpha Jet experienced engine problems. Spares had to be flown over from France, and the *Patrouille* finally left to meet an important time slot over the Champs Elysées — saluting the arrival of the new Tour de France champion, Britain's Chris Froome.

The theme was Sky Guardian, covering everything from airborne early warning and air interception to maritime patrol, search and rescue and humanitarian taskings. The Brazilian Air Force fielded an Embraer R-99 'multi-intel' aircraft, incorporating a forward-looking infra-red turret and a synthetic aperture radar incorporated into the belly and cheeks of an ERJ-145 airframe. The Hellenic Air Force's equally rare contribution was an ERJ-145H AEW&C, with Saab's Erieye radar mounted on top, and the Portuguese Air Force deployed a very new C295MPA with a FLIR turret.

But a particularly rich array of older hardware caught the discerning eye. There was a glorious Estonian Air Force An-2, not destined for retirement any time soon, and two French Air Force Mirage F1CRs which certainly were. Likewise, the show would never again be graced by a VC10, the No 101 Squadron K3 offering a

departure day treat when it was briefly juxtaposed on the runway with the Breitling Super Constellation. Having only just flown in civilian hands, the short-lived Midair Squadron's Canberra PR9 XH134/G-OMHD made its race against the clock to add another classic to the line-up.

Aircraft content was not, by any means, the show's best. A much higher-than-usual number of civilian flying acts bore out the circumstances — straitened budgets, ongoing and expensive military commitments — in which the Air Tattoo now seemed to be existing. But, against that, the event needed to start getting the public back through the gates in larger numbers, and this it did. Now, the challenge was to find fresh ways of keeping them on side.

Air Tattoo Memories: David Higham

David, a former RAFCTE director trading and finance, has been Air Tattoo souvenir programme editor since 2014.

"Having joined the finance department in 1997 of what was then the RAF Benevolent Fund Enterprises, and after only a month with the company, being asked to jointly oversee RIAT's trading operation around the showground, little did I know it at the time but my RIAT rollercoaster ride had only just begun and would last for over 20 years! Unsurprisingly, there have been a few challenges along the way. Yes, all of these were met and overcome by grit and determination, — but, without exception, by great teamwork from an amazing collection of board members, colleagues, staff and volunteers I've had the privilege to work with, many of whom remain friends to this day.

"Successfully overcoming challenges can often then turn into highlights. The 'fast balls' (for which RIAT is legendary!) a small but dedicated team had to face in assisting with the Royal Military Tattoo on the Mall and Horse Guards Parade in 2000 being one classic example. Despite inclement weather and long hours, the significant financial end result for RAFBFE did, however, make it all worthwhile. Having to find and finance a new building in 1999, Paul Bowen's sad passing in 2004, the formation of a new charitable parent company in 2005 and the cancellation of RIAT in 2008 were significant individual challenges — all of which were successfully overcome.

"Following my official retirement in 2013, this amazing chapter in my life continues today as a RIAT volunteer and as a trustee for the Flying Scholarships for Disabled People. One of my many lasting happy memories occurred in 2013 when I headed the arrival of the Super Constellation in the back of a RIAT 'Follow Me' vehicle along with my trusty Canon. As Paul Simon might have summed it up, 'Still crazy after all these years!'"

13

PHOTO: SVEN MARQUARDT

In reviewing the 2013 show, aviation journalist David Halford remarked upon the Lockheed Martin F-35 being the centrepiece of the year's poster artwork, without ever being scheduled to participate. "Maybe the artwork will be reused on next year's RIAT programme", he mused, "or possibly 2016's". How prophetic that proved. The saga of the planned trans-Atlantic deployment by RAF and US Marine Corps F-35Bs, which would have given the Air Tattoo the scoop of the Lightning II's European public debut, was the sole topic of conversation — and consternation — in the lead-up to 2014's show, after a severe engine fire on a US Air Force F-35A at Eglin Air Force Base grounded the whole fleet. From that moment, on 23 June, all plans were thrown into serious doubt. Would the grounding be rescinded in time? Could the visit to Fairford and Farnborough go ahead? It turned into quite the soap opera.

In the end, time simply ran out. A decision to allow all F-35s to resume flying within tight restrictions was being made as the Air Tattoo wound down. Cancellation of the trans-Atlantic deployment was announced late on the subsequent Tuesday evening at Farnborough, to no-one's great surprise. Scratch one star item.

Having announced that he would be retiring after RIAT 2014, outgoing chief executive Tim Prince deserved much better than to see the year's major plan fall to bits, even if the circumstances were out of anyone's hands. At least the American

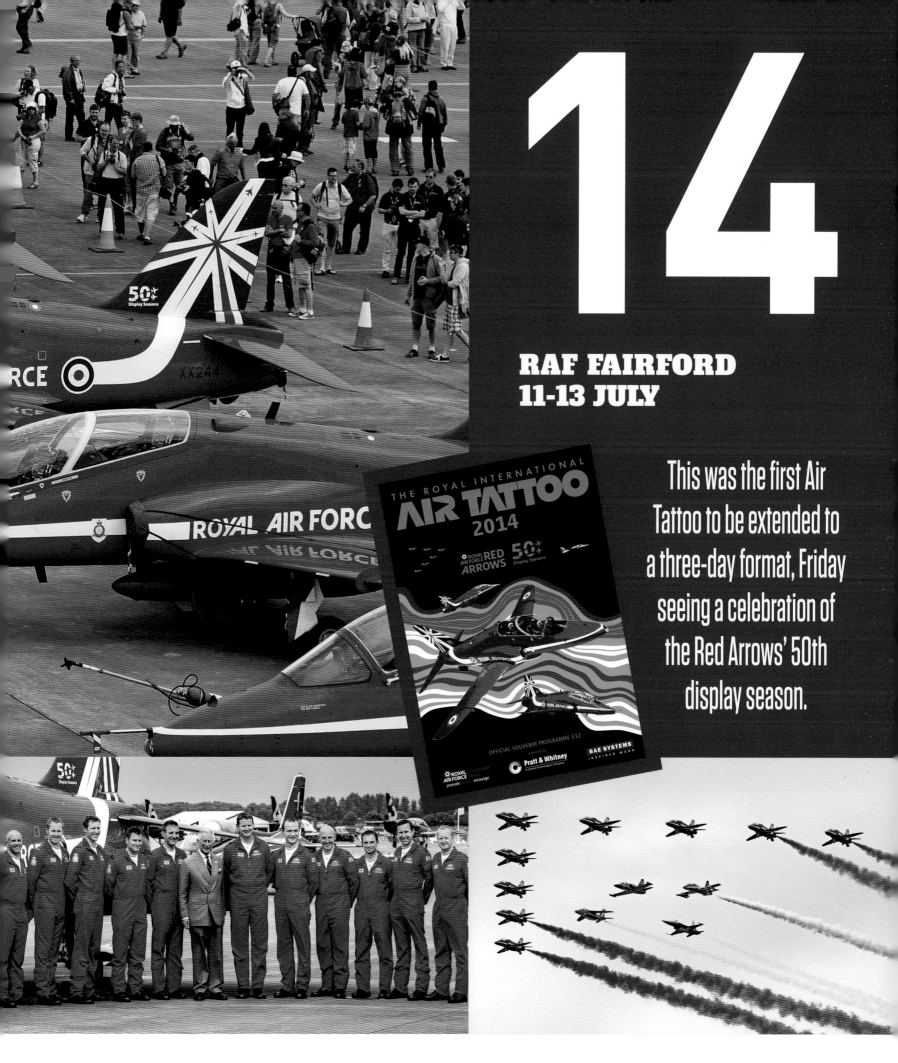

14

RAF FAIRFORD
11-13 JULY

THE ROYAL INTERNATIONAL
AIR TATTOO
2014

ROYAL AIR FORCE RED ARROWS   50 Display Seasons

OFFICIAL SOUVENIR PROGRAMME £12

ROYAL AIR FORCE   Pratt & Whitney   BAE SYSTEMS

This was the first Air Tattoo to be extended to a three-day format, Friday seeing a celebration of the Red Arrows' 50th display season.

was back, a USAF F-15E and KC-135R, and — for the first time at Fairford — a US Navy P-8A Poseidon, complete with Project 'Seedcorn' RAF co-pilot, all featuring in the static display. So soon after sequestration, this was a pleasing effort. Against that, it could hardly go unmentioned that the total of RAF aircraft on static display numbered precisely 14, two being Viking gliders from the Air Cadets, which were not considered airworthy at the time due to a fleet-wide grounding order. The weekend's flying programmes saw five Italian Air Force flying items against six from the RAF, two of which were historic. What a sign of the times. Still, the Aeronautica Militare's contribution was outstanding, superb displays from the Reparto Sperimentale Volo's A-200 Tornado, F-2000A Typhoon, C-27J Spartan and increasingly rarely seen AMX International A-11 backing up the *Frecce Tricolori*.

This was the first Air Tattoo to be extended to a three-day format, Friday seeing a celebration of the *Red Arrows'* 50th display season — as opposed to 50th anniversary — with close-up 'Pit Day' access to the gathered teams and a shortened flying schedule. It proved an innovation from which lessons would be learned, several of the display team aircraft still having their covers on, and few pilots on hand for a chat. Later there was a special 'birthday' formation when the *Reds*, led by Sqn Ldr Jim Turner, flew their 'Big Battle' formation with a four-ship diamond — billed as being piloted by the leaders from the three national military jet teams and the *Breitling Jet Team*, though the *Patrouille de France* were, in reality, represented by their operations officer

Star status this time went to the two-ship Polish Air Force Su-22M4K team. The tactical display by the 'Fitters' won them the FRIAT As The Crow Flies award.

— tucked in behind. It was a pity a repeat performance on Saturday, before the French left on Sunday morning for a commitment at Le Bourget Airport's centenary show, was not possible, in lieu of the planned formation of the *Reds* and the F-35B.

Celebrations of the F-16's and the Hawk's 40th anniversaries passed off without much of note, though mention must go to the Belgian Air Component's solo 'Viper' pilot, Cdt Avi Renaud 'Grat' Thys, on top form in his final display season. Not only did he win the Sir Douglas Bader Trophy for best individual flying display, but 'Grat's' flat show in awful conditions on Sunday morning was an exemplary demonstration of bad-weather fast jet display flying.

Star status this time went to the two-ship Polish Air Force Su-22M4K team from 40. elt at Świdwin, flown by Maj Bartłomiej Mejka and Capt Radosław Leszczyk. The muscular tactical display by the 'Fitters', with the two aircraft tightly paired before 'attacking' the airfield on opposing vectors, won them the FRIAT As The Crow Flies award. Two similarly old machines were unquestionably the pick of the static park: Hellenic Air Force A-7E and TA-7C Corsair IIs, making their final appearance at a British event. The 'SLUF' was to be retired in October 2014 and both were in special markings for the occasion, those on the single-seat A-7E being the more eye-catching, the mountain motif in its design highlighting the fact that 336 Mira — the world's last Corsair II operator — was named 'Olymbos'. It took the show's best livery prize. The two-seat TA-7C was more understated, having been repainted in the original wrap-around camouflage applied when first the Greek A-7s were delivered.

Through these classic jets, RIAT 2014 rekindled memories of great days gone by, when aircraft of that era were the show's staples. In particular, the Su-22s recalled the early years of détente at the Air Tattoo in the wake of the fall of the Berlin Wall and the break-up of the Soviet Union. Suddenly, aircraft only occasionally glimpsed in fuzzy photos were sitting barely yards away, while crews from NATO and the former Warsaw Pact shared their perspectives. On this, and much more, Tim could reflect as he prepared to hand over the reins to his successor Andy Armstrong. He told the author, "I've learned a huge amount from a lot of people — people I'd count as friends — from all walks of life. Where I'm really wiser is that, after my training as an air traffic controller, I sat at my radar tube and I was the centre of the world. I told aeroplanes to go up and down and turn left or right, and they did what I said — in the main, anyway. I now realise that if anything's going to work, everybody's got to be on-side, everybody's got to feel good about it. I'm wiser through sharing and listening. I've still got a lot to learn, but I probably haven't got time to learn it!"

In fact, those learning opportunities continued. Tim was made an honorary vice-patron of the Air Tattoo, and has carried on playing a very active role. Those directly connected with RIAT 2014 showed their appreciation at the Sunday-evening hangar party, but there were many others keen to add their thanks for 40-plus unforgettable years.

PHOTO: RONNIE McDONALD

PHOTO: TIM FELCE

PHOTO: ADRIAN PINGSTONE

15

RAF FAIRFORD
17-19 JULY

There was perhaps no more potent illustration of how the Air Tattoo has fostered relationships than the sight, in the static park, of a Japan Maritime Self-Defense Force Kawasaki P-1 maritime patrol aircraft alongside the US Navy's P-8A Poseidon.

It might have been the start of a new era, as Andy Armstrong's inaugural show as chief executive, but RIAT 2015 was every inch a classic Air Tattoo. A very high-standard assembly of aircraft, flying displays that were spectacular and emotive, beautiful weather — the planets aligned, and made for some of the finest Fairford moments of the 21st century to date.

It also dispelled any doubts that having RIAT, and RAFCTE, headed up by someone with a non-aeronautical background — Andy had previously been a senior European executive with Sony — might lead to a dilution of the event's essential ethos. He had been to the 2014 show, 'shadowing' Tim Prince and meeting staff, volunteers and enthusiasts. He also had a long-standing interest in aviation, this resulting in no small part from his father, a vicar, having been corps chaplain to the Air Training Corps. Having obtained an RAF flying scholarship, Andy got his private pilot's licence and was a member of the Universities of Glasgow and Strathclyde Air Squadron before deficient eyesight put paid to his wish to become an RAF pilot. So, he was no stranger to the environment.

There was perhaps no more potent illustration of how the Air Tattoo has fostered relationships than the sight, in the static park, of a Japan Maritime Self-Defense Force (JMSDF) Kawasaki P-1 maritime patrol aircraft alongside the US Navy's P-8A Poseidon. Even better, a second P-1 was to be seen in the flying programme, the shapely four-jet machine hailing from air development squadron VX-51 at Atsugi, and in the hands of a crew headed by Cdr Ken Yasuoka. The list of 'firsts' being notched up was quite

The Battle of Britain 75th anniversary flypast involved no fewer than 16 aircraft — nine Spitfires, five Hurricanes, one Seafire and one Buchón — with Air Transport Auxiliary veteran Joy Lofthouse joining Fighter Command veterans Geoffrey Wellum, Tony Pickering and Ken Wilkinson in taking the salute.

something: this was the international debut of the P-1, the first trans-Atlantic flight by the JMSDF, the first flying display by the Japanese military in Europe, and the debut of the JMSDF at a European event. It was an impressive show of strength on the part of Japan's military and its aerospace industry.

There was rarity value aplenty in the static line-up. The two Spanish Air Force SF-5Ms from Ala 23 at Talavera la Real were virtually impossible to beat in that regard, long sought-after — with just 19 left in service as lead-in fighter trainers — but only now secured. Time was when US Air Force A-10s were to be expected every year, but with the 'Warthog's' withdrawal from Europe, no longer. However, a Theater Security Package deployment to the continent by the 355th Fighter Wing from Davis-Monthan AFB had brought it back, and two of its A-10Cs came to Fairford.

The historic element created some of RIAT 2015's most indelible images. One of Andy's aims for the year was to put on a Battle of Britain 75th anniversary set-piece worthy of the occasion, and that it certainly was. The main flypast involved no fewer than 16 aircraft — nine Spitfires, five Hurricanes, one Seafire and one Buchón — with Air Transport Auxiliary pilot Joy Lofthouse joining Fighter Command veterans Geoffrey Wellum, Tony Pickering and Ken Wilkinson in taking the salute. While they formed up, the returning Bf 109G-4 from the Flugmuseum Messerschmitt and the Aircraft Restoration Company's newly restored Blenheim, now configured as a MkIF night fighter, performed solo. Leading the whole display was, suitably enough, the Battle of Britain Memorial Flight's (BBMF) 1940 combatant Spitfire IIa P7350, with another veteran of the battle, Peter Vacher's Hurricane I R4118, on one wing; over from the USA for the summer's commemorations, the Historic Flight Foundation's Spitfire IX SL633 was on the other. Behind, a Hurricane quartet allowed five of the Hawker fighters to be seen in close proximity. Interspersing the 'Balbo' flybys, Richard Lake's Spitfire XVIII and the Buchón operated by the Aircraft Restoration Company broke out to perform a close-range dogfight, Ian Smith and Steve Jones at the controls. This was 'Theatre of the Air' in the old RIAT tradition.

Co-ordinated by the officer commanding the BBMF, Sqn Ldr Dunc Mason, the entire routine was awarded the King Hussein Memorial Sword for best overall flying demonstration. However, by the Sunday night prizegiving all the aircraft and pilots involved had gone home, except for Spitfire IX MH434 and Brian Smith, who duly stepped up to collect the trophy on behalf of the mixed military and civilian group. Brian participated in many Battle of Britain commemorations that year but says of RIAT's, "That was a memorable one. I flew with 'Milli' [Andy Millikin, then the BBMF's OC-designate] and 'Parky' [Antony Parkinson, then the BBMF operations officer]. I suppose it came naturally to 'Parky', being ex-*Red Arrows*, but his wingtip appeared to be buried somewhere between 'Milli's' tailplane and his aileron. I thought I'd better try and match this... The first day I think was a bit tentative, but on the second day we all realised we could cope. I've been around the track a bit over the years, but flying with those two and being accepted by the military side of things was one of those experiences that gave me a jolt and made me think, 'Yes, that means something to me'."

A later warbird was responsible for the weekend's most dramatic flying. Who will ever forget Vulcan XH558's flamboyant low-level turn during Saturday's take-off, or indeed its wingover well past the vertical at the apex of its concluding zoom climb, prior to forming up with the *Red Arrows*? This truly dazzling performance earned XH558's crew, headed by Kev Rumens, the As The Crow Flies Trophy from the Friends of RIAT (FRIAT), under whose noses the take-off happened. FRIAT clearly felt the sheer effort of keeping the Vulcan in front of the public for so long should be rewarded before 'her' retirement at the end of the 2015 season.

Air Tattoo Memories: Air Chief Marshal Sir John Cheshire

Sir John Cheshire was chairman of the Royal Air Force Charitable Trust from 2008 to 2013.

"Thanks to my old friend Sir Mike Knight, I followed him as chairman of the RAF Charitable Trust in 2008. The next five years were rewarding and enormous fun. Why? Because my fellow trustees and I had the challenge of ensuring that we donated Trust funds to the worthiest of youth-related causes. Also, as president of RIAT, it was a privilege to host a huge spectrum of air-minded supporters including royalty, politicians, air chiefs from around the world and the captains of industry who generously sponsored our charitable endeavours.

"Every year I was staggered by the selfless and hugely professional support we had from our myriad volunteers. Thanks to their immense efforts and to the outstanding work of the permanent staff in Douglas Bader House, RIAT was unquestionably a success story. I salute each and every one of them. The fact that I always seemed to be in the right place at the right time during the hectic RIAT weekends was almost entirely due to the efforts of the renowned 'Speedbird Bob' Taylor who masterminded my programme flawlessly for five years.

"My Air Tattoo experience started as a display pilot in 1976, then as a Russian interpreter in the early '90s. But, it was my term as chairman that my late wife, Sam, and I remember with the greatest affection. May the next half-century bring great success and happiness to future RIATs and hence to the worthy endeavours of the RAF Charitable Trust."

RAFCTE CEO Andy Armstrong (pictured centre) with Tornado crews celebrating the 35th anniversary of the initial Tornado deliveries to the Tri-National Tornado Training Establishment (TTTE).

Somehow this was a year of particular charisma among the fast jet sequences. The French Air Force Mirage 2000N pair display by the *Ramex Delta* team from the Istres-based Escadron de Chasse 2/4 'La Fayette', glued to each other at high speed, reminded spectators what an impressive aircraft this was. The old Mirage 2000 fighter solos had portrayed the aircraft as a lithe dogfighter, but this tactical display by the 2000N nuclear striker showed it in thunderous 'mud-moving' guise, heavy and powerful, yet still possessed of considerable agility. *Ramex Delta*'s first UK display proved well worth the wait, even when a fly-by-wire system problem reduced it to a single-ship on Sunday.

Much more sedate, but interesting nonetheless, Tornados from the RAF, Italy's Aeronautica Militare and the German Luftwaffe appeared in some brief three-ship flybys to mark the 35th anniversary of first deliveries to the Tri-National Tornado Training Establishment. This rather unusual theme was also reflected in the static park, three further aircraft receiving special anniversary tail markings in the form of vinyl wraps. Applied after the Tornados arrived at Fairford, they were removed again before departure.

Among the solo jets, the Polish Air Force's MiG-29, in the hands of Capt Adrian Rojek, was undeniably

Fashion model and TV personality Jodie Kidd flew into RAF Fairford for the show's media launch.

Who will ever forget Vulcan XH558's flamboyant low-level turn during Saturday's take-off? This truly dazzling performance earned XH558's crew the As The Crow Flies Trophy from the Friends of RIAT.

outstanding, this ageing fighter starting a tremendously punchy sequence with the best 'reheat rotation' take-off seen since the days of the RAF's Lightnings. The Hellenic Air Force debuted its Demo Team 'Zeus', flying an attractively schemed F-16C Block 52+ complete with conformal fuel tanks, thus providing a new variation on a familiar theme.

One of the rotary-wing acts took visitors of a certain vintage back to Air Tattoos past, as Hptm Torsten Möbius flew the German Army MBB Bo 105P1 through a quite brilliant sequence of aerobatics. This was an item not seen at Fairford for 30 years, since the legendary 'Charly' Zimmermann last flew at IAT 85, when it earned him the Sir Douglas Bader Trophy. Möbius departed with the same prize in 2015.

The US Air Force made its comeback to the flying, and with a debut to boot:

a recently delivered CV-22B Osprey from the 7th Special Operations Squadron at Mildenhall, giving an effective demonstration of tilt-rotor manoeuvring. It had been some years since the Air Tattoo last saw a Czech Air Force 'Hind' display, and this year's Mi-24V routine was an excellent example. The static park contained a second 'Hind' from the 221st Helicopter Squadron, painted to resemble a wartime Consolidated Liberator of No 311 (Czechoslovak) Squadron, part of RAF Coastal Command. Both Mi-24s departed in formation with a US Army UH-60A+ Black Hawk and AH-64D Apache, themselves uncommon Air Tattoo visitors at the time.

Securing the Skies: Past, Present and Future was RIAT 2015's theme, and this it reflected admirably across the board, even if the 'Future' part was represented on the posters and programme by the absent F-35. It wouldn't be long, though, until we got our chance to see it.

After the disappointment of two years earlier, the Lockheed Martin F-35 Lightning II loomed large at RIAT 2016, with fully six aircraft present and a lot of global attention.

16

RAF FAIRFORD
8-10 JULY

This time, they made it. After the disappointment of two years earlier, the Lockheed Martin F-35 Lightning II loomed large at RIAT 2016 — very large, in fact, with fully six aircraft present and a lot of global attention. So long had its inaugural British public outing been awaited that the significance of the event perhaps became rather lost. This was the most important new combat jet for many years making its debut on these shores, not something that happens too often. And the Air Tattoo made a great deal of it.

The historic inaugural F-35 landings on British soil took place well in advance of the show, on 29 June. A trio of F-35Bs, the STOVL (short take-off and vertical landing) derivative, touched down at Fairford following the trip from Marine Corps Air Station Beaufort, South Carolina. All three were officially on the strength of US Marine Corps (USMC) fighter/attack training squadron VMFAT-501, but they included one of the UK's first examples of the new Lightning, ZM137, as well as two of the USMC unit's own jets. At the controls were RAF pilot Sqn Ldr Hugh Nichols and USMC aviators Col Richard Rusnok and Maj Jack Cronan, who would between them share flying duties at RIAT and then Farnborough.

A feature of the F-35B's display was, for the first time, to be a vertical landing, making use of specially laid AM-2 matting on the north side of the runway. Wednesday's rehearsals threw up one issue, namely

One of the F-35Bs opened Friday's programme with a one-off air-to-air refuelling flypast, tucked in behind a USMC KC-130J Hercules tanker.

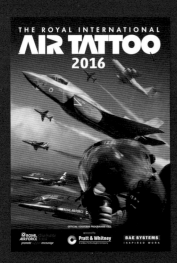

the amount of grass dust thrown up by the Rolls-Royce LiftSystem element of the propulsion system while the STOVL Lightning was in the hover, creating an obvious FOD (foreign object damage) hazard. It was a lesson learned, and each time the aircraft flew thereafter, the show's fire crews dampened down the surrounding ground with their hoses. This, though, could not prevent some of the display line markers going for a burton during Saturday's performance!

Opportunities to see the F-35B flying were not lacking. One of the USMC aircraft opened Friday's programme with a one-off air-to-air refuelling flypast, tucked in behind a KC-130J Hercules tanker from VMGR-252. Another UK first, this was, remarkably, the debut of the Marine Corps in an Air Tattoo flying programme. Apart from each day's solos, performed alternately by the RAF and USMC jets, there was a formation pass with the *Red Arrows* and a pair of Typhoon FGR4s. With each day's display duties complete, one of the F-35Bs was towed over to the south side to enable close-up views, a quite fascinating sight for those able to witness the aircraft being 'put to bed', seemingly endless doors and covers closing automatically in a sort of computerised ritual.

Not to be outdone, the US Air Force's 56th Fighter Wing at Luke AFB, Arizona, sent a trio of conventional take-off and landing (CTOL) F-35As to make up the six-strong Lightning II contingent. Aside from solo displays by Maj Will Andreotta, the intention was to stage a three-ship Heritage Flight, accompanied by a P-51D Mustang and the 1st FW's F-22A Raptor demo aircraft. This was not to be, the weather preventing the Mustang from making it across from Duxford until Sunday, when the F-22 suffered a technical snag.

However, the combination of the P-51 — Robert Tyrrell's *Miss Helen*, flown by Dan Friedkin — and the F-35A was an attractive one nonetheless.

There was an extra degree of scrutiny on this RIAT's flying displays, an inevitable consequence of the previous August's tragedy at the Shoreham Airshow. For the Air Tattoo's chief executive Andy Armstrong, coming into his second show at the helm, the challenge was considerable. His first RIAT, after all, had been a smooth-running delight. "One of the things I was very keen to do was learn how the whole organisation worked", says Andy. "I didn't want to come in with size-10 shoes and stomp all over everything. That's not my style anyway. I looked at what needed to be done, and encouraged everybody to bring forward their actions. That, combined with good weather during the site build, meant I kept on bumping into people and in response to, 'How's it going?', there was almost a surprised look on their faces: 'Actually, we're in a good place'. The more you can do beforehand the easier the show will become, but it suddenly became a very serious job in the post-Shoreham world.

"We took safety extremely seriously and knew we ran a safe show, but what we wanted to do was evidence that and make sure everything was properly documented and we could show that we were following those behaviours. We probably, as a team, spent at least two days a week 'kicking the tyres' of everything to do with safety in that year, to ensure that the show was run successfully. RIAT is so big, and — heaven forbid — if we'd had a major incident, particularly in that immediate aftermath, I think it would have had very significant ramifications for the whole industry, never mind RIAT.

"We put the focus in, we subjected our work to third-party external experts, and we brought onto our full-time staff

somebody with 'safety' in their job title. Right at the end, Chris Murray [RIAT's director of operations] and I went to see one of the country's leading experts in aviation safety and asked him to 'mark our homework'. We explained everything we had done, all of our work. At the end of that session, he said, 'You've done everything I would have expected you to have done. Indeed, you have done more than I would have expected you to do. But what *else* can you do?' That was an important learning experience for me. You cannot be complacent about safety. You have to continually challenge yourself and those around you, to see what else can be done without stifling the organisation, finding different ways of doing things and checking everything to make sure you're in the best possible position to run the event."

One of the new MAA and CAA (Civil Aviation Authority) requirements stipulated the designation of a display area, defined as the ground area footprint of the airspace in which displaying aircraft can be manoeuvred below standard military and civilian minima. With such a focus on the need to minimise or remove so-called secondary crowds — gatherings of spectators outside display venues — some local campsites, which previously had served as popular off-airfield gathering places, were affected. "We put the display area we had selected over the local geography", says Andy. "That had consequences, and we had conversations with the police, the local authority, Highways and local landowners to ensure we were able to manage third-party crowds appropriately and within the regulations."

In order, Andy puts it, "to validate the display area", a company called Aveillant generously supported the show by deploying to Fairford a 3D radar tracking system. This was primarily employed not as a monitoring tool, but to build a picture of the ground 'footprint' covered by individual displays throughout the Air Tattoo week. The following year, the display area was tweaked based on this data.

Air Tattoo Memories: Ben Dunnell

The editor of *Aeroplane* magazine, Ben has been on the Air Tattoo commentary team since 2009, and the show's senior commentator from 2013.

"Boscombe Down, Air Tournament International, June 1992. My first Air Tattoo-organised show, and what an introduction. I'd been to many air displays before, but nothing on that scale. It was somewhat overwhelming. On that hot weekend nearly three decades ago now, I would never have imagined how my involvement would develop.

"It was as a member of the Air Tattoo photographic team, headed by my great friend Peter March, that I started out. What memories there are from those years. Anatoly Kvochur's Su-27 arrival at Boscombe in 1992 set the tone; the Tu-95 'Bear' the following year, 1995's Victory Finale, the Tracor F-100 in 1997 and 2006's RAF Canberra PR9 farewell are all, to me, equally indelible. But begin going down that road of reminiscence, and it's impossible to stop.

"On a personal level, the Air Tattoo made possible nothing short of a major change in my life. Asking Tim Prince if I could be considered as a member of the new commentary team in 2009 seemed a bit ridiculous at the time — after all, I had zero broadcasting experience. But he was kind enough to say 'yes'. I could scarcely believe it. As part of the team under Dan O'Hagan for four years, and then as senior commentator, I've been privileged to help guide the RIAT audience through some of the modern airshow scene's most impactful spectacles, not a responsibility ever to be taken lightly at such a prestigious event. And, following on from my commentary baptism at Fairford, I've been fortunate enough to be entrusted with the microphone at many other venues in the UK and overseas. That first opportunity, thanks to Tim and the Air Tattoo, has led to some of the most enjoyable aspects of my professional career. I'll forever be grateful."

The Croatian Air Force aerobatic team's imaginative and immaculate sequence
set a very high standard, the likes of formation spins and hammerhead stalls,
and a triple mirror formation, offering something genuinely different.

Adding further lustre to the Croatian Air Force's debut, the Krila Oluje support aircraft, a Mi-171Sh helicopter, was a star of the static park.

PATRON'S PAVILION

Fast jet power dominated the skies at RIAT 2016. Apart from the two F-35s and the F-22, there were four Typhoons, a bombed-up BAE Systems jet in the hands of test pilot Nat Makepeace joining the RAF, Italian and Spanish examples, and four F-16s, the Polish Air Force's new Tiger Demo Team with a Block 52+ F-16C joining the better-known Belgian, Greek and Turkish 'Vipers'. A poignant note was added by the magnificent Mirage 2000Ns of the French Air Force's *Ramex Delta* tactical display pair, which on the Sunday performed its last ever public display. Taxiing back beneath the arcing water jets of two fire tenders seemed a suitable send-off 'à l'Anglaise' to one of the Armée de l'Air's finest display teams, both in terms of pilots and aircraft. By contrast, it was also the final outing for the German Army's aerobatic Bo 105 display, Hptm Torsten Möbius again at the controls of the exceptionally nimble helicopter.

But perhaps the most notable item, Lightning IIs aside, was the Croatian Air Force aerobatic team, *Krile Oluje* (Wings of Storm). On six Pilatus PC-9Ms, its imaginative and immaculate sequence set a very high standard, the likes of formation spins and hammerhead stalls, and a triple mirror formation, offering something genuinely different. On the first visit to a British show by both team and air arm, the award of the King Hussein Memorial Sword for the best overall flying demonstration was extremely well deserved. The trophy win was big news back home in Croatia, a MiG-21 escort being put up for the PC-9s on their return to Zagreb airport, where the defence minister and several high-ranking military officials were on hand for a VIP welcome.

Adding further lustre to the Croatian Air Force's debut, the *Krila Oluje* support aircraft, a Mi-171Sh helicopter, was a star of the static park. There the other main newcomers were to be found among the 'heavies', such as the Royal Australian Air Force KC-30A, or the Royal Air Force of Oman C295. But the returning Pakistan Air Force C-130E was not to be ignored, No 6 Squadron again applying tail artwork especially for the show, and nor were the Hellenic Air Force F-4Es from 339 Mira, chances to see operational Phantoms on these shores now being few and far between.

That in itself was a point to reflect on. For years, many other fast jets than just the F-4 had dominated NATO's operational inventories. As those inventories become smaller, with multiple capabilities embodied in single aircraft, the F-35 will be one of far fewer front-line types in those air forces' arsenals for a long time to come. It was the embodiment of RIAT 2016's theme, 'The Next Generation', but this very high-quality show had again illustrated the potency of generations past as well.

PHOTO: SLAWEK KRAJNIEWSKI

Alan Smith
Reflections from RAFCTE's Chairman

Having been connected in one form or another with the International Air Tattoo for over 40 years, Alan Smith reflects on his relationship and involvement with the Air Tattoo's team of volunteers, RAFCTE's permanent staff and its parent charity. At the same time, he acknowledges the immense support received from the event's sponsors, the great British public, the United States Air Force and the Royal Air Force. His incredible journey has seen changes in personnel, challenges by the bucket load, but also many memorable, never to be forgotten moments.

Early in 1976, I made a bold but self-interested decision. At the time, I was Marketing Manager for a national brewery company with a large financial budget at my disposal. Being a military aviation enthusiast, I thought why not therefore sponsor an aerobatic team? Indeed, why not sponsor the Royal Navy *Blue Herons* with their Hawker Hunters? I might even get a flight. So, I did (well, the lager brand 'Arctic Lite' did!) The Blue Herons' leader, Derek Morter (Mort), invited me to attend the International Air Tattoo at RAF Greenham Common on 31st July 1976 and it feels like I have never left since!

Over time my relationship and involvement with the Air Tattoo team, especially with Paul Bowen and Tim Prince, gradually increased — first as a sponsor, then as an unpaid advisor and subsequently as a Non-Executive Director, finally taking on the role of Chairman of the Board of the Royal Air Force Charitable Enterprises (RAFCTE) and Trustee of the parent charity. So, 45 years after that brave decision (and I did get two rides in Mort's Hunter) I am still involved and have loved every minute (well, almost!).

There have been many highlights. Those early Greenham shows with massive line-ups of the same aircraft type (Hunters, C-130 Hercules and F-4 Phantoms); some people used to say that was boring. If only! The first visit of the Russian

Tu-95 'Bear', the flypast of Concorde with the *Red Arrows* and the attendance of the South Korean *Black Eagles* are special memories — as is the arrival of 'Del Boy' in a yellow 'Trotters Independent Trading Co' helicopter which he then tried to sell to the Chief of the Air Staff!

In those early years, the Air Tattoo was run in support of the Royal Air Force Benevolent Fund (RAFBF) where the Deputy CEO of Lloyds Bank, Fred Crawley, was Honorary Treasurer and a company Non-Executive Director. Fred was unusual as a banker as he had a generous heart and was a huge aviation enthusiast, having served in the RAF during National Service.

In 2004, the RAFBF decided that they no longer wanted to be responsible for a major airshow, leaving the company Board of Directors with a dilemma; having a great product but no charity to receive the financial benefit.

Fortunately, there already existed a dormant charity, the RAFBF Development Trust, the aim of which was to organise airshows to promote the RAF. It was a perfect home for RIAT but required a very complicated process to make it happen under a new and independent name, the Royal Air Force Charitable Trust. Many people in the RAF, ex-RAF and civilians helped us bring this transition about. It was 'touch and go' for a few months and failure would have meant the demise of the Air Tattoo for good. Fred played a key role during this changeover, handling it brilliantly with his amazing diplomatic and negotiating skills. Sadly, over time, Fred's health deteriorated and he and the Trustees invited me to take over as volunteer Board Chairman. Whilst I was keen to do this, Fred had left big shoes to fill, but I was greatly helped by Tim Prince, especially in those early years.

Unlike Fred, who had Tim available as his CEO after the death of Paul Bowen, I was dreading the day when Tim would tell me that he planned to retire with his 12 months' notice. That day duly arrived, and a new CEO was needed. Given that it is a very unusual role, the Trustees and I decided we should use a head-hunter to search for Tim's successor. As expected, this proved difficult and we had to go through many interviews before eventually finding Andy Armstrong, who proved

to be a perfect fit for the role. In 2019, after five very successful years, Andy, in turn, decided to step down, so we went through a similar process to appoint Paul Atherton, the current CEO. I have no desire to go through it a third time!

I guess one of the most unusual aspects of the organisation is that RAFCTE has very few employees but thousands of unpaid volunteers, including the Chairman and Non-Executive Directors. I am asked many times why I and my fellow volunteers do it. Perhaps we all have different reasons, but for me there are four main ones. I love military aircraft and people (but never really wanted to join the military!), I enjoy the challenges that are presented (and there are many), and the benefits derived by the Charitable Trust make the effort and time put in worthwhile. Perhaps most important though is the camaraderie generated amongst all the volunteers, many of whom I have known for 20 years and more.

The Air Tattoo is the beneficiary of support not only from its volunteers, but also from so many other people and organisations. Outstanding amongst these is the United States Air Force. It never ceases to amaze me that the USAF is happy to hand over the huge airfield at Fairford to a bunch of mainly part-time volunteer airshow organisers. OK, they keep a watchful eye over us but, beyond that, let us get on with it. On top of that, they send numerous aircraft and very senior USAF officers to the show. They are happy to do this despite world events meaning that RAF Fairford might be urgently needed for other purposes.

This generosity seems to get passed from one USAF Chief of Staff to another. Maybe it's covered in their job interview! We should never forget that when Greenham Common was closed, the USAF said "Well, we've got this big airfield in the Cotswolds, why don't you use that?"; and, yes, it was as simple as that!

Occasionally, Fairford has been unavailable for long-term maintenance reasons and the challenge has been 'Where do we go?' The answer was Boscombe Down in the early '90s and RAF Cottesmore at the start of the new millennium. The latter was a real test because of its distance from Fairford but, as ever, with some fantastic support from the RAF, we pulled it off and had two successful shows. Nevertheless, it was a relief to get back to RAF Fairford.

In fact, this fantastic level of RAF support occurs every year. Occasionally, I have to remind myself and others that providing aircraft and people is not the RAF's main purpose in life. Sometimes we have to push, and the RAF always comes through in the end.

When the Cottesmore shows were held, interestingly, the people of Fairford seemed to miss us whilst we were away. Each year, the Air Tattoo makes for an exciting but frustrating few days for the residents of Fairford and the surrounding area. Yes, it brings in welcome revenue for the local businesses, but also lots of noise and disruptive traffic. Nevertheless, we get very few complaints and lots of thanks for the benefits the show brings to the local community.

We are also immensely grateful to the providers of our two main sources of income — the paying public and our sponsors. Our income is split approximately 50:50 and ensuring that both sets of supporters get what they expect can be a tricky balance. How do we have the hospitality chalets in the right place without interfering with the customers' view? How do we get the VIP military chiefs from around the world in without causing traffic jams? One way or another, we usually find a way even when a badger sett closed the main approach road to Fairford (the badgers agreed to move).

So, how would I reflect on 45 years of involvement with the Air Tattoo and RAFCTE? There have been some amazing experiences and the odd disappointment (none greater than the two cancellations). Overall, I consider myself very lucky to have taken part in such a fantastic event.

On reflection, I would miss the feeling of anticipation about what would be in the aircraft participation list; the arrival at an empty airfield on the Wednesday morning in an R22 helicopter with the registration G-RIAT; even better, flying in on a Saturday morning with the airfield full of hundreds of aircraft. On the other hand, there is that empty feeling on a Monday evening when driving into RAF Fairford for what is known as the 'Survivors Dinner'. All the aircraft have left. All the people have gone and only a few flapping marquees remain. All that effort and all that energy have dissipated, but what is left behind is a lot of satisfied customers and a lot of pound coins for the RAF Charitable Trust.

So, what of the future? RIAT and airshows in general will have a future because people love aircraft and the pilots who fly them. RAFCTE staff and volunteers love organising the best airshow in the world. Will it be the same? No, because it changes every year anyway. Compare the first shows at North Weald, Greenham Common or Fairford. RIAT is very different now.

Most importantly though, the RIAT team loves a challenge and overcoming whatever problems they face. I know of no other organisation with a greater 'can do' approach to the world. If the request came in to 'Please organise RIAT at RAF Mount Pleasant in the South Atlantic', the loudly shouted response would be 'OK. Next week or next year?' Mind you, can Air Ops get an A-4 Skyhawk to attend? That seems to be much more difficult!

Alan Smith Chairman RAFCTE

17

RAF FAIRFORD
14-16 JULY

Modern-day airshows don't often contain the unexpected, it's true. As B-2A *Spirit of Pennsylvania* ran in during the Sunday of RIAT 2017, F-15C escorts in close attendance, it rather disproved the theory. The Spirit's appearance had gone unannounced beforehand, its arrival remaining a surprise to all but the best-informed few. Two curving passes ensued, the 509th Bomb Wing aircraft engaged in a 23-hour 'Global Power' sortie from and to its home at Whiteman Air Force Base. It was certainly the highlight of the Air Tattoo's 70th anniversary tribute to the US Air Force. It was, indeed, among the stars of the entire show.

All major USAF-led events have two prime ingredients, the six F-16C/Ds of the *Thunderbirds*, back in Britain for the first time in six years, and the Heritage Flight, this one flown by Dan Friedkin in Comanche Fighters' P-51D Mustang *Frenesi* with an F-22A Raptor, in the hands of Maj Dan 'Rock' Dickinson, tucked in alongside. Preceding this were displays from B-17G *Sally B* and Peter Teichman's P-51D *Tall-in-the-Saddle*, the latter's landing circuit interrupted on Sunday by the B-2's arrival. A very welcome feature on all three days was the US Air Forces in Europe flypast, involving F-15C/Es from Lakenheath, Spangdahlem-based F-16CMs, one of Mildenhall's KC-135R/Ts and a C-130J-30 out of Ramstein. In the case of the fast jets, 'flypasts' is more appropriate, multiple passes being offered with dynamic zoom climbs to close.

Having the *Thunderbirds* in a British show brings its own particular pre-requisites, not least in regulatory terms. RIAT chief

The Spirit's appearance was certainly the highlight of the Air Tattoo's 70th anniversary tribute to the US Air Force.

executive Andy Armstrong presented the team with his CEO Award for an outstanding contribution, leading *Thunderbird 7*, director of operations Lt Col Kevin Walsh, to comment, "There was a great team effort just to get the whole team overseas and in the air — to get us to put on a different demonstration out here we had to change our rules and change our display a little bit to fit the mould here. We thought we did well with it". There was value to be gained from interaction with the *Red Arrows*, too, the *Thunderbirds*' pilots flying in the back of the Hawks during an in-season practice, and

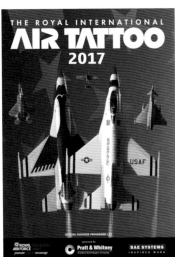

Red 4 going along for the ride on Friday in the two-seat F-16D.

As is hopefully to be expected of an anniversary occasion, the USAF contingent in the static park was especially sizeable, 14 aircraft in all. Having both a B-52H and B-1B on hand, 2nd and 28th Bomb Wing examples respectively, harked back a few years. So did the 9th Reconnaissance Wing U-2S, one of numerous examples seen staging through Fairford on deployment during the RIAT week. An historic American aircraft, Tony de Bruyn's OV-10B Bronco, attracted an unexpected visitor in the form of Gen Tod Wolters, commander of US Air Forces in Europe. The general was a Bronco pilot at Sembach, West Germany, early in his career, and later an instructor on the type.

We were also taken back to a past era by the Ukrainian Air Force, but while its Su-27s will remain deeply redolent of the Cold War, their so-called 'digital' camouflage reflected the fact that these examples from the 831st Guards Tactical Aviation Brigade at Myrhorod had been much-upgraded. Getting the 'Flanker' back in the flying display was not the work of a moment — the RIAT flying control committee chair, Wg Cdr Jonathan Nixon, visited Myrhorod to observe and validate the solo display. The single-seat Su-27P1M duly performed at Fairford, Col Olexsander Oksanchenko giving the first 'Flanker' demonstrations at a British event since the great Anatoly Kvochur flew at Jersey in 2001. As a piece of sheer brute force, they could barely be bettered. The graft put in by RIAT, and the Ukrainians, was well worthwhile.

The French Air Force had earlier marked the centenary of the arrival of American forces in France during 1917 by

Right: The RIAT Crew Challenge, open to all air and ground crews participating in the Air Tattoo, features a range of competitive activities.

The show's other big surprise, B-2 aside, was the presence of an Israeli Air Force C-130J-30 Hercules. Its attendance, the first by an Israeli aeroplane at the Air Tattoo in 17 years, was kept a very closely guarded secret.

PHOTO: TOM GIBBONS

PHOTO: TIM FELCE

PHOTO: ADRIAN PINGSTONE

The BBMF's 'Thompson Formation' was a nod to the flight's founder, Wg Cdr Peter Thompson DFC, in the 60th anniversary year of its establishment.

sending the *Patrouille de France* on a six-week tour of the USA. To that end, the *Thunderbirds* joined the Bastille Day flypast over Paris on RIAT's opening Friday, returning for a formation pass at Fairford with the *Red Arrows*. But the Armée de l'Air paid further tribute, both to that critical event and the 100th anniversary of the squadron SPA 85 'La Folie', with one of two Alpha Jet Es from Tours. It had various figures painted on its tail, including that of Eugene J. Bullard, who from May 1917 was the first and only African-American pilot to fly operationally in World War One.

Meanwhile, the 30th anniversary of the Armée de l'Air's second major attack on Wadi Doum in Libyan-occupied northern Chad in January 1987 was commemorated in markings on the desert-camouflaged Mirage 2000D of the *Couteau Delta* pair, one of the show's stand-out display teams. The two-ship, newly formed on the conventional strike jet by Escadron de Chasse 3/3 at Nancy-Ochey, carried on where *Ramex Delta* had left off, providing a superbly choreographed sequence of tactical-style manoeuvres that contrasted markedly with the familiar solo fast jets.

Apart from reintroducing the Lancaster following a major overhaul and application of new markings, the Battle of Britain Memorial Flight added an elegant fighter foursome of Hurricane LF363 and three Spitfires, their extended 'dumbbell' tailchase covering the full crowdline. With the Lancaster they made up 'Thompson Formation', a nod to the flight's founder, Wg Cdr Peter Thompson DFC, in the 60th anniversary year of its establishment.

The show's other big surprise, B-2 aside, was the presence of an Israeli Air Force C-130J-30 Hercules — locally designated Shimshon in Hebrew — operated by 103 Squadron. Its attendance, the first by an Israeli aeroplane at the Air Tattoo in 17 years, was kept a very closely guarded secret. It was part of a static park larger than the show had assembled in recent times, and spearheaded by a more sizeable RAF contingent. The sparing of two Atlas C1s and a Voyager by Brize Norton's hard-pressed units was a good effort; the sight of the desert pink-painted No 12 Squadron Tornado GR4, about to be grounded at the end of its service life, was one for sore eyes. The same might be said of the Hellenic Air Force F-4Es, for the two specially marked examples from 338 Mira are, to date, the last Greek Phantoms to have graced the Fairford tarmac.

The Royal Canadian Air Force, meanwhile, went to great lengths. A CH-147F Chinook from 450 Squadron was flown to Brize Norton aboard a 429 Squadron CC-177 Globemaster III, reassembled there and flown to Fairford, while another CC-177 made the trip purely as a RIAT static exhibit. The Royal Australian Air Force's E-7A Wedgetail airborne early warning and control platform brought something new to the show — and, as it's turned out, a portent of things to come for the RAF. Indeed, it departed Fairford for Waddington, where it spent a day on a demonstration visit. Affinity Flying Services, one of the partners in the UK's Military Flying Training System contract, exhibited the brand-new T-6C Texan

II, Phenom 100 and G120TP Prefect in RAF markings but still with civilian registrations prior to delivery.

But perhaps the single most outstanding aeroplane on the airfield was far-removed from all this modern metal. If the B-2 and the myriad multi-role combat jets represented the state of the art as regards the striking ability of air power, the Airco DH9 of the Historic Aircraft Collection showed something of its beginnings. Restored to airworthiness by Retrotec in East Sussex but, at this stage, yet to fly — that happened in 2019 — the DH9, E8894, was brought by road to Fairford and reassembled as part of the BAE Systems heritage static display. The pioneering First World War strategic bomber made quite the impression on its public debut, not least by being parked a stone's throw from the B-52. This delighted the Stratofortress crew from the 2nd Bomb Wing, for its direct ancestor, the US Army's 1st Day Bombardment Group, had flown American-built DH-4s in France during 1918. Guy Black and his team from Retrotec/HAC went away with the trophy for best civilian aircraft at RIAT 2017.

In marking the USAF anniversary, and in putting together a first-class array of aeroplanes overall, this Air Tattoo set the bar very high. What would the following year, and the RAF's centenary, bring?

Scampton Airshow 2017 9 & 10 September

A new venue, but an historic location: the first Scampton Airshow, held at the famous former RAF bomber station in Lincolnshire — and, of course, home to the *Red Arrows* — on 9 & 10 September 2017 was a different challenge for RAFCTE. This was not intended to be a northern equivalent of RIAT, nor a direct replacement for the Waddington shows. Rather, the idea was to stage a show of broad appeal, more of a military/civilian mix than the Air Tattoo, and with something of Scampton's heritage to the fore.

It certainly had the feel, from the outset, of a well-established event. Off-base parking with a shuttle bus link ran smoothly, the traffic flowed freely, and Scampton felt like it had been staging this show for years. Airshows with a dedicated static park, as opposed to the positioning crowd-side of flying display aircraft, are rare these days, so the effort here was especially commendable. The Swedish Air Force Historic Flight brought its J 29F 'Tunnan', SK 35C Draken, AJS 37 Viggen and, most notably, J 32D Lansen, the latter only recently returned to flight on the civil register and making the type's first appearance in Britain since IAT 94. However, it did not prove possible to resolve the issue of pilot display authorisations for the Swedish jets before the show, so they remained ground-bound. A Royal Canadian Air Force CF-188, on deployment to Europe, added further international flavour, while Scampton-based defence contractor HHA provided its Hunter F58, Buccaneer S2B, Su-22M4K 'Fitter' and F-4F Phantom to create a unique line-up. A dedicated Heritage Hangar, featuring many exhibits from regional aviation heritage organisations amongst others, won a lot of plaudits.

The flying programme had its issues. The *Red Arrows* were down to eight Hawks anyway, *Red 5* being on paternity leave; when, on Saturday, *Red 3's* mount went unserviceable on the runway, the rest of the team's 'Enid' section had to scrub too, leaving only four jets to perform. Not what was intended, but it was unique! Still, the eight aircraft had earlier been able to give a formation flypast with a No 5(AC) Squadron Sentinel R1, and Sunday saw an eight-ship display. Perhaps the best sight of the weekend was the Battle of Britain Memorial Flight's Lancaster in the skies over Scampton, the station where the type had first entered service. It followed a period of several weeks' grounding for the BBMF's Merlin-engined aircraft, due to reduction gearbox issues. However, Sunday's windy weather kept the flight on the ground back at Coningsby. The list of stand-out performers was suitably eclectic: the solo French Air Force Alpha Jet truly danced around the sky in a stunning routine; the BAE Systems Heritage Flight's Avro XIX Anson and Mark Stott's Pembroke, in the hands of Peter Kosogorin and Jon Corley respectively, were flown individually in sparkling fashion; and Dan Griffith and crew aboard the T2 Aviation/Oil Spill Response Boeing 727-2S2F(RE) doused the airfield with water from its spray bars. But the crowd of some 50,000 was about 75 per cent of what RAFCTE had hoped for, and the decision was taken not to stage a Scampton Airshow the following year. Thus far, it has not returned.

PHOTO: GARY PARSONS

18

RAF FAIRFORD
13-15 JULY

This was the big one: the Air Tattoo's celebration of the Royal Air Force's centenary. Planning for the occasion had gone back a long way — as Andy Armstrong explains, his involvement started as soon as he got the chief executive's job back in 2014. "We were thinking about the centenary right from the start — for me, personally, it was four years in the planning. It started getting serious within two years of the event, and it wasn't just RIAT — it was a series of events throughout the year, including the RAF100 Centenary Gala at the Royal Albert Hall on 31 March. That was an incredibly proud moment, to hire the Royal Albert Hall, fill it, and put on such an amazing show. With the feedback at the end, that was a tremendous day at the office."

Speaking to the author around that time, Andy stressed the nature of RIAT's own place in the celebrations. "The London event [on 10 July] we see as the national celebration of the centenary", he said. "It then flows into RIAT, which is the international celebration". As for the historical element, while it would of course be reflected, this was not foremost in the Air Tattoo's mind. "I think that others can do that better", Andy commented. Reminiscing now, he reflects, "Lots of other activities were happening around the UK, and we needed to maintain that focus so we maximised all of the natural support."

The much-praised London flypast, staged 100 days after the actual anniversary date on 1 April, and early appearances by the RAF100 National Aircraft Tour kept the occasion very much in the public mind. So did other airshows with an RAF centenary theme. Before RIAT, the Shuttleworth Collection at Old Warden and the RAF Cosford Air Show presented unique arrays of historic aeroplanes juxtaposed with present-day counterparts. In September, IWM Duxford staged its Battle of Britain Air Show, the year's most comprehensive aerial cavalcade of historic RAF types, again with strong modern involvement. In between came RIAT, with its ceremonial and international focus. "We had the world's air forces coming, which they did en masse to celebrate with the RAF", says Andy.

For the first time, RIAT became a full three-day event in 2018, the Friday being expanded in size to equal Saturday and Sunday. It made the Air Tattoo literally a whole week long, when measured from Tuesday's first arrival to Monday's last

For the first time, RIAT became a full three-day event in 2018, the Friday being expanded in size to equal Saturday and Sunday. "We had the world's air forces coming, which they did en masse to celebrate with the RAF."

departure. And, make no mistake, this was the largest the show had been for a good many seasons. Hardstandings that had recently accommodated car parking were once again given over to aircraft, not least present-day RAF aircraft, as the service made its most sizeable contribution of the era.

The ceremonial day passed off well, and reflections on the RAF's past produced many of RIAT 2018's best moments.

There was an added element scheduled for that opening day, too: an RAF Review, staged while the rest of the event went on around it. In fact, this was the first time a Royal Review had taken place at a full public event. Once the new Queen's Colour for the RAF in the United Kingdom had been paraded, HRH The Duke of Kent and the Chief of the Air Staff, Air Chief Marshal Sir Stephen Hillier, carried out their tour of the RAF and Commonwealth static display, while HRH Prince Michael of Kent and the RAF's Air Marshal Sir Stuart Atha, deputy commander operations, were taken around the international contingent.

And, of course, there was to be a flypast: 50 aircraft in all, with three Pumas and a Chinook leading the Lancaster, a Hurricane and four Spitfires from the BBMF, an Atlas, five Tornado GR4s, three F-35Bs, 22 Typhoons in the '100' formation that had so wowed the masses in London, and the nine Hawks of the *Red Arrows*. Unfortunately, Friday the 13th lived up to its billing, and the elements did their worst. "Who would have thought", says Andy, "after all that planning and with such a lovely day, that we would have an electrical storm over Swindon and the aircraft flying north-south, as was planned, would go straight into it? That was hugely frustrating. But, having lived safety for so long in the run-up to the flypast, there was absolutely no chance that it could go ahead, sadly". The call to cancel came with the BBMF aircraft about to roll for take-off. The disappointment was palpable, the decision understandable.

Still, the ceremonial day otherwise passed off well, much to Andy's satisfaction, for it had been quite far outside the Air Tattoo norm. "Once we got to the gala dinner on the Friday evening, which remained a very special event to mark the centenary and which was attended by HRH The Princess Royal, I felt we were on familiar territory again. I was very proud of what we'd been able to deliver". There was still much more to come.

Reflections on the RAF's past produced many of RIAT 2018's best moments. There was in fact an extensive historic static display, the BAE Systems Heritage Flight exhibit forming a large part of it. A BE2e reproduction from the World War One Aviation Heritage Trust and a very rare outing by Bianchi Aviation Film Services' Sopwith Camel replica helped recall the service's pre-1918 origins. Seldom seen away from Duxford, the Historic Aircraft Collection's Hawker Fury I added one of the finest examples of an original 1930s front-line biplane, while the Shuttleworth Collection offered a sizeable contribution of Avro Tutor, Tiger Moth, recently restored Spitfire LFVc and the BAE Systems Heritage Flight's newly RAF-schemed Avro XIX Anson. Martin-Baker and Hawker Hunter Aviation bolstered the historic jet side, with Meteor T7 and two Hunter F58s respectively. One of the Hunters sported a new, aggressor-esque splinter camouflage scheme, and gave some low passes on arrival as a visual height check for the flying control committee.

But all were eclipsed by the Flying Bulls' Sycamore, this sole airworthy example of the Bristol-built helicopter coming towards the end of a short UK tour, and making for a marvellous sight parked alongside Andrew Whitehouse's Whirlwind HAR10.

A typically immersive 1914-18 air combat tableau by the *Bremont Great War Display Team*, and the very elegantly flown Vampire duo from the Norwegian Air Force Historical Squadron, in the hands of Kenneth Aarkvisla and Finnish Air Force chief test pilot Jyri Mattila, helped reflect RAF100 in the air. But this was the BBMF's weekend. For the anniversary season, it had worked up a formation dubbed 'Trenchard' in honour of the first Chief of the Air Staff, bringing together Dakota, Lancaster, Hurricane and Spitfire. On the Saturday of RIAT we saw, as a one-off, a seven-ship — Dakota, Lancaster, two Hurricanes and three Spitfires — otherwise referred to as 'Trenchard Plus'. Its execution was of the highest order, producing

what many felt was the best BBMF display of all time, and a major contributor to the flight's award of the King Hussein Memorial Sword.

The other element of its contribution saw the Lancaster breaking off from the formation to join the weekend's most special mixed flypast. While a diamond nine of Typhoons flew by, the Avro bomber linked up with two of its No 617 Squadron successors. The resulting trio of Lancaster, Tornado GR4 and F-35B Lightning paid tribute to many strands running through the year — RAF100, of course, but also the 75th anniversary of the Dambusters raid and the RAF's impending retirement of the Tornado, provided here by No 31 Squadron. A wings-swept, afterburning pass into a zoom climb by the GR4, and the F-35B's hover, made for a potent illustration of the baton being handed on.

So, in a different way, did an event on Thursday evening. The arrival of an

PHOTO: PENGUIN/RAFCT

Air Cadets
Northern Ireland Wing

THE ROYAL INTERNATIONAL
AIR TATTOO
The
Patron's Pavilion
Sunday 15 July
2018

G550

DONATE **FUNDRAISE** VOLUNTEER
RAF100 APPEAL

babcock
QinetiQ
FUJITSU
M&S

RAF
100
APPEAL

RAF
100

**COMMEMORATE
CELEBRATE
INSPIRE**

ROYAL
AIR FORCE

ROYAL
AIR FORCE

" The most complete airshow I've ever been to. "

Al Worden Apollo 15 Astronaut

HHA

AL WORDEN

MQ-9C SkyGuardian marked the inaugural trans-Atlantic flight by this medium-altitude, long-endurance unmanned air system, and the first time a UAV had flown to the show. For the Air Tattoo, making this happen brought a whole new set of challenges to overcome, but — in partnership with manufacturer General Atomics, and numerous airspace and regulatory authorities — happen it did. The 4,000-mile flight started at Grand Forks, North Dakota, where the SkyGuardian's crews were located. Turning up early in British airspace, it was put into a holding pattern before touching down exactly on time, 24 hours and two minutes after setting off. Not long after it had cleared the runway, the Camel replica followed it in. Now *there* was an embodiment of 100 years of air power.

Once on the ground, the civilian-registered airframe had RAF markings applied, specifically those of No 31 Squadron, which will become the first RAF unit to operate what the service will dub the Protector RG1. It completed a notable array of RAF assets present and future, among them a trio of Waddington-based ISR (intelligence, surveillance and reconnaissance) types that had never before been shown together at RIAT: Sentry AEW1, Sentinel R1, and the latest RC-135W Rivet Joint. Though their Shadow R1 stablemate was not represented, No 14 Squadron did bring a civilian-registered King Air 350C crew trainer.

The rarity tally was high in the rest of the static park, too. The European debut of a Japan Air Self-Defense Force Kawasaki C-2 airlifter, provided by 403 Hikotai, allowed for an intriguing comparison with Embraer's KC-390 demonstrator. The NATO SAC (Strategic Airlift Capability) initiative made a first British show outing with a C-17A from its Heavy Airlift Wing, stationed at Pápa, Hungary. Another Globemaster III, the Royal Canadian Air Force CC-177, brought in its hold a CH-146 Griffon helicopter operated by 430 Squadron at CFB Valcartier near Quebec City, and in an immaculate special scheme to boot. Part of a strong US Air Force contingent to make the trans-Atlantic trip included a 920th Rescue Wing HC-130N Combat King based at Patrick AFB and a 305th Rescue Squadron HH-60G Pave Hawk from Davis-Monthan AFB, the latter flown into Fairford inside a USAF C-17A. The Royal Australian Air Force E-7A went unserviceable en route and missed the Royal Review, but the No 2 Squadron crew was not to be deterred, and the Wedgetail duly pitched up on Friday evening. From closer to home, QinetiQ supplied its very new, very attractive PC-21, flown in from Boscombe Down by legendary test pilot Dave Southwood.

Looking its best against the clear blue, the Royal Canadian Air Force CF-188 demo

Air Tattoo Memories: Air Marshal Sir Kevin Leeson

Sir Kevin Leeson was chairman of the Royal Air Force Charitable Trust from 2013 to 2020.

"When I was appointed chairman of the RAF Charitable Trust in 2013, this followed over 20 years as a RIAT volunteer. It felt a great privilege to become the senior RIAT host and chair of the Trust. All the great work the RIAT team and my predecessors as chair had done meant I inherited leadership of a treasured international event that was on a sound financial footing. My tenure as chair would present the opportunity to further build the event's following with our loyal visitors, the excellent team of volunteers, the RAFCTE permanent staff and the world's air forces. The income to the Trust gave us scope to initiate many scholarships to further young people's careers in aerospace and flying. We also sought to make considerable investments in the showground, to enhance visitors' enjoyment.

"The show has a great reputation for its themes, which linked flying and ground spectaculars to the role of the Royal Air Force and its fellow air arms. We also sought to mirror important national and international aerospace and aviation events in the display. It was great fun to be part of bringing those ideas together.

"My first RIAT as chairman saw the thrilling appearance of the newly delivered first British Airways Airbus A380 in perfect formation with the *Red Arrows* — a RIAT 'world first' (which we always worked hard to invent!). Amongst my most memorable will be the Battle of Britain 75th in 2015, where we brought together a huge showing of Spitfires, Hurricanes and a Messerschmitt Bf109 to the delight of the crowd, but also to a large assembly of veterans, which was unlikely to be repeated. In 2014 we also had a go at achieving the first European appearance of the F-35, but an engine issue dashed our hopes at the last minute.

"The extremely sad accident at Shoreham in 2015 gave us a period of reflection, but RIAT's safety rules were judged to be of the highest order. Of course, we learned everything we could from that tragic event, to make sure we delivered air displays at the leading edge of safety.

"In 2016 we saw the RAF's first F-35 fly over the Atlantic using five nail-biting air-to-air refuelling brackets, to make its maiden RIAT appearance. Its arrival on the pan at RAF Fairford was greeted by a magnificent rainbow — a real tear-jerker of a moment if ever there was one! In 2016 we also had a visit by Their Royal Highnesses The Duke and Duchess of Cambridge accompanied by Prince George — attending his first public engagement. It was a great privilege to host two future kings. RIAT having hosted Her Majesty The Queen and HRH The Prince of Wales previously, it was great to get the full set!

"RIAT 2018 was the pinnacle of my time as chairman, when we

celebrated the RAF's 100th anniversary in the air and on the ground. The static line-up of RAF aircraft representing that illustrious 100 years was inspiring. We intended to repeat the flypast that had taken place in London earlier in the week, but the biggest thundercloud ever seen over Fairford blocked the approach of the 50 aircraft flypast that was ready to run in. That's the joy of organising airshows!

"In 2019 one of our celebrations was 100 years of British Airways and 50 years of the Boeing 747, featuring another spectacular joint flypast with the *Reds*. The 747 was in the old colours of BOAC, evoking wonderful memories for many of us watching. As we looked up and admired the perfect formation, no one would have believed the situation that would pertain when RIAT 2020 came around, with British Airways retiring their entire fleet of 747s earlier than planned. It was with enormous sadness that I handed over the chairmanship as we dealt with the cancellation of RIAT 2020.

"Nonetheless, the joy of aviation is that there is always something new to admire and celebrate, so all the more reason to look forward to the next RIAT as a glorious celebration of 50 years of Air Tattoos."

---

aircraft marked the 60th anniversary of NORAD, the North American Aerospace Defence Command, and put on a stylish show in the hands of 3 Wing pilot Capt Stefan Porteous. With a lot of the other fast jet items having been seen at recent RIATs, an exception was the two-ship French Navy Rafale M tactical routine. It acted as a pleasing counterpoint to its French Air Force equivalent, the returning *Couteau Delta* Mirage 2000D duo. Col Oleksandr Oksanchenko gave a gracefully dynamic demonstration of raw power in the Ukrainian Air Force Su-27P1M. All too often, the ever-loyal *Royal Jordanian Falcons* can seem a little lost amid such heavy metal, but a switch to the new Extra EA330LX changed that, the variant's greater power adding a fresh degree of dynamism to an always professional aerobatic display.

An extremely welcome international nod to RAF100 came courtesy of the USAF Heritage Flight, an F-35A being surprisingly accompanied by not one but

two of Comanche Fighters' warbirds off its wings. To the expected P-51D Mustang, this time *The Hun Hunter\Texas* flown by Dan Friedkin, was added Steve Hinton in desert-camouflaged Spitfire LFVc JG891, in the markings of No 249 Squadron, RAF. Another USAF contribution was a single flypast from a B-2A, statutory F-15C escorts in attendance. No global salute to the RAF's history could have been complete without such strong American involvement, and RIAT 2018 certainly enjoyed that.

How does Andy look back on 2018? "Because 2017 worked so well, we followed the same pattern and got senior 'buy-in' at an early enough stage to make sure it was delivered well." Just as Andy had gone to the States and spent time with the USAF chief in the run-up to that air arm's big anniversary show, so he and his colleagues discussed RIAT 2018 with the RAF's top brass well in advance. The result was testament to those efforts.

British Airways Boeing 747-436 G-BYGC, painted in the colours of an early 747-100 of the British Overseas Airways Corporation, joined up with the RAF's Red Arrows for two beautiful flybys, the first a curving affair against a fine skyscape.

19

RAF FAIRFORD
19-21 JULY

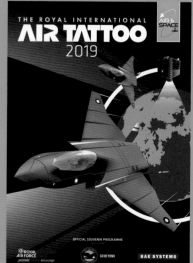

A tale of two airshows. That might be one way of summing up RIAT 2019. Or maybe even three. As much of Friday's display again fell victim to the weather, spirits could not help but drop. The Belgian F-16 fast-taxied, the RAF Typhoon took off and went straight into the circuit to land. It was all they could do. Most of the NATO 70th anniversary flypast was scrubbed, but the alliance's own E-3A, returning to a British flying programme after a very long absence, still got airborne and gave its own flyby. The effort was appreciated — especially when the Sentry then went unserviceable for the rest of the weekend.

Old adversaries were back in welcome force. The Romanian Air Force MiG-21 LanceR C not only brought the distinctive shape of the quintessential Cold War-era fighter back to UK skies, but did so with notable style. The routine by Col Stancu Gheorghe from Escadrila 861 was of a very high standard, his overshoot into an undercarriage-down roll in afterburner, and a low-level partial knife-edge pass, making the most of the fairly

diminutive, not-that-manoeuvrable interceptor. The new Ukrainian Air Force Su-27P1M display pilot, Lt Col Yurii Bulavka, made his presence felt with a lengthy and hard-hitting showing of the 'Flanker'.

For power and spectacle, little else could match the Spanish Navy duo of EAV-8B Harrier II+s. Not for nearly a decade had the Air Tattoo seen the classic V/STOL jet in action, and the two-ship mounted by Escuadrilla 009 brought the crowd to its feet. Two Harriers standing on columns of thrust from their Pegasus engines could hardly fail to do so. Their attendance allowed pilots from across the generations to gather in the 50th anniversary year of the type entering RAF service, as Sqn Ldr Tom Lecky-Thompson, who won his class in the *Daily Mail* Transatlantic Air Race in 1969 with an early Harrier GR1, met the Spanish Navy aviators. One of them, squadron boss Cdr Manuel Rodríguez Giner, made his last Harrier flight on the Sunday of the show.

Air Tattoo Memories: Chris Murray

Chris Murray is a former director operations RIAT and current RAFCTE company secretary.

"After nearly 35 years' service in the RAF, I joined RAFCTE in 2008 as deputy director ground operations, company secretary and secretary to the RAF Charitable Trust, having worked in the airshow's showground operations centre as a RIAT volunteer. Thereafter, I was to enjoy the friendship and supportive atmosphere that exists in the Air Tattoo's HQ at Douglas Bader House in Fairford. From the outset I was extremely impressed by the strength of purpose that existed and still exists within the RAFCTE board. The contribution made by the non-executive directors — without remuneration — is simply astounding, and the company's success owes much to their influence, particularly its successive chairmen. In March 2009, I became an executive director with responsibility for air ops, ground ops, safety services and health and safety. I was blessed with some very able people at all levels, and I valued throughout my time the contribution made by the volunteer teams in every discipline; without their contribution there would be no airshow.

"The Shoreham incident in 2015 became a 'game changer' for all of us throughout the airshow industry. The impact was significant and I personally became heavily involved in all aspects of the total review that we undertook of all our aviation activities. This included crowd safety, secondary gatherings of spectators, risk ownership, flight profiles, tracking devices and display areas. Whilst the Shoreham incident was undoubtedly tragic, on reflection the industry as a whole, including RIAT, has benefitted from the subsequent review and changes that have since been introduced.

"Of course, my time within the company was not all so operationally focused. Significantly, in 2008 I met a volunteer, Kim, who is now my wife. Also, those who know me may recall that I enjoy fancy dress – including wearing a tie! From Darth Vader to Arabian sheiks, to Chinese mandarins, Santa Claus and numerous Halloween related ghouls, I felt able to display my full repertoire of costumes before the unsuspecting staff in DBH! I particularly recall having catering-sized cans of beans poured over me after the voting in a 'Red Nose Day' charity effort was rigged!"

"I look back with immense pride on my contribution to the company and with huge affection for an organisation that I was privileged to be part of."

RAFAT's Sqn Ldr Martin Pert with British astronaut Tim Peake.

" It was wonderful to see, first hand, so many young people inspired and excited by what the Air Tattoo had to offer. By delivering an exciting blend of entertainment and education, the Air Tattoo is helping to bring science and technology to life and encouraging the next generation of pilots, engineers, scientists — and astronauts! "

Tim Peake UK Astronaut

All three of the Belgian Air Component's Fighting Falcons present, the 'Dark Falcon' display aircraft and two in D-Day 75th anniversary colours, joined up to open Saturday's proceedings.

The number of special flypasts was very notable. Serviceability and operational requirements conspired to cut back the NATO salute somewhat, but the sight of four F-16s from different nations — Belgium, Denmark, the Netherlands and Norway — in formation, and an ultra-rare French Air Force C-135FR appearance, was not to be sniffed at. All three of the Belgian Air Component's Fighting Falcons present, the 'Dark Falcon' display aircraft and two in D-Day 75th anniversary colours, had earlier joined up to open Saturday's proceedings.

The *Red Arrows*' Hawks and the eight Alpha Jets of the *Patrouille de France* came together in their respective Concorde formations as a nod to the 50th anniversary of the Anglo-French supersonic airliner. The first flight of 'British' Concorde 002, G-BSST, ended at Fairford, which was used by the British Aircraft Corporation as its main flight test base for the type until 1977. Accompanied by the British and French national anthems, the multiple flybys were an excellent piece of airshow theatre. That they were rescheduled for Saturday, having been weathered-out on Friday, was an added bonus.

Retiring RAFCTE CEO Andy Armstrong welcomes his successor, Paul Atherton.

The *Red Arrows* were also involved in Saturday's most imposing spectacle. Throughout 2019, British Airways marked the centenary of the first regular, scheduled operation by Aircraft Transport and Travel, the oldest of the 'ancestor' companies that, through subsequent mergers, came together to form what is now the UK's flag-carrier. In aerial salute, BA's Boeing 747-436 G-BYGC, painted in the colours of an early 747-100 of the British Overseas Airways Corporation (BOAC), joined up with the RAF Aerobatic Team for two beautiful flybys, the first a curving affair against a fine skyscape. It was the sole airshow appearance by any of the four BA 'retro-jets' in historic schemes — three 747-400s in BOAC and earlier BA liveries, and an Airbus A319 in British European Airways colours. The subsequent premature retirement of the carrier's 747 fleet, as a result of the coronavirus pandemic, rendered the occasion a true Air Tattoo one-off.

It was unfortunate, if unavoidable, that none of these special flypasts — and some other items — could be staged on Sunday, due to operational and overseas display commitments. But the world's air arms, and civilian contractors, had still turned out in strength. Two Turkish Air Force F-4E-2020 Phantoms, from 111 Filo, were the pick of a fine range of specially marked NATO fast jets on static display; the USAF B-52H, a 2nd Bomb Wing example, was pleasingly weathered, in contrast to the immaculate Qatar Emiri Air Force C-17A in its Qatar Airways garb. The new generation of RAF fixed- and rotary-wing training types, procured under the Military Flying Training System initiative, was grouped for the first time: Prefect, Juno, Jupiter, Phenom, Texan and Hawk T2. Likewise the Maritime and Coastguard Agency's corral, comprising F406 Caravan II, AW189 and Sikorsky S-92, proved a popular feature. New to the show, Embraer's smart EMB-314 Super Tucano headlined the industry inputs.

In presenting his special RIAT CEO award to the Spanish Harrier crews, Andy Armstrong brought to a close his last show at the helm, after five very successful years. The 2019 event experienced its difficulties, but such is any organiser's lot, and it still put on an impressive display of air power. As Andy handed over the reins to his successor Paul Atherton, no-one could have imagined what happened next.

USAF Gen David Goldfein presents the US Bronze Star medal to the Chief of the Air Staff, Sir Stephen Hillier, for services in the Iraq war.

PHOTO: PETER REOCH

2020: A VIRTUAL AIR TATTOO

The 2020 Virtual Air Tattoo attracted 362,000 live views with an overall reach of 1.2 million and watched in over 50 countries. The digital show was a huge success and continues to be streamed every day, somewhere in the world, and will be an Air Tattoo legacy for years to come.

We should be ending this 50th anniversary book with a recap of RIAT 2020, of the exciting aircraft secured as part of its themes — Fast Jet Combat Air Power and Intelligence, Surveillance and Reconnaissance — and a weekend of top-class flying displays. But we're not. The COVID-19 pandemic saw to that. On 20 March, just before the British government formally declared a lockdown, the show's cancellation was announced.

"This decision has not been taken lightly and a significant amount of work sits behind this course of action", new RAFCTE chief executive Paul Atherton said in a statement. "The growing COVID-19 crisis, which is worsening by the day, and the implications of which are becoming more profound, has led RAFCTE to conclude that the most prudent course of action is to suspend any further planning to deliver this massive event."

The news was unavoidable. But, very soon, members of the permanent staff at Douglas Bader House began developing the concept of a Virtual Air Tattoo. It emerged as a two-day online event mixing archive footage, live interviews, specially filmed showcases from air arms and aerospace companies around the world, and some outstanding virtual displays — both solo and team — courtesy of the flight simulator community. Hosting the event from a studio set up at Fairford were the author and his regular RIAT flying display commentary colleague, Gp Capt Mark Manwaring; the Air Tattoo's new head of air operations, Peter Reoch, found himself arranging the virtual participation as opposed to the real thing, and directing the day's proceedings behind the cameras; and PlanesTV, headed by Iain Campbell, made the technical side happen. A step into the unknown for most of those involved, but gratifyingly well-received, the Virtual Air Tattoo helped fill a gap — but it was more than that. Might we see more of the concept, in addition to the real show? Time will tell…

Air Tattoo Memories: Caroline Rogers

Caroline joined the organisation in 1990 and is now commercial director of RAFCTE.

"I recall my interview in Paul's office. The curious looks — is this going to be another fluffy luvvie spouting business jargon? 'What can you tell us about how to set up a hospitality operation in a field?' I was asked. 'Where will the loos go and how do we manage the wet waste?' was part of my response. I think this is what the ops boss, Tim, wanted to hear — bogs and drains!

"So began my career at the Air Tattoo. We were a small band of permanent staff then, each with a wide range of responsibilities. In addition to the mixed bag of hospitality, marketing, sales, catering, concerts and guest management duties that came with the role, part of my job also included the admin and co-ordination of the emergency services operation. I recall my first full planning meeting on day three in the job, with all the volunteer managers and external agencies, as we scoped out how things would work for the first show at Boscombe Down. I didn't really understand a word that was said from start to finish. My draft minutes were returned to me with more red pen than printed black type! A good way to learn though.

"I have frequently questioned what it is that has kept my enthusiasm, affection and admiration for this unique and special organisation over so many years, when other paths and challenges have beckoned. It is quite simply the people and the pride. Dedicated volunteers who have been core to our success and taken the ups and downs on the journey with us. Suppliers and contractors for whom nothing is ever too much trouble and who frequently deliver above and beyond what can reasonably be asked. Magnificent sponsors without whom we would not exist, special and exceptional relationships based on trust and friendship. And finally, I have the most supportive and brilliant team around me who achieve so much year after year, the driving force behind the outstanding reputation that we now enjoy.

"Some best times...2005, supporting Tim to secure the survival of the organisation; the RAF100 Gala; the Sunday night omelette; signatures on BAE Systems contracts (thank you Jane!); the wise and wonderful Fred and Alan; meetings in the Pentagon. Too many to list."

Air Tattoo Memories:
RAFCTE CEO Paul Atherton

Rarely in life do opportunities like the one presented to me in 2019 come along, namely to take the helm of the greatest airshow in the world. So, when I was offered the chance to become only the fourth CEO in the Air Tattoo's illustrious history, it was a chance too good to miss.

I was already in awe of what the Air Tattoo team achieved each year, having attended many times during my 34-year career with the RAF. However, it was only when I was offered a glimpse behind the scenes that the sheer scale of RIAT and the incredible effort put in by everyone involved to deliver such a world-beating event year-on-year became apparent — not least my talented, enthusiastic and outstanding permanent team based at Douglas Bader House, pictured opposite with our two RAFCT colleagues.

Although aware of the tremendous help provided by the RAF, US Air Force and the Air Cadet Organisation each year, I was genuinely overwhelmed by just how much support there was for the airshow among the world's air arms and their chiefs, the aerospace industry both here and abroad, the Air Tattoo supporters from around the world and last, but not least, the incredible army of volunteers without whom the event could not take place.

Having to cancel my first RIAT due to COVID-19 was incredibly challenging, deeply disappointing and personally upsetting. Whilst the extent of the pandemic's impact on our plans for RIAT 2021 remains uncertain, the Air Tattoo team will continue to explore the art of the possible against the backdrop of an ever-changing landscape. Not for the first time will we have to be innovative and flexible in order to deliver a great event!

However, the cancellation did provide a clear demonstration of just how much goodwill exists across the globe for RIAT as we planned and delivered our first ever virtual Air Tattoo which took place over the RIAT 2020 weekend. The support from the RAF, global air arms and industry, as we collectively stepped into the unknown for the first time, was again overwhelming and augers well for whatever the future may hold.

To all of you reading this who have attended an Air Tattoo during the past 50 years, I wish to thank you on behalf of all those who have played a part in its success. To those of you who have yet to experience the thrills and excitement of the world's greatest airshow, I hope the stories and photos in this wonderful book encourage you to join us in the future.

O ROYAL AIR FORCE Charitable Trust Enterprises

The permanent staff of the Royal Air Force Charitable Trust Enterprises 2020, together with our army of volunteers and supporters, are the people behind the Royal International Air Tattoo.

Roll of Honour

All the winners of the show's flying display awards — nearly 50 years of Air Tattoo 'top guns'.

BEST SOLO JET DISPLAY

Embassy Solo Jet Aerobatic Trophy

1972	Fg Off Rod Dean, RAF Hunter F6
1973	Flt Lt W. Tyndall, RAF Jet Provost T5
1974	Flt Lt Peter Chapman, RAF Lightning F3
1976	Flt Lt David Webb, RAF Jet Provost T5
1977	Flt Lt David Fitzsimmons, RAF Hawk T1
1979	Oblt Erich Wolf, Austrian Air Force Saab 105OE
1981	Capt Hans Hemmelder, Royal Netherlands Air Force NF-5A
1983	Flt Lt Mike Thompson, RAF Lightning F3

Superkings Solo Jet Aerobatic Trophy

1985	Maj Eric Nedergaard, US Air Force F-15C Eagle
1987	Flt Lt Paul Brown, RAF Tornado F3
1989	Flt Lt Simon Meade, RAF Hawk T1A
1991	Sqn Ldr Ian MacDonald, RAF Harrier GR5
1992	Cdt Avi Dany Payeur, Belgian Air Force Alpha Jet E
1993	Cne Thierry Lang, French Air Force Mirage 2000
1994	Capt Ingemar Axelsson, Swedish Air Force J 35J Draken
1995	Maj Ivan Hulek, Slovak Air Force MiG-29
1996	Col Nikolai Koval, Ukrainian Air Force Su-27
1997	Cne François Ponsot, French Air Force Mirage 2000
1998	Lt Col Ivan Húlek, Slovak Air Force MiG-29
1999	Capt Gyula Vári, Hungarian Air Force MiG-29UB
2000	Capt Anders Eriksson, Swedish Air Force JA 37 Viggen
2001	Capt Jyri Selvenius, Finnish Air Force F-18C Hornet
2002	Flt Lt Tony Cann, RAF Harrier GR7
2003	Cne Yann Vallet, French Air Force Mirage 2000

Paul Bowen Solo Jet Trophy

2004	Cdt John Vandebosch, Belgian Air Component F-16A MLU Fighting Falcon
2005	Capt Olli Siivola, Finnish Air Force F-18C Hornet
2006	Capt Michael Reiner, Swiss Air Force F/A-18C Hornet
2007	Capt Thomas Peier, Swiss Air Force F/A-18C Hornet
2009	Capt Thomas Peier, Swiss Air Force F/A-18C Hornet
2010	Maj Dave Skalicky, US Air Force F-22A Raptor
2011	Cne Michaël Brocard, French Air Force Rafale C
2012	Sqn Ldr Scott Loughran, RAF Typhoon FGR4
2013	Flt Lt Jamie Norris, RAF Typhoon FGR4
2014	Flt Lt Noel Rees, RAF Typhoon FGR4
2015	Capt Ville Uggeldahl, Finnish Air Force F/A-18C Hornet
2016	Cne Jean-Guillaume Martinez, French Air Force Rafale C
2017	Maj Dan Dickinson, US Air Force F-22A Raptor
2018	Capt Serdar Doğan and Capt Erhan Günar, Turkish Air Force F-16C Fighting Falcon (one pilot per day)
2019	Lt Col Yurii Bulavka, Ukrainian Air Force Su-27P1M

BEST OVERALL FLYING DEMONSTRATION

Shell (UK) Oil Trophy

1976	Peter Phillips, Britten-Norman BN-2 Defender
1977	Royal Navy Blue Herons, Hunter GA11s (team leader Derek Morter)
1979	Swiss Air Force Patrouille Suisse, Hunter F58s (team leader Hptm Hans-Rudolf Beck)
1981	Royal Netherlands Air Force Grasshoppers, Alouette IIIs

Sir Douglas Bader Trophy

1983	Hptm Karl 'Charly' Zimmermann, German Army Bo 105M
1985	Sqn Ldr Jolyon Maclean, RAF Sea King HAR3
1987	Royal Netherlands Air Force Grasshoppers, Alouette IIIs
1989	Lt Col Giovanni Ammoniaci, Italian Air Force G222
1991	Cne Laurent Fournier, French Air Force Mirage 2000
1993	Chilean Air Force Halcones, Extra EA300s

1994	Swiss Air Force Patrouille Suisse, Hunter F58s (team leader Maj Frans Ramseier)
1995	Czech Air Force 'Hind' Team, Mi-24Vs (team leader Lt Col Stefan Jasso)
1996	Swedish Air Force Team 60, Saab Sk 60s (team leader Maj Mats Lindskoog)
1997	Maj Enrico Scarabotto, Italian Air Force G222
1998	French Air Force Voltige Victor, Mirage F1Cs (pilots Cne Pontaillier and Ltt Berlinson)
1999	Alan Wade, Joint Elementary Flying Training School T67M-260 Firefly

King Hussein Memorial Sword

2000	Swiss Air Force Patrouille Suisse, F-5E Tiger IIs (team leader Hptm Jan Frasa)
2001	Hunter 50th anniversary display (team leader Rod Dean)
2002	French Air Force Voltige Victor, Mirage F1s (pilots Ltt François Breton and Ltt Guillaume Coeffin)
2003	RAF Red Arrows (team leader Sqn Ldr Spike Jepson) & USAF F-117A Nighthawk (Sqn Ldr Richie Matthews, RAF)
2004	Ricardo Traven, Boeing F/A-18F Super Hornet
2005	Italian Air Force Frecce Tricolori, MB339As (team leader Capt Massimo Tammaro)
2006	Pavel Vlasov and Mikhail Beliaev, RAC MiG MiG-29M OVT (one pilot per day)
2007	Royal Navy/FR Aviation Black Seahawks, Hawk T1s and Falcon 20s (team leader Martin Stoner)
2009	Royal Navy Fly Navy 100 'Balbo' (leader Lt Cdr Mike Pamphilon)
2010	Maj Dave Skalicky, US Air Force F-22A Raptor
2011	Maj Murat Keleş, Turkish Air Force F-16C Fighting Falcon
2012	Republic of Korea Air Force Black Eagles, T-50B Golden Eagles (team leader Maj Wook Cheon Jeon)
2013	Swiss Air Force PC-7 Team, Pilatus NCPC-7s (team leader Capt Martin Vetter)
2014	WO1 Mick Kildea and Capt Neill Posthumus, Army Air Corps Lynx AH7
2015	Battle of Britain 75th anniversary flypast (leader Sqn Ldr Dunc Mason)
2016	Croatian Air Force Krila Oluje, PC-9Ms (team leader Lt Col Damir Barišić)
2017	Cne Jean-Guillaume Martinez, French Air Force Rafale C
2018	RAF Battle of Britain Memorial Flight 'Trenchard Plus' formation
2019	Capt Peter Fallén, Swedish Air Force JAS 39C Gripen

BEST INDIVIDUAL FLYING DEMONSTRATION

Sir Douglas Bader Trophy

2000	Col Peter Wey, Swiss Air Force Super Puma
2001	Andy Sephton, Rolls-Royce Spitfire PRXIX
2002	Capt Richard Buijs, Royal Netherlands Air Force F-16AM Fighting Falcon
2003	Capt Martin Birkfeldt, Swedish Air Force JAS 39A Gripen
2004	Will Curtis, Honda Dream Team Su-26M2
2005	Maj Wandert Brandsen and Capt Raymond Laporte, Royal Netherlands Air Force AH-64D Apache
2006	Alan Wade, Defence Elementary Flying Training School T67M-260 Firefly
2007	Flt Lt Jim Walls, RAF Typhoon F2
2009	Cne Cédric Ruet, French Air Force Rafale B
2010	Flt Lt Steve Kenworthy, RAF Harrier GR9
2011	Maj Severino De Luca and Maj Francesco Ferreri, Italian Air Force C-27J Spartan
2012	Cne Michaël Brocard, French Air Force Rafale C
2013	Flt Lt Paul Farmer, RAF Chinook HC2
2014	Cdt Avi Renaud Thys, Belgian Air Component F-16A MLU Fighting Falcon
2015	Hptm Torsten Möbius, German Army Bo 105P1
2016	Capt Peter Fallén, Swedish Air Force JAS 39C Gripen
2017	1st Lt Andrej Fiorelli, Slovenian Air Force PC-9M
2018	Capt Lauri Mäkinen, Finnish Air Force F/A-18C Hornet
2019	Capt Arto Ukskoski, Finnish Air Force F/A-18C Hornet

BEST DISPLAY BY AN OVERSEAS PARTICIPANT

International Display Sword

1977	Hptm Karl 'Charly' Zimmermann, German Army Bo 105M
1979	Maj G. E. C. 'Boy' Soons, Royal Netherlands Air Force F27-300M Troopship
1981	Maj G. E. C. 'Boy' Soons, Royal Netherlands Air Force F27-300M Troopship
1983	Hptm Karl 'Charly' Zimmermann, German Army Bo 105M
1985	Hptm Karl 'Charly' Zimmermann, German Army Bo 105M
1987	Royal Netherlands Air Force Grasshoppers, Alouette IIIs
1989	Chilean Air Force Halcones, Pitts S-2A Specials
1991	Capt Reinder Zwaart, Royal Netherlands Air Force F-16A Fighting Falcon
1993	Maj Jan Fröjd, Swedish Air Force JA37 Viggen
1994	Cne Pierre Pougheon, French Air Force Mirage 2000

Lockheed Martin Cannestra Trophy

1995	Royal Jordanian Falcons, Extra EA300s (team leader Capt Omar Bilal)
1996	French Air Force Raffin Mike, Jaguar Es (pilots Ltt Praud and Ltt Boutron)

1997	Irish Air Corps *Silver Swallows*, Fouga Magisters

1997 Irish Air Corps *Silver Swallows*, Fouga Magisters
1998 Lt Col Alexiy Vaneev, Ukrainian Air Force An-72
1999 Capt Anders Eriksson, Swedish Air Force JA 37 Viggen
2000 Maj Ken Burch, US Air Force C-17A Globemaster III
2001 Maj Gyula Vári, Hungarian Air Force MiG-29UB
2002 *Royal Jordanian Falcons*, Extra EA300s (team leader Capt Omar Hweij)
2003 *Apache Jet Team*, L-39C Albatroses (team leader Jacques Bothelin)
2004 Cne Yann Vallet and Ltt Fabrice Camliti, French Air Force Mirage 2000 (one pilot per day)
2005 Cne Yann Vallet and Cne Fabrice Camliti, French Air Force Mirage 2000 (one pilot per day)
2006 Capt Henrik Holm, Swedish Air Force JAS 39A Gripen
2007 Capt Tommi Heikkala, Finnish Air Force F-18C Hornet
2009 *Royal Jordanian Falcons*, Extra EA300s (team leader Maj Mohammad Quol)
2010 Cdt Michel Beulen, Belgian Air Component F-16A MLU Fighting Falcon
2011 Maj Roland Blankenspoor and Capt Paul Webbink, Royal Netherlands Air Force AH-64D Apache
2012 Lt Col Artur Kałko and Capt Adrian Rojek, Polish Air Force MiG-29 (one pilot per day)

Cannestra Trophy

2013 Tony Flynn and Karl-Heinz Mai, Airbus A400M
2014 Italian Air Force *Frecce Tricolori*, AT-339As (team leader Maj Jan Slangen)
2015 1st Lt Andrej Fiorelli, Slovenian Air Force PC-9M

RAFCTE Trophy

2016 French Air Force *Ramex Delta*, Mirage 2000Ns
2017 Capt Ivo Kardoš, Czech Air Force JAS 39C Gripen
2018 *Royal Jordanian Falcons*, Extra EA330LXs (team leader Col Jamil Zayyad)
2019 Italian Air Force *Frecce Tricolori*, AT-339As (team leader Maj Stefano Vit)

BEST DISPLAY BY A UK PARTICIPANT

UK Display Sword/Trophy

1993 Army Air Corps *Silver Eagles*, Lynx AH7 and Gazelle AH1s (team leader Capt Colin Dunscombe)
1994 Fg Off Mark Discombe, RAF Tucano T1
1995 Flt Lt Don Ritch, RAF Hawk T1
1996 *Rover Group Aerobatic Team*, Extra EA300s (pilots Brian Lecomber and Alan Wade)

Steedman Display Sword

1997 Flt Lt Andy Lewis, RAF Hawk T1
1998 Alan Wade, Joint Elementary Flying Training School T67M-260 Firefly
1999 Sqn Ldr Terry Cairns, RAF Canberra T4
2000 Flt Lt Antony Parkinson, RAF Tornado F3
2001 Alan Wade, Joint Elementary Flying Training School T67M-260 Firefly
2002 Lt Cdr Rob Schwab and Lt Will Hynett, Royal Navy Sea Harrier FA2 pair
2003 Lt Mark Scott and Lt Jamie Coulton, Royal Navy Lynx HAS3S pair
2004 Flt Lt Tim Freeman and Flt Lt Neil Crawley, RAF Tornado F3
2005 Flt Lt Carl Zarecky, RAF Chinook HC2
2006 Sqn Ldr Matt Elliott, RAF Typhoon T1
2007 *Team Guinot*, Boeing Stearman Model 75s (team leader Vic Norman)
2009 Sqn Ldr Scott Loughran, RAF Typhoon F2
2010 Sqn Ldr Dunc Mason and Flt Lt Rich Walton, RAF Spitfire LFIXe and Typhoon T1 'synchro pair'
2011 Mark Bowman, BAE Systems Typhoon FGR4
2012 Flt Lt Paul Farmer, RAF Chinook HC2
2013 Flt Lt Andrew Fyvie-Rae, RAF Tucano T1
2014 RAF *Red Arrows*, Hawk T1/T1As (team leader Sqn Ldr Jim Turner)
2015 Flt Lt Antony Parkinson and Flt Lt Ben Westoby-Brooks, RAF Spitfire IIa and Typhoon FGR4 'synchro pair'
2016 Nat Makepeace, BAE Systems Typhoon FGR4
2017 Flt Lt Ryan Lawton, RAF Typhoon FGR4
2018 RAF *Red Arrows*, Hawk T1/T1As (team leader Sqn Ldr Martin Pert)
2019 RAF *Red Arrows*, Hawk T1/T1As (team leader Sqn Ldr Martin Pert)

BEST OVERALL DISPLAY AS JUDGED BY THE FRIENDS OF RIAT

As The Crow Flies Trophy

1997 Cne François Ponsot, French Air Force Mirage 2000
1998 Capt Gyula Vári, Hungarian Air Force MiG-29UB
1999 Capt Gyula Vári, Hungarian Air Force MiG-29UB
2000 Capt Péter Kovács, Hungarian Air Force MiG-29UB
2001 Maj Gyula Vári, Hungarian Air Force MiG-29UB
2002 Lt Cdr Rob Schwab and Lt Will Hynett, RN Sea Harrier FA2 pair

2003 Capt Zoltán Szabó, Hungarian Air Force MiG-29
2004 Ricardo Traven, Boeing F/A-18F Super Hornet
2005 Maj Wandert Brandsen and Capt Raymond Laporte, Royal Netherlands Air Force AH-64D Apache
2006 Pavel Vlasov and Mikhail Beliaev, RAC MiG MiG-29M OVT (one pilot per day)
2007 Flt Lt Jim Walls, RAF Typhoon F2
2009 Cne Cédric Ruet, French Air Force Rafale B
2010 Maj Dave Skalicky, US Air Force F-22A Raptor
2011 Maj Severino De Luca and Maj Francesco Ferreri, Italian Air Force C-27J Spartan
2012 Republic of Korea Air Force *Black Eagles*, T-50B Golden Eagles (team leader Maj Wook Cheon Jeon)
2013 Maggiore Fabio De Michele, Italian Air Force C-27J Spartan
2014 Maj Bartłomiej Mejka and Capt Radosław Leszczyk, Polish Air Force Su-22M4K pair
2015 Kev Rumens and Martin Withers, Vulcan to the Sky Trust Vulcan B2
2016 Maj Dan Dickinson, US Air Force F-22A Raptor
2017 Col Oleksander Oksanchenko, Ukrainian Air Force Su-27P1M
2018 French Air Force *Couteau Delta*, Mirage 2000Ds
2019 Capt Arto Ukskoski, Finnish Air Force F/A-18C Hornet

Best of the Best

Two pilots share a unique distinction in Air Tattoo history: that of being five-time victors in the show's flying awards.

One is Gyula Vári, the outstanding Hungarian Air Force MiG-29 solo exponent. The former MiG-21 pilot was in the vanguard of the Hungarian air arm's entry into the post-Warsaw Pact era, as it aligned itself closely with western procedures and structures. Having converted to the MiG-29 he began taking part in NATO's Tactical Leadership Programme exercises and undertook leadership training at Maxwell AFB in the USA. Based at Kecskemét with the then 59th Tactical Fighter Wing, Vári's first season as a 'Fulcrum' display pilot was 1996. His debut at RIAT came in 1997, and thereafter he was among the Air Tattoo's familiar performers, giving some of the most professional and exciting MiG-29 demonstrations on the circuit. Vári took a year out for 2000, his former student Capt Péter Kovács flying in his stead, but he returned in 2001 and, at the Cottesmore show, achieved a double award win with his best displays yet, firing decoy flares spectacularly during lengthy tailslides. That was his final Air Tattoo, Vári retiring from the Hungarian Defence Forces in 2002 to become a parliamentary representative for the Hungarian Socialist Party. However, he has continued his aviation activities in the civilian world, not least as a regular competitor in aerobatic contests.

The other is one of Britain's most seasoned airshow exponents, the late Alan Wade. The former RAF pilot made a tremendous name for himself on the display scene during the 1980s and 1990s, initially with the CAP 10 and Cranfield A1, and then as a member of Brian Lecomber's Firebird Aerobatics équipe on the Pitts S-2B and Extra EA300. His first RIAT trophy win, indeed, came in 1996 as Lecomber's number two in the Extra-mounted *Rover Group Aerobatic Team*. When the civilian-operated, tri-service Joint — later Defence — Elementary Flying Training School was established, employing the Slingsby T67M-260 Firefly, Wade joined its instructor cadre, making use of his vast experience in the role. He was also a natural choice to perform solo displays in the Firefly, and the capabilities of the 260hp version allowed Alan to exhibit his talents to the full. The sheer precision of his aerobatics had to be seen to be believed, and four more Air Tattoo trophies, all judged by the flying control committee, were the result. Wade was also a regular pilot for The Fighter Collection, and in 2004 displayed the FM-2 Wildcat at RIAT as well as the Slingsby. After the disbandment of JEFTS, he carried on as a Ministry of Defence flying instructor, now on the Grob Tutor, and in early 2017 was awarded the Queen's Commendation for Bravery in the Air after safely landing one of those aircraft — with a student on board — following a total electrical failure, its cockpit full of smoke. Alan died in September 2019.

Acknowledgements

The Royal International Air Tattoo has many strands, which, carefully managed and woven together, contribute to its ultimate success. So too, we hope, will be the case with this specially commissioned anniversary book which, as editor, it has been a privilege to have been involved in. My sincere thanks go to many people, without whose help this book would not have been possible.

First and foremost, my thanks go to Tim Prince for the many hours he spent searching through his archives of Air Tattoo ephemera and photographs, discussing the history of the event with the author and proof-reading all the pages throughout the production process.

My sincere gratitude goes to the author of this book, Ben Dunnell — now also the regular Air Tattoo commentator. Ben's many years of involvement with RIAT and his encyclopaedic aviation knowledge have produced the Air Tattoo's story, ensuring it is both authoritative and interesting for the reader.

My thanks also go to my friend and colleague Graham Finch, steeped in the event's history since 1973, for creating the outstanding high-impact, quality layouts which make up this book. Such a combination of knowledge and talent in one person is indeed rare. Many of you will already be familiar with Graham's work as he has been the designer of the Air Tattoo show programme since 1989, and having been part of the photo team for many years, he was also able to contribute previously unseen images from his files.

We have trawled through thousands of archived photographs in making the final selections, and I make no apology for the vast number of images reproduced over the 300 pages. High-quality digital images were only possible around the turn of the century and we are therefore indebted to renowned aviation photographer Peter R. March, an Air Tattoo volunteer since 1971, for providing many images from his vast personal resource that document the early years of the show, and through the subsequent decades.

I am grateful also for the photographic contributions made by long-time volunteers Rich Cooper, John Dunnell, Kev Storer, Paul Fiddian and Frank Mormillo, as well as Tim Prince and Ben Dunnell, and those external people who have been individually acknowledged alongside their supplied photographs.

Additionally, I would like to thank the following talented photographers for their significant contributions: long-time RIAT friend and volunteer Katsuhiko Tokunaga, in particular for his amazing air-to-air overhead shots; Paul Morrison and his RIAT media liaison group team, who have taken thousands of images of the show over a number of years, many of which now justifiably appear for the first time in the public eye; and Paul Johnson, editor of Flightline UK, who provided many outstanding aircraft images for the book from his RIAT archives.

In compiling an accurate and comprehensive record of the history of what is universally acknowledged as the greatest military airshow in the world and the participating aircraft, author Ben Dunnell expresses his gratitude to Richard Arquati, Andy Armstrong, Mark Ashley, Ian Black, Geoff Brindle, Denis J. Calvert, Rod Dean, Dick Gilbert, Bruce Hales-Dutton, Seán Maffett, Joe Maxwell, Floyd Nelson, Jim Salminen, Brian Smith, Dave Southwood, Bruno Stocker, Brian Strickland, Gyula Vári, Pavel Vlasov, Ken Whitehead and Phil Wilkinson for their personal contributions. His special thanks go to David Halford, without whose input compilation of the chapters from 2009 onwards would have been much more difficult.

Finally, my thanks go to the RAFCTE permanent members of staff who have assisted me with this amazing project from the outset and contributed to its successful production, and those who will continue to be involved in the coming weeks.

I hope this book gives everyone who reads it as much pleasure as I have had being involved in its production and publication as its editor.

David Higham Editor

November 2020

Publisher:
The Royal Air Force Charitable Trust Enterprises,
Douglas Bader House, Horcott Hill, Fairford, Gloucestershire, GL7 4RB, United Kingdom
Tel: +44 (0)1285 713300
Email: enquiries@rafcte.com
Web: airtattoo.com

First published November 2020
Reprinted January 2021
ISBN: 978-1-8382604-0-8

Printed by:
Hampton Printing, Bradley Road, Royal Portbury, Bristol BS20 7TT
Text printed on Essential Silk 150gsm
Endpapers printed on UPM Fine 140gsm